Global Images of Peace and Education

Transforming The War System

Edited by
T. M. THOMAS
DAVID R. CONRAD
and
GERTRUDE F. LANGSAM

PRAKKEN
PUBLICATIONS, INC.
1987

GLOBAL IMAGES OF PEACE AND EDUCATION:
TRANSFORMING THE WAR SYSTEM
Edited by T. M. Thomas, David R. Conrad,
and Gertrude F. Langsam
First Published 1985 by Prakasam Publications, Kottayam, India
Republished 1987 by Prakken Publications, Inc.,
Post Office Box 8623, Ann Arbor, Michigan 48107
© The Society for Educational Reconstruction 1985
Transferred to Prakken Publications, Inc., 1987
ISBN 0-911168-67-2
Library of Congress Catalog Card Number: 86-63413
List Price - $15.00

To

Theodore Brameld

Teacher

Scholar

Friend

PREFACE

In the Spring of 1984, the Executive Committee of the Society for Educational Reconstruction asked the editors of this volume to prepare a book of essays in honor of the distinguished educational philosopher, Theodore Brameld, who recently completed his eightieth birthday. Through his scholarship, teaching and lifetime of struggle for justice and peace, Brameld dared to dream of a world far different from today's world which is torn by constant preparation for war and dehumanizing social, racial and economic injustice. It seemed appropriate that a book dedicated to Theodore Brameld would focus on "Global Images of Peace: Transforming the War System".

Many manuscripts were received as a result of an announcement in the Society for Educational Reconstruction *Newsletter* as well as personal invitations from the editors. All manuscripts were reviewed carefully and those appearing on the following pages were selected for inclusion in this volume. As editors, we exercised our responsibility to produce a high quality book which we hope the reader will find informative, challenging and provocative.

It is our belief, shared by Brameld, that we are living in a time of crisis, and hence face both threats and promises of an unprecedented nature. We live in fear as violence and war permeate our social fabric. In the opening chapters of this volume several authors discuss the nature of the present war system and search for alternative ways to live in peace. For us, peace is more than prevention of war; peace means *shalom* or human well–being which suggests transformation both at personal and societal levels. The war system entangling us must be transformed to achieve world peace.

A global perspective is needed to transform the war system. Modern technological advancements make it possible today to realize a much higher level of fulfillment for all people throughout the planet. Since our lives are becoming increasingly interdependent, worthwhile social achievements in the future will be global in nature. Peace in the emerging age must be global in scope; only then it is relevant to our nuclear age. Thus, education for global consciousness will be examined in several chapters. This leads to a discussion of different perspectives on world community toward the end of the book. The last chapter explores the contributions of Theodore Brameld, a world citizen, as seen by three of his former students and friends.

The co-editors believe that individuals who are committed to peace and are engaging in various forms of peace action can benefit much from this book. We stand for "thinking globally and acting locally" and hence local action can be enriched by broadening a person's perspectives on peace. We also have in mind concerned undergraduate and graduate students in colleges and universities. Courses in peace studies are offered at a growing number of colleges where this book may be adopted. We have tried to present a scholarly volume for use in these courses without becoming too technical or abstract. Relevant sources are cited by each author at the end of every chapter.

Most essays selected for this volume were written specifically for this publication and therefore appear here for the first time. We believe there is unity in the diversity of ideas. All authors are committed to the cause of peace and justice, though each has a unique perspective. We are appreciative of their distinctive contributions.

The co-authors of this book have presented a vision of tomorrow – the creation of a just and peaceful world – so that humankind will not perish. In the urgent hope that future generations will reject warfare in all forms and live in global peace, we proudly dedicate this book to Theodore Brameld, a world citizen whose ideas become more urgent with each year.

Spring 1985

T. M. T.
D. R. C.
G. F. L.

TABLE OF CONTENTS

PART III

PERSPECTIVES ON WORLD COMMUNITY

CHAPTER 1

Introduction: From a Warring World to a Peaceful Global Order

T. M. THOMAS

University of Bridgeport

We live at the most critical time in human history. Our achievements in recent years are so remarkable that living today is totally different from the past. What makes the present so critical is the future prospects, the possibility of creating a new world. A new age is emerging leaving behind the industrial era of the last approximately three hundred years. The emerging age shows both promises and threats. On one side it promises a fulfilling life to people all over the world while on the other it threatens even the existence of human life upon this planet.

Both the promises and threats of an emerging civilization are to be recognized and directed. As Alvin Toffler remarks, "the dawn of this new civilization is the single most explosive fact of our lifetimes."[1] This new age that is emerging in our times has not earned an accepted name since it is so new. Sociologist Daniel Bell describes the coming of a "post–industrial society". Soviet futurists call it the "scientific–technological revolution". Space–Age, Information Age, Electronic Cottage, Global Village, Age of Automation Cybernetics, Computer Age are other widely used terms. Toffler, after using the term "super–industrial society" for a while, has come up with a popular concept, the "Third Wave", to describe the emerging civilization.[2]

The Future

We live at the dawn of a new civilization or "in–between times" when the challenges of the present cannot be met either by the answers of the non–relevant past or the dim future. Hence our task is to strengthen the conception of the future so that it can exert an influence on the present. In periods of rapid social change such as ours, past solutions of problems do not guide us. Hence we have to shape the present based upon our idea of the future or what we want to become.

By recognizing either the promise or the threat, people tend to seek simplistic answers to serious questions about the emerging age. Hence on the one side we see naive optimism in anticipating a bright future while on the other we hear doomsday forecasting that tells of no future at all. For example, the 19th century optimism that relied on the progress of science was too naive because it admitted only the goodness of people. Many prominent thinkers, starting with Rousseau in the previous century, argued that human nature is good and that human beings are on their way to a paradise. They failed to note the evil in human nature and the possibility of world wars in the 20th century. Therefore, any responsible view of the future should take into account both the good and evil forces in human nature.

There is a paradox when we say that the future holds both promises and threats. Indeed, most fundamental truths about life are seen as paradoxes which should be resolved at a deeper level. Brameld argues that "genuine paradox invites far–reaching resolution and transcendence". He notices both promise and threat in the emerging world: "This is the paradox that civilization itself is fraught both with fearful omens of global destruction and with magnificent opportunities for global reconstruction."[3] Though both possibilities will remain in the future, human beings have the capacity to choose one path over the other. Our challenge is to strengthen the process of global reconstruction.

The present generation has a great choice to make regarding the future. The decisions we make – or fail to make – today will determine humanity's tomorrows. Human achievements of the past, especially in the field of science and technology, have brought us to the most critical time. We have reached a situation in which human extinction is a possibility, if a third world war takes place. The other possibility is human survival and growth to higher levels of existence by creating a new global community. In the past, human beings had "histories in the plural", while in the future there is a common life in a "one world". The leading spokesman of "hope theology", Jurgen Moltmann, anticipates the emergence of "one world" for the first time in history. "Since in the future we will either perish together or survive in a new community, we have a future in the singular. We have many pasts but only one future."[4] With the creation of a global community, human beings enter into a new stage. Moltmann continues: "... past and future today no longer appear in one and the same continuum. We have arrived at the leap from the quantities of history to a new quality of history."[5]

Such a leap to a higher stage is explained by Teilhard de Chardin from an evolutionary perspective. Homo sapiens have reached the highest stage in evolution by a distinctive type of consciousness, namely, reflection or the ability "to know that one knows."[6] Teilhard believes that the ability opens up greater scope for transformation which culminates in Point Omega. At Omega, consciousness has greatly increased its depth and distinctiveness. "The world is only interesting when one looks forward", was a favorite saying of De Chardin.[7] Aurobindo, the great Indian philosopher and *yogi*, anticipates the emergence of a supermind as the next stage in evolution. To him consciousness is already released with the formation of life and then mind; the next step is the development of a "supermind."[8] For its development Aurobindo advocates the life of meditation along with social action.[9]

The ability to transform is a unique aspect of human nature. The creation of a global community presupposes transformation both at personal and social levels. New elements in values, attitudes, human relationships, social structures and others should be created for the formation of a future world. A human being is both a creator and a creature. While creating new elements, human beings need help and guidance from the Creator. The emerging one world is nothing less than the dream of "heaven on earth." If we lack a utopia (secular or religious) or a vision for one world, we may perish as a world.

The Destructive Forces in a Warring World

The human ability to turn from destructive to constructive, or creative, behaviour is quite remarkable. Both destructive and constructive forces are always present in the human condition. In today's world, destructive forces are expressed at maximum in militarism, racism, sexism, and poverty. World military spending is rising at an alarming rate. Racial groups are discriminated against everywhere and even genocide is not uncommon in the world today. No part of the world has completely recovered from discrimination based on sex; women are treated as inferior. It is ironic that poverty remains as a very serious issue of our times when technological progress is expected to solve human problems. Death by starvation in Ethiopia now and ongoing malnutrition suffered by millions of people around the world are realities that we should find shameful. Unjust conditions of living are so forceful that we have to work desperately for the creation of a just and peaceful society. The guiding factor of the emerging world must be justice and peace, conditions we rely on for constructive human development.

The destructive forces of human nature have established a central place in modern social life. Crime and violence in various walks of life are becoming ordinary affairs about which there is growing concern. Many social scientists in recent years struggled hard to study this central phenomenon of modern living. Bertrand Russell, the leading philosopher of the century, examined the question, "Why do people fight?", while engaging in peace activist movements in England. He sought answers, not in the rational life of people, however important it is, but in the impulsive side of human nature.[10] Erich Fromm, one of the foremost American social scientists of the last several decades, spent much time and effort during the last years of life studying the issue of human destructiveness. After showing the central place of destructiveness or "love of death" in modern life, Fromm hoped that mankind might choose "love of life" for its survival.[11]

We live in a world dominated by "warthinking". There is a "mind–set" which seeks security in the number and efficiency of weapons. Even when security is not found in making more efficient arms, there is a compulsive force that clings to conventional notions of national security without seeking alternative ways. Along with this mind–set, a "war system" is emerging which encompasses all major institutions of social life including politics, industry, education and others. Such a system makes huge military spending possible indeed necessary. National governments do not meet major opposition in obtaining approval for a huge military or defense budget. As theologian Edward Long shows: "The Nations continually prepare for war as a way of preserving their national rights and security.... Military strength come to be seen, not as something that deals in death and destruction, but as something to preserve national rights and security."[12]

Toward Peace Thinking

A shift in the warring world from its characteristic mode of thinking to "peace thinking" is one of the greatest challenges of the emerging world. Soon after the entry of the human race into the atomic age with successful testing of a new kind of bomb in 1945, the pioneer of this new age, Albert Einstein, reminded us of this challenge: "The unleashed power of the atom has changed everything save our mode of thinking and we thus drift toward unparalleled catastrophe." Since we are caught up in warthinking, the world is drawing closer to an "unparalleled catastrophe", a third world war which would destroy civilization. When someone asked Einstein about the nature of the third world war, he gave the following insightful answer: "I do not know what weapons will be used in the next war, but the one after that will be fought with bows and arrows."[13]

Progress in peace thinking is slow because we are caught up in a war system. Hence we think that peace can be kept by mastering the techniques of war and we make them increasingly precise and accurate. Indeed, we consider military preparedness as a form of peacekeeping and fail to search seriously for efficient alternatives. As peacemakers, we have to come up with different approaches so that people may realize that the use of warfare as a means to keep peace has become increasingly precarious in the nuclear age. Throughout history war was seen as the ultimate arbiter of differences between groups. Hence war and preparations for war became an integral part of human culture.

Today we live at a time when conventional war can become nuclear and, if so, it is suicidal. A nuclear war would destroy civilization and, eliminate precious human life from this planet. Authors, such as Jonathan Schell, vividly describe the consequences of a nuclear blast and show the possibility of a "second death" which is the death of mankind. [15] They urge us to make a responsible choice by selecting the path of life and not the path of death. [16] The advent of nuclear weapons has posed a new challenge to mankind and an urgency for action. Russell expresses this urgency: 'The problem is that of abolishing large–scale war, not at some distant future date but quickly." [17]

Many people continue to think of nuclear war and nuclear weapons in ways not very different from ways they view conventional warfare. We have to learn that the nuclear threat is not just quantitatively different. Lutz and Folk in *Peace Ways*, for example, "view nuclear weapons and the possibility of nuclear war as qualitatively different from conventional weapons and war." [18] The reasons are: 1) Using nuclear weapons makes it impossible to limit destruction to combatants; 2) Using nuclear weapons makes it impossible to limit destruction to the present generation: 3) using nuclear weapons makes it impossible to speak of winners. [19] Perhaps when people recognize this difference, they will shift increasingly to peace thinking.

Fear by itself will not generate longstanding results, but it can be an incentive for some immediate action or for taking the first step. The pursuit of peace, however, must be based on an understanding of human potentialities. The developmental framework of Abraham Maslow and other humanistic psychologists focuses on the growth possibilities or self-actualization of psychologically healthy people. After studying highly developed or self-actualized persons throughout history, Maslow presents a hierarchy of needs starting with physical needs and culminating in being or meaning needs which include the human need and capacity for knowledge, understanding, beauty, truth, goodness, wholeness, justice, peace and others. "These meta or meaning needs are synonymous with the deeper spiritual values and goals of the world religions as well as with humanist aspirations." [20] The process of becoming more fully human involves growth that is inward as well as outward by its universal dimension. Maslow shows the relationship between personal human development and the human world order in this way: "There is a feedback between the Good Society and the Good Person. They need each other... By Good Society I mean ultimately one species, one world." [21] To relate personal transformation and global transformation is a difficult task, but a challenge which must be faced.

The Emerging World Order

The emerging world order has already shown certain features to which many others should be added for the sake of human survival. The central feature of the world today is its interdependence made possible by modern science and technology. Technological advancements in the modern era have brought the world from its isolated units of the past to greater closeness and oneness.

The network of travel and communication is so comprehensive and encompassing that no one part of the world remains isolated. Economic interdependence is growing fast due to the present trade pattern and spread of multinational corporations. Some of the national resources and industrial products of one area are becoming so essential to life in certain other parts that living becomes almost impossible without them. The so–called "oil crisis" of the early 1970's helped the United States and some other countries realize how much they depend upon the production of oil in Arab countries. Many Third World countries depend upon the United States and other industrialized nations to supply machinery for their development and economic advancement.

In this interdependent world, the place of independent sovereign nations remains problematic. Today people are organized as nations with a primary loyalty to these large units. Nations promise security and in turn make great demands from people, including their wealth and even their lives. The national security of the state, as expressed in constant mobilization of leadership, institutions, resources and values, is beginning to dominate all nations whether rich or poor, capitalist or communist. [22] The three national security imperatives discussed by global educators Gerald and Patricia Mische are balance–of–weapons competition, balance–of–payments competition, and competition over scarce resources. All nations are expected to compete for these imperatives in order to provide the security guaranteed by them. [23]

The failure of nations to provide the security noted above is becoming a fact of modern living. However, people still look to their own nations for security in spite of the failure. In place of our present loyalty to nations, a loyalty to the world must be developed. Today the notion of world citizenship is not very real to most people but this situation can change. An awareness that we are world citizens while continuing our citizenship in particular nations is a revolutionary concept to be developed in the emerging age. As Finnerty says in his book *World Citizen*: "We are bound by our economy, our technology, our yearning to learn and to communicate, into a global framework that demands of us an expanded citizenship." [24]

A world citizen sees the world as one with its interdependent units of regions and nations. His/her primary

loyalty is not to sovereign nations with the
ration from one another, but to earth itself
form of human life has evolved. People li
of this planet, irrespective of all their din
language, beliefs, knowledge and values, form one
in which all are treated as brothers and sisters.
are considered as necessary and healthy, not occasio..
fights or genocide which has happened throughout history.
world citizen, more than anything else, maintains a global
perspective while dealing with local and national issues because
the motto is "thinking globally and acting locally." The global
nature of present human problems is noticed and action is
taken in specific smaller spheres.

The above description of a world citizen is only a dream
for most people today. However, for some people it is real
because of the urgency for developing new concepts to live
in an emerging world. People such as Theodore Brameld have
taken the notion of world citizenship seriously because of their
interest in the future. With eagerness, they have devoted
their time and energy to create a better society with a global
outlook and active local participation. They form the "creative
minority" in Arnold Toynbee's sense; to this outstanding historian, the turning points of history come from a creative
minority. Brameld and others are promoting this future society in which many people acknowledge their primary loyalty
to the human race and live as world citizens. [25]

Global Issues : Economic Injustice

The major problems that people try to solve at local or
national levels have assumed a greater global nature in the
contemporary world. Such problems, if we select a few, are:
1) poverty or economic injustice; 2) war or nuclear armaments; 3) racism or human rights denial; 4) sexism or sex
discrimination and 5) pollution or environmental destruction.
Those who take world citizenship seriously devote time and
energy to resolving these issues we confront. To the extent
that we succeed in solving these problems, we are creating a
suitable world order that the future demands of us. The
emerging world will have a strong foundation if the present

ration treats the major problems it faces from a global
spective. From the five problems mentioned above, we will
lect one, economic injustice, for further discussion.

Economic injustice is considered the leading problem in
all developing Third World countries, while peace gains
priority among problems in advanced industrialized nations.
Instead of contrasting justice and peace by associating them
with the two hemispheres of the world, we shall treat both of
them as necessary qualities in all parts of the world. Both
justice and peace can be seen as two sides of the same coin.
Justice is the precondition for achieving peace. As Edward
Long maintains, "There can be no genuine peace in human
affairs unless individuals and groups are treated properly and
fairly by others and in turn feel themselves obliged to treat
others with respect and righteousness." [26] It is impossible to
think about peace without regard for justice; by building a just
society, people can live in peace.

A global understanding of economic injustice must take
into account the current debate between the industrialized
North and the developing South. The disparity between rich
nations and poor nations is tremendous, as shown in the
differences between per capita income; while in countries such
as the United States the per capita income is more than seven
thousand dollars, in developing countries, like India, it is less than
two hundred dollars. Two thirds of the world population lives
in developing countries with low income and many people face
hunger everyday. The developed countries, with nearly thirty
percent of all people living today, consume a disproportionate
amount of resources; for example, 89 per cent of the tractors
and 92 per cent of the world's automobiles are used by the
industrialized countries. [27] In advanced countries, refrigerators,
television sets and other appliances are considered necessities
of life while in many developing parts of the world they are
treated as luxury items.

The growing disparity between the rich North nations
and the poor South nations presents a serious threat to peace
because peace is jeopardized when an unjust system gains
strength. Today the rich nations find more and more avenues

to exploit the poor nations, and this exploitation gains greater acceptance because of the trend in all nations to act on the basis of self–interest. Any behavior of one country is justified so long as it brings gains, whether money or power. Moral issues are not raised while serving national interests. The crucial question of what is good for the world and humanity at large is completely ignored in the present pursuit of national self–interests. In the past, colonial powers exploited the colonies. Though the colonies are free countries today, they have not gained economic freedom. Even after the demise of the "colonial political order" the "colonial economic order" remains.[28] It is unfortunate that the United States, though not a former colonial power, acts like one in exploiting the Third World countries; the multinational corporations are given a free hand in making profits by following whatever means they desire.

When inequality or injustice is built into the social structure there will emerge two opposing groups, one the beneficiaries of injustice and the other its victims. The oppressors and the oppressed have contrasting interests. Brian Wren argues that "the beneficiaries of injustice almost always have a psychological need to believe that the victims are inferior."[29] Even today there are people who believe that poverty is caused by the inferiority of poor people. The victims of injustice have to unite and work for change by becoming aware of their position as a group. This new awareness is a function of critical consciousness a process which Brazilian educator, Paulo Freire, calls "conscientization".[30] Education has a central role to play in promoting such an awareness among oppressed people. This innovative function focusing on social transformation is one of the central concerns of reconstructionism, the philosophy of education formulated by Brameld.[31]

Though inequality between rich and poor nations remains a major problem, many nations, both rich and poor, are in the process of solving injustice within their national boundaries. For example, in the United States pockets of poverty have been recognized in the last two or three decades and several projects are initiated to solve problems of the poor. Also,

American women who receive lower wages than men for the same work are now struggling to attain equality.

We select a developing country to illustrate the problem. India, the largest democracy in the world, officially subscribes to a socialist pattern of society and tries hard to solve its many inequalities. During the last half century the conditions of the lower castes, the former untouchables, have improved considerably. By granting "protective discrimination", the problems of these lower castes are being solved. Seats are reserved for lower castes (scheduled castes and tribes, the terms used in India) in professional colleges and government jobs. Many have made use of this opportunity in protective discrimination and enjoy middle or upper class status in society. Though the caste situation has improved considerably in India, the class problem is a serious one because millions of people in the lowest class have to face major hardships in their daily life. While many people suffer from extreme poverty, some citizens lead a luxurious life at the other end of the class division. Hence the achievement of economic and social justice is a major issue in India.[32] Though the goal of justice and economic freedom is the motto of independent India, the country has to go a long way to attain them. The force of the "revolution of rising expectations" is so noticeable in India, as in many other Third World countries, that something tangible has to be achieved on the question of injustice without further delay.

A new sense of equality and justice, following higher notions of freedom, is on the rise during the present century all over the world. This deeper understanding of freedom and justice has brought several revolutions or structural changes to many societies. Most Third World countries, after obtaining political freedom, are in the process of implementing economic freedom which is justice in action. No doubt, some Third World countries become reactionary under totalitarian regimes and turn away from justice which they need. In general, however, most nations are taking some steps to implement justice within their boundaries.

What is at stake now is the practice of justice between nations. An understandable cause behind this lag is the lack of a global structure. Hence the greatest need of the immediate future is to find a global structure or order so that justice can be practiced in relationship between nations. If the emerging world fails to implement global justice through a new world order and the necessary laws that accompany that order, there will be impending dangers such as a major war. The growing sense of equality and justice must find ways of implementation at national and global levels. From an awareness level or conscientization, we can move on to strategies or the practice of justice within and between nations in a new world order. We must find ways of achieving global resource–sharing and other forms of world community life. A world citizen accepts the challenge of global justice as the first priority and earnestly works for the creation of a better future.

Shalom: A Broad Meaning of Peace

The above emphasis on justice in peacemaking efforts is summarized in the Hebrew word shalom. The meaning of shalom is so comprehensive that this concept gains wide acceptance among people interested in peace studies. In the Hebrew Scriptures shalom means "such things as wholeness and health, prosperity and security, political and spiritual well–being".[33] It is much more than absence of war or inner serenity. Shalom has to do with a security that is physical as well as spiritual: "Action to alleviate world hunger is peacemaking; seeking to reverse the arms race is peacemaking; working for an economic order that narrows the disparities between rich and poor is peacemaking. Whatever enhance the well–being of the human family is peacemaking, the spreading of shalom."[34]

This spreading of shalom has been undertaken by many prominent Christians of our era, among them Pope John XXIII and Reinhold Neibuhr who "believed that the path to peace is found in the struggle for justice".[35] Today increasing number of Christians take an active role in peacemaking by recognizing Christ as the "Prince of peace" One of the final "gifts" of Jesus to his disciples was peace: "Peace is what I leave with you; it is my own peace that I give you".[36] Peace-making is also given due importance in the Sermon on the Mount "Happy are those work for peace: God will call them his children."[37] Throughout these centuries Christian saints prayed for peace, for example, the well–known prayer of Saint Francis: "Make me an instrument of Thy peace..."[38]

To secure peace is a central concern of other religions as well. The very word Islam means peace along with another meaning, submission to God. In Hindu worship *shanti* (peace) is a term that is much repeated. *Shanti* refers to the supreme blessing that a person can receive in this world from the divine. Buddhism preaches the "gospel of peace"; it was because of missionary effort of Asoka, the great Indian emperor of 3rd century B. C., who gave up war and sent missionaries with the message of peace, that Buddhism found its acceptance in southeast Asia and other places.

Yet, the two great dangers of our contemporary world, divided into an advanced North and poor South, are the possibility of war and the prevalence of injustice as manifested in poverty and discrimination. Hence the greatest need of our times is the creation of a just and peaceful world order.

Notes

1.   Alvin Tofler, *The Third Wave* (New York: Bantam Books, 1980), p. 9.
2.   *Ibid.*
3.   Theodore Brameld in David R. Conrad, *Education for Transformation: Implications in Lewis Mumford's Ecohumanism* (Palm springs. CA : ETC Publications, 1976) p. iii.
4.   Jurgen Moltmann, *Religion, Revolution and the Future* (New York : Charles Scribner's Sons, 1969), p. 201.
5.   *Ibid.*
6.   Teilhard de Chardin, *Phenomenon of Man* (New York : Harper Torch Books, 1959), p. 165.
7.   Joseph Kopp, *Teilhard de Chardin*; *A New Synthesis of Evolution* Deus Book, 1964), p. 29.
8.   Robert McDermott, *The Essential Aurobindo* (New York: Schocken Books, 1973), p. 29.
9.   T. M. Thomas and J. B. Chethimattam, *Images of Man: A Philoso-, phic and Scientific Inquiry,* (Bangalore : Dharmaram Publications 1974). p. 99.

10. Bertrand Russell, *Why Men Fight?* (New York: The Century Co., 1917).
11. Erich Fromm, *The Anatomy of Humam Destructiveness* (Greenwich, CT. Fawcett Crest Book, 1973). p. 406.
12. Edward LeRoy Long, Jr., *Peace Thinking in a Warring World* (Philadelphia: The Westminster Press, 1983), p. 14.
13. Einstein in Karl Jaspers, *The Future of Mankind* (Chicago: University of Chicago Press, 1961), p. 2.
14. E. Long, *op. cit.*, p. 28.
15. Jonathan Schell, *The Fate of the Earth* (New York: Avon Books, 1982), p. 115.
16. *Ibid.*, p. 231.
17. Bertrand Russell, "The Prevention of War" in Morton Grodzins and Eugene Rabinowitch, *The Atomic Age* (New York: Basic Books, 1963), p. 100.
18. Charles P. Lutz and Jerry L. Folk, *Peace Ways* (Minneapolis: Augsburg Publishing House, 1983), p. 15.
19. *Ibid.*, p. 16.
20. Gerald and Patricia Mische, *Toward a Human World Order* (New York: Paulist Press, 1977), p. 26.
21. Abraham Maslow, *The Farther Reaches of Human Nature* (New York: Viking Press, 1971), p. 19.
22. Gerald and Patricia Mische, *op. cit.*, p. 47.
23. *Ibid.*
24. Adam D. Corson-Finnerty, *World Citizen* (Maryknoll: Orbis Books, 1982), p. 5.
25. Theodore Brameld, *Teacher As a World Citizen* (Palm Springs, CA: ETC Publications, 1976).
26. E. Long, *op. cit.*, p. 30.
27. Adam Corson-Finnerty, *op. cit.*, p. 25.
28. *Ibid.*, p. 25.
29. Brian Wren, *Education for Justice* (Maryknoll, New York: Orbis Books, 1977), p. 73.
30. Paulo Freire, *Pedagogy of the Oppressed* (New York: The Seabury Press, 1970),
31. Theodore Brameld, *Toward a Reconstructed Philosophy of Education* (New York: Holt, Rinehart and Winston, 1956).
32. Annamma Thomas and T. M. Thomas, *Kerala Immigrants in America: A Sociological Study of St. Thomas Christians* (Cochin: Simons Printers and Publishers, 1984), pp. 65–66.
33. Robert M. Brown, *Making Peace in Global Village* (Philadelphia: The Westminster Press, 1981), p. 14.
34. *Ibid.*, p. 15.
35. *Ibid.*
36. John 14:27.
37. Matthew 5:9.
38. St. Francis quoted in Kenneth Boulding, *Stable Peace* (Austin: University of Texas Press, 1978), p. 5.

PART I

FROM A WAR SYSTEM TO PEACE AND JUSTICE

Introduction

War is the logical outcome of a certain mode of thinking. Since our modern social structures promote such a lifestyle, we constantly live in the shadow of another world war which can totally eliminate our civilization. People live in fear and they are not confident of a future. How can we transform this planet of fear to a world of hope and peace? What changes are to be made in our way of thinking?

In these chapters, war is explained as a system for organizing and institutionalizing violence in intergroup relations. War has become a legally recognized mode for resolving conflicts between groups. Throughout history, nations have engaged in wars as a means of arbitrating controversies. But in modern life, war has become obsolete because of the destructive power of nuclear weapons. If we resort to war for resolving conflicts, we may end up with a nuclear disaster that eliminates the human race. The global nature of nuclear warfare is a new phenomenon we face. Hence we must look at alternative ways of resolving conflicts rather than wage war against each other. The authors of Part I examine the nature of the present warring world and show that an ideology of militarism is deeply ingrained in present social structures. They try to seek ways of creating a peaceful and just society.

The path of nonviolence is shown as a superior way to peace by T. M. Thomas in the opening chapter. Thomas discusses war as a social institution and recognizes the force of militarism in the present society. Dangers of the arms race, with special reference to nuclear arms, are reviewed and the question of morality in relation to war is explored at length.

Nuclear deterrence is the topic of discussion in Robert Nash's chapter. Since the arms race is justified by the superpowers on the basis of a deterrence policy, it is important that the ethical implications of this concept be carefully examined. Though political leaders practice deterrence, theoretical justification comes from several Christian scholars. Nash examines the arguments of these scholars and urges people to be "co-creators" in peacemaking efforts.

Military spending is an expression of the war system. Kevin Cassidy shows how huge military expenditures ruin the economy of both advanced and developing countries. Economic conversion, an alternative, is discussed in detail. Cassidy argues that more jobs are provided with economic conversion than with the present military economy. So our global economic condition will be substantially improved if we turn swords into plowshares, he concludes.

Another manifestation of the war system is economic injustice, a topic explored by Richard Lyons. Economic injustice is studied by focusing on work inequality and alienation. Theory of work, as formulated by Frederick Herzberg, is examined in detail. Economic justice is achieved worldwide, the author concludes, when society is committed to growth achieved through meaningful, satisfying work.

Part I ends with a case study in nonviolent civil disobedience. As a participant observer, David Conrad gathered detailed information of events that took place in Winooski, Vermont, in the office of a U. S. senator. By examining the three day occupation of the senator's office and the eventful trial that followed, the author shows that civil disobedience, with its long history in America, continues to be a force for social change today.

CHAPTER 2

War as a Social Institution: From Militarism to Nonviolence

T. M. THOMAS

University of Bridgeport

Our contemporary world accepts contradictory beliefs on the question of war. The almost universal yearning for peace stands in contradiction to present preparations for war. Though we know that a third world war will destroy modern civilization, we carry on our daily lives as if there is no such danger. While we profess that there is no winner in a nuclear war, the possibility of a secret first attack is found deep in the hearts of many leaders. Even when an over stock of strategic weapons can destroy the world several times, we continue building more weapons of every kind as if we do not have enough. In spite of our knowledge that nuclear war is different from all previous wars, we prefer the darkness of ignorance as we assume that it is just another war. In these contradictions Trotsky's aphorism about the dialectic of war comes true: "You may not be interested in war, but war is interested in you." [1]

We have become entangled in a war system. Military institutions are formed by modern nations for the purpose of providing security to people. Even when that purpose is not met, these institutions continue to grow and become stronger every day. As peace educator Betty Reardon argues: "The

U. S. is probably the most heavily armed nation in the world. In spite of this emphasis on 'national security' and military preparedness, we are a nation lacking fundamental human security."[2] In fact, other nations are in the same predicament since security is getting weak while militarism becomes stronger. As William Boyer remarks, in *"Education for Annihilation* ... institutions may even work counter to the original objective ... One of the ironies of history is that societies develop institutions to serve people and soon find people serving these institutions."[3]

Militarism as an Ideology

Security is found in "order", but the present highly militarized world order does not meet this human need. Today the violent alternatives make their appeal to people. Of the two dimensions of violence, direct and structural, the former is easily recognized as overt and dramatic. The second dimension, structural violence, is less readily visible because it is subtly linked with existing social structures. In his peace research, Johann Galtung gave due attention to the structural aspect of violence. When some people are forced to live in conditions of poverty and deprivation, they are the victims of structural voilence. However, education for peace is concerned with both the direct and structural dimensions of violence.[4]

Militarism evolved as an ideology during the nineteenth century. Prior to this time, armies and navies were comprised mainly of recruited seamen, mercenaries, and aristocrats. They were supported by monarchies to serve special interests. "During the nineteenth century", according to Boyer, "nations developed a permanent officer corps dedicated to the management of violence, and military academies were created to develop the art, science and philosophy of war."[5]

The chief theoretician of modern military ideology was Karl Von Clausewitz, director of the General War Academy in Prussia (1780–1831). His influential book, *On War*, deals with all aspects of warfare — political, social and personal — and it is quoted by modern military leaders throughout the world.[6] The military ideal of Clausewitz was total destruction of the enemy: "War is an act of force ... which theoretically can have no limits."[7] The idea of war carries with it the idea of limitlessness and hence no moral codes will be added to it: "We can never introduce a modifying principle into the philosophy of war without committing an absurdity."[8] War to Clausewitz became the pursuit of politics by other means, the other means being the use of organized violence.[9] The Clausewitzian idea of limitlessness is found in General Sherman's burning of Atlanta and the famous march through Georgia.[10]

Militarism as an ideology has been well established during the twentieth century. It is marked by some of the most tragic events in all human history: two world wars, the Holocaust in Europe, holocaust in Japan and several major regional wars. These alarming human tragedies have not prevented us from war preparations. The presence of large quantities of nuclear bombs, huge military spending by all nations and an arms race which gets worse every year are all indications of the force of militarism in contemporary culture. Even after recognizing the dangers, people adhere with an irrational force, to a mode of consciousness and set of behaviors. The words of philosopher Berdyaev come true: "War is possible only in a certain psychological atmosphere."[11] The growing military ideology of our times creates a suitable psychological atmosphere which makes war possible, even probable if present trends continue.

The Arms Race and Nuclear Danger

The most dangerous course in human history is found in the present arms race of the superpowers and in the military build-up of all modern nations. For the first time, the world is threatened by total elimination of human life. Stockpiles of nuclear arms have created a fearful situation. The possibility of nuclear arms has become the central terror of our time. The United States has about 30,000 bombs: over 9,000 strategic and 21,000 tactical nuclear weapons. The Soviet Union is not much behind in the number of weapons or in its nuclear capability. The number of weapons on both sides is far greater than the number of targets to be hit.

The atomic age began in 1945 with the successful testing of an atomic bomb in July of that year and its use as a weapon on August 6 and 9 over two populated cities in Japan, Hiroshima and Nagasaki. In Hiroshima a fission bomb with a yield of twelve and a half kilotons was detonated nineteen hundred feet above the ground. The centre of the city was flattened, and every part of the city was damaged. Tens of thousands of people were burned to death. Other tens of thousands suffered injuries of every description.[12]

The Hiroshima bomb was a very small one compared to the powerful bombs in our arsenal today. What happened there was less than a millionth part of the present levels of world nuclear armaments.[13] In his influential book, *The Fate of the Earth*, Jonathan Schell describes the effects of a one megaton bomb and a twenty–megaton bomb if dropped on New York City. The twenty–megaton bomb has one thousand six hundred times the yield of the Hiroshima bomb. The fireball would be about four and a half miles in diameter. People caught in the open within twenty three miles from ground zero would be burned to death. The mushroom cloud would be seventy miles in diameter.[14]

If a third world war would occur, bombs such as the one described above will be used, but with one major difference. There will be an exchange of such powerful weapons from both sides, while in Hiroshima only one country had the bomb. It is hard to conceive exactly what would happen in a nuclear war when both parties possess a large number of the most powerful weapons. The Hiroshima bombing does not provide an adequate model for future nuclear wars because of the qualitative difference: Schell calls it "a difference in kind" along with magnitude.[15] Changes caused by destruction of ozone layer in a powerful nuclear exchange must be studied through use of human insight and imagination along with reason.

The failure of an attempt in 1946 to bring atomic energy under international control was a great loss to humanity. Bernard Baruch, United States Representative to the United Nations Atomic Energy Commission, presented an American plan to the Commission in June 1946. The proposal had been worked out under State Department auspices by a Board of

Consultants whose leading member was Robert Oppenheimer, an opponent of atomic weapons development after directing the Manhattan project which built the atomic bomb. The Baruch plan states categorically: "The United States proposes the creation of an International Atomic Energy Authority, to which should be entrusted all phases of development and use of atomic energy, starting with the raw material and including... ownership of all atomic energy activities'... power to control, inspect... to detect misuse of atomic energy."[16] Though proponents hoped that the nuclear issue could be isolated from traditional power politics, they proved to be wrong. Deterioration of East–West relations dictated the fate of this subject of paramount significance to the security of mankind. The Soviet Union opposed the plan by raising questions about veto power, inspection procedures and others. In short, efforts to control the new weapon failed and the superpowers entered into an ever–escalating nuclear arms race.[17]

The nuclear monopoly of the United States continued until 1952 when the Soviet Union created an atomic bomb. The period of 1953 to 1966 was marked by American nuclear dominance. Since 1967 a period of "Essential Equivalence", a term used by Bruce Russett, had begun.[18] The nuclear arms race in the last two or three decades shows that the United States creates a new type of weapon or delivery system and very soon the Soviet Union catches up with the invention. Though these superpowers have a huge arsenal of nuclear weapons, other countries also possess these weapons or a nuclear capability. This group includes Great Britain, France, China and India. Development of nuclear capability is possible, if not already achieved, in several countries such as Israel, South Africa and Brazil. In short, the nuclear threat remains the major danger of the contemporary world.

Militarism as a Cultural Problem

In the last two sections we have seen that militarism is being established as an ideology and that nations are engaged in an arms race that includes nuclear weapons. Here we argue that the dominance of weapons in our society and human reliance on arms can be explained as a cultural problem.

Robert Musil agrees when he says that "nuclear weapons are a cultural problem" and they are "produced by a particular culture."[19] Hence we have to study the "tangled root of society's most prolific and most poisonous growth."[20] Efforts for arms control or disarmament, with its ups and downs, cannot succeed fully until we come to grips with this cultural problem.

Since we live in an age of science and technology, our modes of consciousness and forms of behavior are influenced, or even dictated, by the trend of our times. While on the one side we are products of existing social conditions, on the other we can transcend these conditions and change the course of history. To be a creature as well as a creator is one of the blessings of human living. By recognizing how much we are shaped by our culture, we can take steps to change the present directions of this culture. The weapon–producing culture in which we live needs a transformation to become a just and peaceful culture. The social or cultural transformation advocated by Theodore Brameld and others should receive greater attention so that we can create a better future and live in peace.

Positivism is recognized as the dominant world–view of this age according to educational historian Douglas Sloan who explains: "The central positivist claim is that science provides our only way of knowing and our only source of genuine knowledge."[21] This claim implies that all problems are scientific and technological and that quantitative science provides an adequate all–embracing picture of the world.[22] Positivism is formed around the assumption that objective understanding and coherent social life can be grounded only by the scientific method of inquiry.[23] "Fundamental to the positivist vision of the true and the good is the assumption that objectivity free from political interests and other biases can be obtained by a radical segregation of knowledge from subjectivity, of object from subject, and of fact from value, by assuming that facts can be directly apprehended as sense data.[24]

Hence the "cultural problem" of our present world is that it is dominated by a positivist mode of consciousness leading to militarism. The approaches to reality recognized by the humanities, art and religion are ignored. The human being today becomes "encapsulated" or "one dimensional man", to use Marcuse's popular term.[25] Accordingly, realities not understood by "technical reason" are rejected and we fail in our peace–making efforts.

Human sensitivity, empathy and care, usually associated with the humanities, are very essential for the creation of a just and peaceful social structure. Imagination and creativity of an artist help us to "see" the unity and oneness of the world instead of the fragmented analytical approach of scientific method. To see the whole with intuitive eyes is different from seeing the material world part by part with our senses. Reality is not confined to matter because human beings have the capacity to understand moral and spiritual realms of reality.

The challenge to peace can be accepted as a human response to God's call. When the Roman Catholic bishops say that "the global threat of nuclear war is a central concern of the universal church", they focus religious perspectives and principles on peace in the modern world. Their Pastoral Letter urges people to go beyond an examination of weapon systems or military strategies and probe the meaning of choices because "peace is the setting in which moral choice can be most effectively exercised."[27]

Morality of War: Just–War Theory

Man is a moral being. Human choices based on a sense of right strengthen a person's humanity. The positivism of our age of science and technology ignores the moral dimension of human life in favor of technical rationality. Peace efforts will be more effective if we see the person as a moral and spiritual being and if we try to change the social structures to create a world which recognizes human worth and dignity of all. Human rights are better achieved when all human beings are seen as brothers and sisters. It is the God of love that unites all into one, bringing unity in the world. Present disunity and war can be handled better with the dream of a "one world." Moral issues form the core for the creation of such a world.

After criticizing the Clausewitzian use of force and the total destruction of the enemy, Michael Walzer advocates that moral questions be considered as part of any war. He believes that the moral reality of war includes both "justice of war", which refers to the causes, and "justice in war" that considers the means adopted in a war. [28] By presenting illustrations from throughout history, including the recent Vietnam War, Walzer brings to our attention many moral issues to be considered in the context of war.

The morality of war issue is debated at length by raising the question whether war is justified under certain conditions. The two major positions or theoretical perspectives that have emerged out of this debate are "just–war theory" and "pacifism". Let us consider the first theory in this section.

Hugo Grotius (1583–1645), the renowned Dutch scholar and "father of international law", inquires whether war is justified in his book, *Prolegomena to the Law of War and Peace.* An affirmative answer is given by rejecting the pacifist views of many esteemed Christian thinkers. Grotius holds that nothing but injury forms the just cause for war and the types of injury are 1) self–defense, 2) protection of property, 3) enforcement of a duty owed and 4) punishment. Grotius asserts that war itself is but an instrumentality of law. When once undertaken it should be carried on only within the bounds of law and good faith.[29]

The just–war theory has been the accepted policy of the Christian church for every century except the first and second when pacifism was practised. It was St. Augustine who formulated the tenets of the just–war theory. In his view, war was both "the result of sin and a remedy for sin in the life of political societies." St. Augustine believed that: "War arose from disordered ambitions, but it could also be used, in some cases at least, to restrain evil and protect the innocents."[30]

This Augustinian insight is the central premise of the just–war theory, even when it has been modified in the history of Catholic theology. Today the Church allows war if it is for self–defense. According to the Pastoral Letter, "As long as the danger of war persists and there is no international authority with the necessary competence and power, governments cannot be denied of the right of lawful self–defense, once all peace efforts have failed."[31]

The just–war theory or limited war doctrine holds that a war can be considered just only if the following conditions are present. It must: 1) be declared by a legitimate authority; 2) be carried out with right intention; 3) be undertaken only as a last resort; 4) be waged on the basis of the principle of proportionality; 5) have a reasonable chance of success; 6) be waged with all moderation possible.[32] By applying these conditions to a nuclear war, Betty Reardon argues that "nuclear warfare would be immoral."[33] By contrast, Theologian Paul Ramsey argues that a just–war is possible in the modern age.

Nuclear Deterrence

A nuclear arms race between the superpowers is raging today on the assumption that it is a justifiable policy to deter war. Most people support the doctrine of deterrence for practical reasons while opinion is divided when moral arguments are raised. The Catholic Bishops, after much debate on the moral issue of deterrence, have arrived at a conditional acceptance of the policy.

Deterrence is explained as a policy to prevent war. When a nation recognizes that the enemy has the military power to inflict total destruction it will start a war. "Mutually Assured Destruction", MAD, is the cornerstone of this policy. Nations are allowed to build arms so long as these weapons are for second–strike capability. According to Russett, "Under conditions of stable deterrence, each side has only a second–strike (retaliatory) capability, not a first–strike force."[34] However, the recent approval of MX missiles in the United states is a shift from this policy because this new weapon secures a first – strike capability. This is an irony since the MX missile system has been approved at a time when the Freeze movement has gained momentum all across the country and won its response in the Congress.

Paul Ramsey, a protestant theologian who wrote much on ethical issues, argues in favor of a justifiable nuclear deterrent strategy. He claims that it is possible to prevent nuclear attack without threatening to bomb cities in response. He argues that "the collateral civilian damage that would result from counterforce warfare in its maximum form "would be sufficient to deter potential agressors. The civilians likely to die in such a war would be the "incidental victims of legitimate military strikes."[35]

Joseph Fahey strongly opposes deterrence doctrine by showing that it is "a morally bankrupt philosophy whose continual development will not prevent war but in fact will cause it".[36] Deterrence assumes that the only ultimate way nations can solve difference is through violence or threat of violence. It is based on the fallacious assumption that "might makes right" and that "armed strength will guarantee security". The most dangerous aspect of deterrence, to Fahey, is "the naive assumption that such weapons will never be used. Of the thousands of arms races in history only a few have not ended in war".[37]

The question of intention is raised by Bryan Hehir who argues that the intention to do evil carries the same culpability as the doing of evil. "The policy of deterrence today is based upon a declared intention to do what just–war ethics could never legitimize", he writes.[38]

These arguments against nuclear deterrence must receive greater attention. The rationale used for just–war theory is not applicable to deterrence. As David Hollenbach points out, "The great danger in the present moment is that moral judgments about the use of nuclear weapons will be adjusted to fit the logic of a favored deterrence posture".[39]

non–harm, a longstanding principle in the religions of Hinduism, Buddhism and Jainism. The vegetarian food habit of people belonging to these religions is a result of this emphasis on *ahimsa* or non–killing. In a conflict, Gandhi seeks the co–operation and friendship of the opponents by self–sacrifice rather than inflicting any injury on them or humiliating them. The process of nonviolent action for Gandhi is essentially a quest for truth. He sees God as truth. Nonviolence involves a firm grasping of the truth and an active feeling of respect for the opponent. The final test of this feeling of respect or regard is self–suffering.[44] The sacrifice and love of enemy found in Christ was a model for Gandhi to practice nonviolence under conditions of modern political life. Martin Luther King Jr. stands in the same tradition; to him the essence of non-violence is found in the Greek concept of agape, the disinterested love which seeks to preserve and create community. To King, nonviolent action "is based on the conviction that the universe is on the side of justice. Consequently, the believer has a deep faith in the future".[45] For both these radical leaders nonviolence provides the basis for social change. As Robert Woito puts it in *To End War*, they have brought "into the political arena the long tradition of religion and personal witness."[46]

Nonviolence is far more than a method of resolving conflicts or changes made in the personal attitudes and values of people. These are necessary steps for the creation of a new social structure and relationship. Gandhi clearly visualized a radical social development in his notion of nonviolence. It calls for "a decentralization of authority from the top of an organization and a taking of power from below at the same time."[47] It implies that rights and privileges are shared among all people. The social development ultimately results in a fundamental alteration of reality as it is defined in the daily life of people.[48]

The new society that Gandhi visualized has been developed further by his followers in the concept of *sarvodhaya* which means total transformation. In it human freedom has to permeate all walks of life from the political realm to the economic, social and others. Vinoba Bhave, a true follower of Gandhi, walked from village to village throughout the vast country of India in the 1950's and 1960's urging landlords to give land to the poor. Following political freedom, he recognized the need for achieving economic freedom and justice. The dream of a new society and total transformation involves continuous change in the person and in the social structure.

The philosophy of nonviolence as advocated by Gandhi as well as Tolstoy includes the following assumptions about the nature of man and society. They are: 1) a faith in the inherent goodness of man; 2) a faith in the ultimate moral constitution of the universe; and 3) a faith in the final realization of human destiny on the terrestrial plane and within universal history.[49]

The practice of nonviolence in our contemporary world is manifested in different actions. After identifying 198 such actions, peace researcher Gene Sharp has grouped them into three principal categories: protest and persuasion, noncooperation, and intervention.[50] Staughton Lynd, while presenting a documentary history of nonviolence in America, discusses the following overlapping but distinct elements: 1) refusal to retaliate ("pacifism", "nonresistance"); 2) deliberate lawbreaking for conscience's sake ("civil disobedience"); 3) acting out of conviction by demonstrative action ("direct action").[51]

Conclusion

We are caught up in a war system while we yearn to live in peace. If the emerging world is not built on just and peaceful structures we cannot anticipate a future at all. The transition from one to the other is the greatest challenge that we face today.

There is growing fear about the possibility of war between nations and violence or crime within a country. Human needs for safety and security are not met; rather people are exploited by nations which build more weapons on the assumption that nuclear weapons insure security.

Crime and violence, either physical or structural, prevail in all civilized societies. As Galtung shows, structural violence is located in the organization of society. Physical violence can be reduced by changing structural violence found in the organization of society.[52]

Militarism has evolved as an ideology which in its original use has an association with false consciousness. Many subscribe to a psychological atmosphere that makes war possible. But the human ability to transcend social trends can and must be used for the creation of new social conditions and ideologies.

Today's mode of thinking is directed by positivism and hence reality is explained from only one point of view. In this situation, the arms race is made possible or becomes inevitable because technical reason occupies a paramount place while other precious human qualities are ignored.

The just–war theory has been influential for a long time in justifying war. At present, the same reasoning used in this theory is applied to formulate nuclear deterrence. The superpowers take advantage of it and increase their nuclear arsenal.

The emerging world requires new approaches to resolving conflicts. In the place of violent answers sought in the past by resorting to war, we advocate nonviolence. Gandhi and King have shown that nonviolent strategies can be effective in modern political and social life. Nonviolence is not just a method to resolve conflict. It has to be accepted as an ideology of the emerging world for its power of transformation. Gandhi has adhered to nonviolence not because it works but because it is right.

Violence which is an expression of "body–force" rises out of fear in people. In its place Gandhi advocated nonviolence which is "soul–force" that appeals to the spiritual need for truth and justice. The *rishis* (seers) of India centuries ago recognized the power of nonviolence or self–sacrifice over the power of violence. A distinguished biographer of Gandhi observes: "Having themselves known the use of arms they realized their uselessness and taught a weary world that its salvation lay not through violence but through nonviolence."[53]

Social and educational reconstructionists can benefit from the philosophy and practice of nonviolence because it integrates both personal and social transformation. Nonviolence acknowledges the evil that is present in our corporate structures as well as in our individual hearts. Dealing with structural evil is not enough and T. S. Eliot was right to warn us of the fallacy of "dreaming of systems so perfect that no one will need to be good."[54] If hearts have to change, so do structures.

The meditative and activist approaches are combined into one in nonviolence as "experimented" by Gandhi and King. This integrated approach is necessary for securing "peace as a social institution" in the emerging world.

Notes

1. Trotsky quoted in Michael Walzer, *Just and Unjust Wars* (New York: Basic Books, 1977), p. 29.
2. Betty Reardon, *Militarization, Security and Peace Education* (Valley Forge: United Ministries in Education, 1982), p. 16.
3. William Boyer, *Education for Annihilation* (Honolulu: Hogarth Press–Hawaii, 1972), p. 2.
4. George Henderson, *Education for Peace: Focus of Mankind* (ASCD Year Book, 1973), p. 15.
5. W. Boyer, *op. cit.*, p. 27.
6. Karl Von Clausewitz, *On War* (Baltimore: Penguin Books, 1968), p. 119.
7. Clausewitz quoted in M. Walzer, *op. cit.*, p. 23.
8. *Ibid.*
9. W. Boyer, *op. cit.*, p. 27.
10. M. Walzer *op. cit.* p. 32.
11. Nikolai Berdyaev, *Slavery and Freedom* (New York: Charles Scribner's Sons, 1944), p. 156.
12. Jonathan Schell, *The Fate of the Earth* (New York: Avon Books, 1982), p. 37.
13. *Ibid.,,* p. 45.
14. *Ibid.,* One megaton means the equivalent of one million tons of TNT.
15. *Ibid.*
16. Morton Grodzins and Eugene Rabinowitch, *The Atomic Age: Scientists in National and World Afairs* (New York: Basic Books, 1963), p. 45.

17. *Ibid.*, p. 93.
18. Bruce Russett, *The Prisoners of Insecurity* (San Francisco: W. H Freeman & Co., 1983), pp. 6–17.
19. Robert K. Musil, "Teaching in a Nuclear Age", *Teachers College Record*, (Vol. 84, No. 1 Fall 1982), p. 79.
20. *Ibid.*
21. Douglas Sloan, "Toward an Education for a Living World", *Teachers College Record, op. cit.*, p, 2.
22. *Ibid.*
23. T. W. Adorno *et al.*, *The Positivist Dispute in German Sociology* New York: Harper and Row, 1976).
24. John M. Broughton and Martha K. Zahaykevich, "The Peace Movement Threat", *Teachers College Record, op. cit.*, p. 154.
25. Herbert Marcuse, *One Dimensional Man* (Boston: Beacon Press, 1964).
26. National Conference of Catholic Bishops, *The Challenge of Peace. God's Promise and Our Response* (A Pastoral Letter on War and Peace, 1983), p. 3 (hereafter called Pastoral Letter 1983).
27. *Ibid.*, p. 21.
28. M. Walzer, *op. cit.*, p. 21.
29. Hugo Grotius, *Prolegomena to the Law of War and Peace*, Trans. Francis Kelsey (New York: Bobbs-Merrill Co., 1957).
30. Pastoral Letter 1983, *op. cit.*, p. 26.
31. *Ibid.*, p. 27.
32. Betty Reardon, *Militarization, Security and Peace Education, op. cit.*, p. 33.
33. *Ibid.*
34. B. Russett, *op. cit.*, p. 24.
35. Paul Ramsey in Michael Walzer, *Just and Unjust Wars, op. cit.*, p. 279.
36. Joseph Fahey, "Pax Christi", in Thomas A. Shannon, *War or Peace: The Search for New Answers* (Maryknoll, New York: Orbis Books, 1980), p. 70.
37. *Ibid.*
38. Bryan Hehir, "The Just-War Ethic" in T. Shannon, *Ibid.* p. 28.
39. David Hollenbach, *Nuclear Ethics* (New York: Paulist Press, 1983) p. 82.
40. *Ibid.*, p. 7.
41. *Ibid.* p. 13.
42. Lewis Coser, *The Functions of Social Conflict* (New York: The Free Press, 1956), p. 8.
43. Kenneth Boulding, "The Power of Nonconflict", *Journal of Social Issues*, (Vol. 33, No. 1, 1977).
44. Joan Bondurant, *Conquest of Violence* (Berkeley: University of California, 1969), pp. 16–33.
45. Martin Luther King, *Stride Toward Freedom* (New York: Harper and Bros., 1958).
46. Robert Woito, *To End War: A New Approach to International Conflict* (New York: The Pilgrim Press, 1982), p. 419.

47.   Severyn T. Bruyn and Paula M. Rayman, *Nonviolent Action and Social Change* (New York: Irvington Publishers, 1981), p. 24.
48.   *Ibid.*
49.   M. M. Thomas, *Ideological Quest Within Christian Commitment* (Madras: The Christian Literature Society, 1983), p. 48.
50.   Gene Sharp, *The Politics of Nonviolent Action* (Boston: Porter Sargent Publishers, 1873), pp. xii–xiv.
51.   Staughton Lynd, *Nonviolence in America: A Documentary History* (New York: The Bobbs-Merrill Co., 1966), p. xvii.
52.   Johan Galtung, "Violence, Peace and Peace Research," *Journal of Peace Research* (1968), pp. 5–6.
53.   Dinanath Tendulkar, *Mahatma: Life of Mohanadas K. Gandhi.* 8 Volumes. (New Delhi: Government of India, 1960–63), Vol. 1.
54.   T. S. Eliot quoted in Robert M. Brown, *Making Peace in the Global Village* (Philadelphia: The Westminster Press, 1981), p. 17.

CHAPTER 3

The Ethics of Nuclear Deterrence: a Religious Perspective

ROBERT J. NASH
University of Vermont

Is it possible for a Christian to believe in, indeed actively espouse, a policy of nuclear deterrence and still remain a believer in Christian principles? Several contemporary pacifists hold that a policy of nuclear deterrence is clearly evil. For example, Joseph Fahey, a member of Pax Christi, believes that deterrence is a "morally bankrupt philosophy" whose continued development will "not prevent war but in fact will cause it."[1] He reasons that a doctrine of deterrence is based on a number of false assumptions, many of them immoral: 1) that the only way nations can settle differences is through the threat of violence. 2) that there will always be hostility among the superpowers precluding any hope of reconciliation. 3) that a military response is the only way to resist injustice, rather than through diplomatic, political and economic initiatives. 4) that armed strength alone will produce national security. 5) that the end justifies the means. 6) that possession of nuclear weapons does not ipso facto guarantee their use. 7) that the Cold War is merely a symptom of deterrence and not its cause.[2] Fahey believes that in light of the entire corpus of Catholic teaching, no Catholic can legitimately support the Salt II treaty because it endorses the doctrine of deterrence, a "mutually assured destruction" philosophy, which genuine Christians can only find abhorrent.

A non–pacifist proponent of just–war theory, Paul Ramsey, as early as 1963, has stated strongly that "it is never right to do wrong that good may come of it. Nuclear weapons have only added to this perennial truth the footnote: it can never do *any good* to do wrong that good may come of it. Neither is it right to *intend* to do wrong that good may come of it. If deterrence rests upon intending massive retaliation, it is clearly wrong no matter how much peace results."[3] Ramsey believes that a reliance on nuclear weapons for deterrence hypothetically commits Christians (as well as others) to murder; if this is true, then a policy of nuclear deterrence can only be wrong, "can never be anything but wickedness."[4] Ramsey's overarching moral principle is a Christian one: if an action is morally wrong, it is wrong to intend to do it. (Ironically, in spite of Ramsey's cogent statement in the first part of his book as to the ipso facto evil of any policy of nuclear deterrence based on an intention to use those weapons, he ends his analysis with a defense of nuclear deterrence which he believes is "morally do–able." I will outline his justifications later.)

In a later statement, 1968, Ramsey contends that the Christian teaching to love one's neighbours, and the concomitant just–war principle that warfare must only be a last resort and when waged must be done compassionately, prudently, and proportionately, forces one to adopt a position of "nuclear pacifism." Because no nuclear war can ever meet the criteria of proportionality and non–combatant discrimination, a policy of nuclear deterrence is, at best, a morally ambiguous strategy, and at worst, a morally disingenuous one. Instead, Ramsey maintains that the United States should adopt a policy of nuclear pacifism: "standing for the possible justice of non–nuclear war ... and to foster and strengthen the means for conducting such a war successfully without resort to nuclear weapons (plan to surrender rather than go to nuclears)."[5]

I wish to explore in this chapter the ethics of nuclear deterrence and the implications for Christians in the 1980's. My analysis will be both historical and descriptive. Because I will focus my analysis on Catholic thinkers predominantly during the last twenty–five years, the content and spirit of my paper will reflect a strong Catholic emphasis (although not exclusively so). For whatever its weaknesses, though, such an orientation will allow me to sharpen the scope of my analysis in a more manageable way.

Richard A. McCormick S. J. raises what he believes are the three main moral questions of deterrence: 1) Does mere possession with no intention to use factually deter? 2) Is it possible to possess weapons which do deter without intending (conditionally) to use them?[6] 3) Is it possible to threaten the use of nuclear weapons as a deterrent policy without intending to use them? And J. Bryan Hehir has identified three morally "insoluble dilemmas" which have emerged in the last twenty–five years in the writings on nuclear deterrence: first, the issue that deterrence appears to be specifically forbidden by traditional Christian morality on the grounds that to intend to do evil is inseparable from the actual doing of evil; and because a policy of deterrence is based on an intention (sooner or later, stated or unstated) to unleash a nuclear response, then deterrence is ipso facto immoral. Second, the issue that it could very well be the threat of nuclear retaliation which has, in fact, prevented the use of nuclear weapons for the last thirty years. Therefore, to condemn a deterrence policy out–right because of the evil intent involved may be to accept a greater evil (possible nuclear war in the wake of unilateral disarmament) than the lesser one which is "a threat which remains unfulfilled." And, third, the issue that any radical or unilateral move to disarm or to build up could produce a "destabilizing" effect on the strategic balance, and increase the chance that deterrence will fail; thus, the moral problem becomes not the threat of nuclear weapons but the use of them.[7]

We will see, in the analysis which follows, that the above dilemmas have produced three kinds of responses over the years to the morality of nuclear deterrence: 1) nuclear pacifism and a condemnation of deterrence, 2) limited nuclear use and acceptance of deterrence, and 3) a prohibition of use but a toleration of deterrence, at least over the short run.[8]

These categories will constitute the major format for the chapter. And as a preliminary response to the question of whether a Christian can sincerely subscribe to a policy of nuclear deterrence in the eighties, the conclusion one reaches after a review of some of the major thinkers in the field is that the third position above appears to be in the ascendancy: prohibition of use but a toleration of a nuclear deterrence policy, until the world powers begin to scrap their arsenals.

Early Church Thinking on Nuclear Deterrence

In 1967, W. V. O'Brien's *Nuclear War: Deterrence and Morality* provided a brief, historical analysis of Papal thinking on the ethics of nuclear deterrence. Early in the book, the author asks the basic moral question which guides his investigations: "Does morality permit the continuance of the nuclear deterrent balance of terror, requiring as it does the credible willingness to wage the nuclear war that none of the nuclear powers wants to wage and which the deterrent is designed to prevent?"[9] (In a sense, this is still the quintessential moral question on deterrence. J. Bryan Hehir, in 1980, contends that "the unique moral problem posed by nuclear weapons is not the *use* of them but the *threat* to use them in a policy of deterrence.[10]) O'Brien's brief review of Papal response to this question is useful.

It must be remembered that the Papal response throughout the fifties and early sixties to the nuclear issue was from within the geopolitical context of stringent anti–Communist sentiment, a sentiment which dominated deterrence policies. Also, while there was abundant discussion on international law and organization in international circles, there was only a modicum of dialogue on the morality of nuclear war. Thus, Pope Pius XII, in 1954, condemned "total war" except in "self–defense." Pius permitted the use of atomic, chemical, and bacteriological warfare but warned that their use should be avoided if at all possible; however, when these weapons are used, they should be employed only within "clear and rigorous" limits (presumably just–war principles), and only for self–defense. While no Pope except Pius XII has explicitly endorsed nuclear warfare since, it is interesting to note that several theologians have. (I will refer to a few of these later.)

Pope John XXIII, in Pacem in Terris, did not openly confront the issue of nuclear deterrence. Although he did not condemn nuclear war outright as immoral, he did assert that nuclear war was unreasonable, and that nations ought to move toward arms control and disarmament. In Mater et Magistra, John observed that "vast human energies and gigantic resources were being employed for destructive rather than constructive purposes." He again condemned the "disproportionate share of revenue" going toward the world–wide build–up of armaments. Vatican II did not openly confront the issue of nuclear deterrence but it did prohibit "total war" and genocide. John's major accomplishment in the late fifties was to break away from the militant anti–Communism of the Church in order to argue for a climate of reconciliation.

Pope Paul VI's 1965 Address to the United Nations included the clause, "no more war, war never again." Paul made a case for disarmament and also condemned the use of nuclear weapons. But, consistent with previous Church teaching on the topic of just war, he asserted that defensive arms were still necessary because self–defense is morally required of all Christians. What most of the early Papal statements have in common, then, is their reinforcement of the just–war principle that a state has a right, indeed a moral obligation, to legitimate defense. Also, Vatican II's Gaudium et Spes argues for a step–by–step approach to nuclear disarmament – gradual, controlled, and guaranteed – even while it excoriates the use of nuclear weapons, based on the principles of proportionality and discrimination. Vatican II did not openly address the issue of nuclear deterrence; it did prohibit genocide and total wars, while endorsing the principle of legitimate self–defense and reiterating Church support for jus ad bellum criteria. While the Papal statements as a whole provide little in the way of explicit policy proposals, they do reflect a political realism regarding the issue of disarmament; and they all make an attempt, no matter how rudimentary, at fostering some type of reconciliation between the super powers.[11]

The Ethics of Limited Use and Deterrence

O'Brien, in 1967, defines deterrence as "a policy of maintaining the capability to do things which a just nation ought not and would not do."[12] He recognizes that just–war theory is fast becoming inapplicable in the nuclear age because of three new conditions: 1) the impersonal nature of modern warfare. 2) non–combatants were now seen as legitimate objects of attack (World War II bombing of cities). 3) the increasing unlikeliness of discrimination in the jus in bello use of nuclear weapons. Despite his skepticism about the applicability of just–war theory in the modern world, however, he remained equally skeptical over the approach of "total pacifists" who eschewed all intentional killing as immoral. O'Brien, like many of his colleagues in the sixties, wrestles with the reality that a nuclear war would probably never be just because of the dangers of escalation, disproportionality, non–combatant deaths and massive collateral damage; but he is even less satisfied with pacifistic exhortations for the United States to eliminate unilaterally both nuclear arms and deterrence policies, relinquish national sovereignty, and work towards creating an international community.[13]

For O'Brien, a policy of unilateral disarmament is unrealistic, immoral, and irresponsible. Such a policy is unrealistic because of the widespread possibilities of cheating and other violations. It is immoral because it rules out a policy of nuclear deterrence, and a "controlled balance of power," necessary if the world is to remain at peace. And it is irresponsible because in a world of suspicions, hostilities and ambitions, scrupulous attention to national security is the only way to prevent the ultimate nuclear conflagration. Life in a world of garrison states must proceed "under the umbrella of nuclear deterrence."[14] In summary, O'Brien's cautious position (in 1967) is that limited nuclear war must remain a possibility, if a policy of nuclear deterrence is to have any realistic impact. Limited nuclear war is accepted only if there is no first use by the United States; no counter–city warfare; and the principle of proportionality is carefully upheld. O'Brien does not hold that the principle of discrimination (not allowing the killing of non–combatants or other collateral damages) is an absolute. In some cases, it can be overridden by an appeal to legitimate self–defense.[15]

In an even earlier statement, in 1963, Paul Ramsey, a Protestant ethicist, argues that a policy of nuclear deterrence and the remote possibility of limited nuclear use is moral under the following three conditions: 1) "Counter–forces" warfare is an acceptable threat mainly because it is highly unlikely that a nuclear war can be so appropriately focused. Ramsey reasons that one can "morally intend" and be "conditionally willing" to engage in such a limited war, depending on the conditions, because the very intention to deter in this fashion is to be oneself similarly deterred. In a sense, then, nuclear warfare is a design for a war which is inherently self–limiting upon rational decision makers. 2) "There may be sufficient deterrence in the subjectively unintended consequence of the mere possession of nuclear weapons."[16] Ramsey reasons that, no matter what the United States says, the enemy is always going to be worried about its cities being destroyed, even though we publicly declare again and again that our targets are enemy forces only. Thus, the weapons themselves will have a powerful deterrent effect. The use of this unintended effect is moral for Ramsey only if the United States continually renounces morally repugnant means (jus in bello) to wage just wars (jus ad bellum): only just or counter–forces war is morally acceptable. And because the "spiral of reciprocal expectations" is a built–in dampener (no matter what we say), Ramsey concludes that the enemy will be similarly constrained not to use its nuclears.

And 3) It is moral to present the *appearance* of attacking cities with nuclears, not the *actuality*. For Ramsey, it is rigidly moralistic to censure even the intention to make do–able what is unthinkable; rather, the moralist must always be careful about irresponsibly disparaging the "argument from bluff" to a morally licit form of deterrence. The most moral policy of deterrence is one which requires an "ethic of restraint, limits and silence,"[17] all the while working toward the implementation of a policy of counter–forces warfare;

this policy alone will afford the deterrence necessary to maintain the peace. Thus, for Ramsey, a public policy of counter–forces warfare plus political diplomacy and restraint is simply good just–war doctrine applied to the problem of nuclear deterrence.

Finally, Francis X. Winters, S. J., argues that nuclear arms can be an acceptable moral instrument of politics, if they can be used defensively—to prevent, diminish, or repel an act of unjust aggression—provided that they do not bring about collateral (intentional) destruction of the society. For Winters, the moral question is: "Short of actual retaliatory strikes against an aggressing society, are there other, legitimate, defensive purposes for which nuclear weapons might be used?"[18] His answer is that nuclear warfare and the threats of nuclear deterrence are morally justified, if and only if the principles of discrimination (Are civilians immune from intentional attack? Surrender is preferable to deliberate targeting of non–combatants), proportionality (is there a scrupulous balancing on a moral scale of costs and benefits, means and ends) and political utility (is there a rigorous balancing on a political scale of costs and benefits, means and ends) are applied. If all of the above conditions hold, and the use of nuclear weapons is related to some achievable political purpose – namely, the defense of a society's internal or external relations – then a policy of nuclear deterrence, based on the real possibility of limited use, is a moral one.

The Ethics of Nuclear Pacifism and a No-Deterrence Policy

In 1965, Justus Lawler, a nuclear pacifist, rejected the position of those thinkers cited above who believe that a limited nuclear war is possible. Lawler argues that a policy of deterrence is morally bankrupt because it implicitly depends on the possibility of use to carry out its implied threats; nuclear use is ipso facto morally reprehensible. For Lawler, a policy of counter–forces warfare is unrealistic because in actuality military installations are located in and around cities and other population centers. Also, it is highly unlikely that any nation on the brink of defeat will not retaliate against cities, if it has a nuclear capacity. And because war is rarely a rational endeavor, a policy of mutually assured destruction will simply not work; when vital interests are threatened, anything goes.[19] Both nuclear threat and use (which alone gives the threat credibility) are immoral because: 1) weapons themselves are immoral. 2) The world–wide psychological strains precipitated by decades of living on the edge of a holocaust only intensify international disharmony and destabilization. 3) Jus in bello means (nuclears) are immoral because they are always non–discriminating and disproportionate in their consequences. And 4) Classical just–war theory is an anachronism because it simply cannot justify nuclear war. It can only realistically justify pacifism in a nuclear age.

For Lawler, the nuclear pacifist qua Christian must realize that it is illicit to deter an enemy by threatening to wage war with illicit means. It is simply immoral (as well as unreasonable) to manufacture and possess weapons for which there can be no conceivable military targets. Any use of nuclears constitutes an act of genocide. A reasonable defense is justified but this defense does not justify the stockpiling of weapons capable of total annihilation of the enemy. Rather, for Lawler, the moral responsibilities of the nuclear pacifist are to: 1) Know and publicly assert the facts about nuclear warfare and their moral consequences. 2) Instead of supporting a suicidal deterrence policy, the Christian should advocate techniques for reducing tensions between the power blocs: these would include arms reduction, adequate inspection systems, readjustments in the warfare economy and foster movement toward a world federation. 3) Work to implement the religious and social programs in Mater et Magistra and Pacem in Terris.[20]

At least one theologian, G. Grisez, holds the extreme position on nuclears that not even the moral legitimacy of national self–defense warrants the use of a nuclear weapon; neither does it warrant the use of a deterrence policy. Grisez reasons syllogistically that because it is always morally reprehensible to intend, even conditionally, to kill the innocent (which certainly would occur in a nuclear war) and because deterrent policies always involve this reprehensible intent (no matter how obfuscatory the apologetics), therefore, a deterrent policy can only be morally wrong. Grisez does not believe that it is possible to deter with mere possession — with no intent to use — because it is only the grisly prospect of millions of non–combatant deaths which gives a deterrence policy any bite. He also rejects the policy of toleration (a temporary toleration of nuclear weapons may be morally acceptable if a nation works toward disarmament, arms limitation, reduction and abolition) because, in effect, such a policy merely perpetuates and intensifies the arms race, even while it attempts to wind it down and to terminate it. It transforms toleration into a justification for deterrence and the very nuclears it is forsworn to abolish. And, finally, Grisez maintains that because non–combatant immunity is an absolute moral principle, never to be overridden, any attempt to justify the killing of innocents on the grounds of proportionality is ipso facto immoral. The judgment (that non–combatant immunity is a sacrosanct principle) must always determine the choice (whether or not to possess, threaten, use nuclear weapons). The answer is clear: possession, threat, and use of nuclears is morally forbidden.[21]

Finally, the pacifist, Gordon C. Zahn, goes several steps beyond even Grisez in his repudiation of nuclear weapons and deterrence policies. He believes that the current debate on nuclear deterrence is the theologian's equivalent of the Rubik cube: "a dazzling display of intellectual dexterity with nothing to show for it when it is done."[22] Zahn advocates an awareness of dependency and a spirit of abandonment on the part of the world's super–powers to the will of God. For Zahn, abandonment is always tempered, not by fatalism, but by the confidence that ultimately good will prevail, in God's own time and way. It is only through the theory and practice of non–violence, and the confidence in the Scriptural promises that God's power is salvific, and that "the gates of hell will not prevail", that the world will gain greater security than reliance on a policy of nuclear deterrence could ever proffer. The dismal alternative, Zahn believes, is a world which has progressed from "thinking the unthinkable about doing the undoable ... to the point where the war Thomas

Merton warned would be a crime 'second only to the Crucifixion' is being discussed as a rational option."[23] The only moral option for Christians, then, is to refrain from taking part in any kind of war. Pacifistic Christians should work toward multi–lateral disarmament and peaceful solutions to international conflicts; refuse to subsidize or in any way engage in the manufacture of instruments of war; speak out against military conscription and training; encourage the practice of conscientious objection among Catholic youth; and publicly repudiate all policies of nuclear deterrence, including possession, production, and preparation to use.[24]

The Ethics of Deterrence With Prohibition of Use

By far, the most representative position in the debate among Christian thinkers today is the position that while nuclear use is forbidden, a policy of deterrence can be tolerated. A non–theological writer, Michael Walzer, lays out the case for nuclear deterrence in an especially compelling way. His argument is cautiously pragmatic in the sense that deterrence is, at this time, the only realistic alternative to be preferred in a world of "sovereign and suspicious states." [25] Walzer claims that although tactical and counter–forces nuclear war loosely meet the formal requirements of jus in bello, such a war makes no moral sense whatever, because of the possible devastating, unintended consequences of "limited". strikes. Therefore, we are left with the paradox that "nuclear weapons are politically and militarily unusable only because and insofar as we can plausibly threaten to use them in some ultimate way." [26] And such threats are clearly immoral. Walzer's solution to the paradox is an agonizing one : because nuclear war is morally unacceptable, the super–powers have a moral responsibility to seek out ways to prevent it. And because deterrence is a bad way, other solutions must be sought. However, for the present time, deterrence, for all its potential and actual criminality, falls under the realm of necessity. "Supreme emergency" forces the world to adopt a flawed political and military solution. Our moral mandate, according to Walzer, is to take risks in order to escape the realm of necessity because this realm is never a stable position, subject as it is to constant historical change. [27]

In a brilliant examination of the ethics of nuclear deterrence — what he calls "the hardest question" — David Hollenbach, S. J. concludes that policies advanced in the name of deterrence should actually decrease the probability of war rather than increase it. Hollenbach is clearly against the pacifist argument that nuclear armaments and deterrence policies ought to be dismantled immediately, regardless of consequences. He is especially critical of Grisez's conclusion that unilateral nuclear disarmament is the only moral option for Christians. According to Hollenbach, such a proposal "does not advance a policy position which assures with any certainty the protection of the lives or freedoms of innocent human beings." [28] Hollenbach is less critical of pacifists such as Zahn because Zahn's pacifism is not dependent on political–military judgments; instead, Zahn is realistic enough to know that his ideal world will only be realized in the city of God, and not in the flawed city of man. In the end, Zahn is a mystic, a meta–historical visionary whose dream transcends human history in the flesh–and–blood, here–and–now.

Hollenbach eschews any attempt to reach a moral judgment about the ethics of nuclear deterrence in the abstract; rather, he maintains that because the nuclear presence is a reality, what must be subjected to ethical scrutiny are specific defense postures involving diverse weapons systems, targeting doctrines, procurement programs, and strategic master concepts. Both normative and prudential political judgments will be necessary. Hollenbach asks that any new policy proposal on deterrence must make nuclear war less likely than the policies presently in effect. [29] Thus, deployment of the new Pershing II missiles in Europe fails the test for a morally legitimate deterrent because they may have the consequence of provoking the Soviet Union to adopt a "launch on warning" policy for their own missiles. And because computers would be making the fateful decisions, the risk of accidental nuclear war would thereby be raised. [30]

The above author also stipulates that any new policy proposal on deterrence should promote the possibility of arms reduction and disarmament. In fact, what is happening today is, that in preparing for tactical nuclear war in Europe, the

United States is constructing a variety of new weapon systems including Pershing II, Cruise missiles, the MX, stealth bombers, and even satellites and orbital space stations capable of conducting nuclear war. Innovations in science and technology now appear to be setting deterrence policy, leading that policy around "by the nose," so to speak. Moral questions are becoming subordinated to complicated war–games scenarios. And the hopes for arms reduction and disarmament are rapidly diminishing.

The question still remains, nevertheless: Is any credible nuclear deterrence really possible at all, if one takes the a priori position that use is immoral? Again, Hollenbach reminds us that, at the moment, thousands of nuclear weapons are already deployed and ready for use by the super–powers. The question is not an abstract one as long as one distinguishes between the will to deter and the will to use nuclear weapons. This distinction prevents deterrence strategies from becoming "war–fighting" strategies.[31] The will to deter minimizes nuclear threats by working toward disarmament; the will to use maximizes the possibility of actually fighting a nuclear war as well as opening up the future to an endless arms race. Deterrence and disarmament, therefore, become complementary concepts. And the Christian's responsibility is to keep public opinion focused on the moral issues of war prevention and arms reduction, rather than on arms buildups which actually weaken national security by increasing the risk of nuclear war, either through accident or design.[32]

J. Bryan Hehir, in 1983, comments that the topic of deterrence is "the key political and moral issue of the nuclear age." He briefly traces the history of the topic in the period from 1978 to 1983, culminating in the publication of the Bishops' *Challenge of Peace* (May 3, 1983). Cardinal Krol's Congressional testimony in 1979 served as a catalyst on the topic of toleration: deterrence is to be tolerated only if it moves the super-powers toward effective arms control and disarmament. Pope John Paul II, in a message to the United Nations, 1982, judged deterrence, "based on balance, and as a step toward progressive disarmament" as morally acceptable. In August, 1982, John

Paul warned that nuclear deterrence can never be a "final goal" or an "appropriate and secure means" for safeguarding peace. And the Bishops' final judgment of deterrence in *The Challenge of Peace* is one of "strictly conditioned moral acceptance."[33]

The Pastoral Letter finds morally unacceptable a policy of deterrence which intends to kill the innocent as part of a strategy of deterring nuclear war. A targeted strike on civilian centers, either intended or unintended, must be morally judged by the principle of proportionality (assessment of consequences) as well as by the principle of non–combatant immunity (assessment of intention). Also, a counter–forces targeting strategy is deceptive in the sense that it conveys the mistaken notion that nuclear war is subject to precise rational and moral limits. The Bishops' Letter, therefore, recommends the following moral propositions regarding deterrence: 1) a policy of nuclear deterrence should exist only to prevent the use of nuclear weapons by others, not to plan for retaliatory and even winnable strikes. 2) "Sufficiency" to deter is the only moral objective; the quest for nuclear "superiority" is clearly immoral. 3) Deterrence is morally justified only as a step toward progressive disarmament. Specific recommendations in the Pastoral include the opposition to first–use, and first–strike weapons (MX and Pershing II missiles), strategic planning and short–range nuclear weapons. In spite of its specific prohibitions and recommendations, the Bishops want it understood that any use of nuclear weapons is probably morally unacceptable.[34]

Finally, in a concise statement, Pierce S. Corden points out the archaic dimensions of just–war theory in a nuclear age. He believes that the "magnitude of destructive power" of nuclear weapons raises questions about the currently dominant political ideology in the United States. He argues that deterrence as a "balance of terror" destabilizes international relations rather than the opposite. He also specifies that technological innovations should be employed to *control* the production of nuclear weapons, not to *proliferate* them. And as more and more countries develop a nuclear capacity, and with it the right to formulate their own deterrence policies, the greater the risk becomes of war by accident or design. Hence, the existence of nuclears probably has made the concept of state independence and national sovereignty an anachronism.[35]

Conclusion

In what sense then can a Christian find a policy of nuclear deterrence morally acceptable ? Those who argue from a pacifistic position believe that deterrence raises significant moral questions for Christians. "Blessed are the peace–makers; for they shall be called the children of God." Many pacifists hold that the determination to be called "the children of God" is the only Christian solution to the nuclear agony. Zahn, for example, sees in the Bishops' Pastoral a "troubled ambivalence and a yearning for a compromise on essentially irreconcilable issues."[36] He advocates instead that Christians cultivate a "pacifist spirituality" which steadfastly resists the manufacture of instruments of death.

Those Christians who argue from a limited–use position, or from a prohibition–of–use position, sometimes share a cautious belief in the pragmatic, if not the moral, acceptability of deterrence. However, Richard McCormick succinctly summarizes the moral dilemmas of this position: "1) The possession of nuclear weapons is at the very best morally ambiguous, and therefore at best only tolerable. It may not even be that. 2) Such possession is tolerable only for the present and under certain conditions. 3) These conditions are: a firm resolve never to use nuclear weapons and a firm resolve to work immediately to assure their abolition, in law and in fact. 4) While unilateral disarmament may not be a clear moral mandate, unilateral steps toward multilateral disarmament certainly are."[37]

The special difficulty for Christians is that norms of Christian morality are rarely absolute; at best they are prima facie principles which require prudential judgment for concrete decision–making. The principles of just–war theory are helpful, but only to a point. In a nuclear age, the norms of just–war theory appear to be militarily and morally inoperative. All Christian principles must continually be interpreted in the light of present and future realities. Karl Barth, the Protestant theologian, remarked in 1959 that the Christian Churches' inability to take an unequivocal position against nuclear war was as great a theological failure as their reluctance to repudiate the rise of Nazism in Germany.[38] Today, this charge no longer applies. In part, the Bishops' Pastoral is evidence that Christian thinkers are taking a strong moral stand against the horrors of nuclear escalation. And Christian manuals such as Ronald Freund's, *What One Person Can Do To Help Prevent Nuclear War*, appear more and more frequently on the bookshelves.[39]

Further, a few critical analysts are attempting to de-mythologize the ideology of the national security state.[40] Writers such as Marek Thee and Michael T. Klare believe that the key to dismantling the nuclear super-structures is to expose the grip which militaristic and nationalistic attitudes have on people's minds. They advocate a kind of reeducation experience whereby people are helped to see how the ideology of militarism has been deeply ingrained in the society's training and indoctrination agencies. This attitude of militarism generates a kind of ethnocentrism, an "us vs. them" view of the world, which results in a society's uncritical support of political, economic, and social programs meant to maintain a country's view of itself as superior to the rest of the world. Today both the United States and the Soviet Union struggle to maintain their ranking as the world's two greatest super-powers by fostering such xenophobia.

The tragic result of international xenophobia is that together the United States and the Soviet Union stand for half of the world's military expenditures, and they command seventy percent of the world arms trade. This world-wide ideology of militarism and national security has produced a chain-reaction of nuclear escalations, military adventurism and sophisticated weapons development. And in the wake of excessive military spending, the social and economic problems of developing nations (and also of the super-powers) grow more and more alarming. The intent of this approach to reeducate people is to break the grip of the national security state on the hearts and minds of its people. Once this process has begun, peaceful steps can then be taken to turn theory into praxis and steps can then be taken to dismantle, step–by–step, the nuclear policies which are grounded in the all–pervasive ideology of militarism.

"I have called heaven and earth to record this day against you, that I have set before you life and death, a blessing and a curse : therefore choose life that both you and your children may live." (Deut. 30 : 19). The harvest of justice is sown in peace for those who cultivate peace" (James 3:18). Of all the material I studied to prepare for this paper, the two essays which moved me most deeply were Gordon C. Zahn's, "Pacifism and the Just War," and John C. Haughey's S. J. "Disarmament of the Heart," in the recently published *Catholics and Nuclear War*. Each thinker is eager to solve the "theologian's equivalent of the Rubik cube" for those Christians who may be dazzled by the erudition often displayed by both proponents and adversaries of deterrence policies in a nuclear age. At a time in the debate when one norm is countervailed by another norm, and when one argument is nullified by another, Zahn and Haughey, each in his own unique way, argue for an authentic abandonment to Divine Providence which recognizes both our powerlessness as well as our responsibility to become co–creators with God in order to work for greater love and justice in the world. Each one of us must listen with a humble and open heart to God's word. [41]

The two thinkers prepare the way for individual Christians to listen to God's word with a kind of "obediential faith." Each writer reminds us that Christ is our basic peace, but it takes an active, determined and probing faith to hear His word. The call for Christ's reconciling power in our lives begins "in the daily, hourly experience of hostility or resentment or any of the negative emotions." As Christians, we must continually break down the walls which we have erected between man and man. The walls are myriad: consumerism, nationalism, elitism, militarism, racism, sexism and nuclearism. As Haughey so eloquently writes: "Since it is unlikely that any of us will be called to Geneva to negotiate an arms accord, it would be better to begin now with the walls that are closer, those in us and between us." [42]

Notes

1.   Joseph Fahey, "Pax Christi," in *War Or Peace?* ed. Thomas A. Shannon (Maryknoll, New York: Orbis Books, 1982), p. 70.

2.   Ibid., p. 70.

3.   Paul Ramsey, *The Limits of Nuclear War: Thinking About the Do-Able and the Un-Do-Able* (New York: The Council on Religion and International Affairs, 1963), p. 46.

4.   Ibid., p. 47.

5.   Paul Ramsey, *The Just War: Force and Political Responsibility* (New York: Scribner's Sons, 1968), p. 272.

6.   Richard A. McCormick, S. J., "Nuclear Deterrence and the Problem of Intention: A Review of the Position," in *Catholics and Nuclear War* (New York: Crossroad, 1983), p. 178.

7.   J. Bryan Hehir, "The Just-War Ethic and Catholic Theology: Dynamics of Change and Continuity," in *War Or Peace,* pp. 27–28.

8.   Ibid., p. 28.

9.   W. V. O'Brien; *Nuclear War: Deterrence and Morality* (Westminster, Maryland: (1967), p. 16.

10. J. Bryan Hehir, p. 28.

11. W. V. O'Brien, pp. 32–73.

12. Ibid., p. 58.

13. W. V, O'Brien, pp. 91–98.

14. Ibid., p. 98.

15. W. V. O'Brien, *Nuclear War: Deterrence and Morality,* pp. 91–98.

16. Paul Ramsey, *The Limits of Nuclear War,* p. 49.

17. Ibid., p. 53.

18. Francis X. Winters, S. J., "Ethics, Diplomacy, and Defense," in *Ethics and Nuclear Strategy?* ed. Harold P. Ford and Francis X. Winters, S. J. (Maryknoll, New York: Orbis Books, 1977), p. 41.

19. Justus George Lawler, *Nuclear War: The Ethic, the Rhetoric, the Reality* (Westminster, Maryland; The Newman Press, 1965), pp. 1–20.

20. Ibid., p. 45.

21. G. Grisez, "Moral Implications of a Nuclear Deterrent," *Center Journal,* 2. 1982–83, pp. 9–24.

22. Gordon C. Zahn, "Pacifism and the Just War," in *Catholics and Nuclear War* (New York: Crossroad, 1983), p. 130.

23. Ibid., p. 124.

24. Ibid., pp. 126–127.

25. Michael Walzer, *Just and Unjust Wars* (New York: Basic Books, 1977), p. 274.

26. Ibid., p. 278.

27. Ibid., pp. 269–283.

28. David Hollenbach, S. J., *Nuclear Ethics*: *A Christian Moral Argument* (Ramsey, New Jersey: Paulist Press, 1983), p. 71.

29. Ibid., p. 75.

30. Ibid., pp. 47–62.

31. David Hollenback, S. J., *Nuclear Ethics*, p. 83.

32. Ibid., p. 85.

33. *The Challenge of Peace: God's Promise and Our Response*. A Pastoral Letter on War and Peace. National Conference of Catholic Bishops, May 3, 1983.

34. Ibid., pp. 51–62.

35. Pierce S. Corden, "Ethics and Deterrence: Moving Beyond the Just-War Tradition," in *Ethics and Nuclear Strategy?*, pp. 168–173.

36. Quoted in Robert F. Drinan, *Beyond the Nuclear Freeze* (New York: The Seabury Press, 1983), p. 113.

37. Richard A. McCromick, S. J. *Catholics and Nuclear War*, p. 180.

38. Robert F. Drinan, *Beyond the Nuclear Freeze*, pp. 151–152.

39. Ronald Freund, *What One Person Can Do To Help Prevent Nuclear War* (Mystic, Connecticut: Twenty-Third Publications, 1983).

40. Marek Thee, "Militarism and Militarization in International Relations," in *The Security Trap: Arms Race, Militarism and Disarmament. A Concern for Christians* ed. Jose-Antonio Viera Gallo (IDOC: 1977); Michael T. Klare, "Militarism: the Issues Today," in *The Security Trap*.

41. Gordon C. Zahn, "Pacifism and the Just War," in *Catholics and Nuclear War;* John C. Haughey, S. J., "Disarmament of the Heart", *Catholics and Nuclear War*, pp. 217–28.

42. John C. Haughey, S. J., p. 227.

CHAPTER 4

Swords into Plowshares:
From Military Spending to Economic Conversion

KEVIN J. CASSIDY

Fairfield University

Economic conversion is the planned use of military production facilities for the manufacture of civilian products. It is the attempt to transfer technical skills, machinery and capital currently committed to war preparation to the production of socially useful items. It is the contemporary effort to fulfill the biblical dictum of Isaiah to beat swords into plowshares.

Economic conversion is fundamental to the struggle to create a new international order based on peace and economic justice. War is caused in part by the excessive production and sale of military weaponry. Not only does this situation increase the likelihood of conflict between the superpowers, it also facilitates local wars among Third World nations who purchase their arms from the developed countries. It is not sufficient, however, to demand an end to excessive military spending. It is also necessary to provide a production alternative, to demonstrate how defense plants can be *converted* to civilian production. Such a transfer is entirely possible, as this chapter will indicate, and it is also healthier for the economies of weapons producing nations. In itself, military spending generates inflationary pressures in these countries and requires the commitment of many scientists and engineers who would otherwise devote themselves to advancement of civilian industry. These problems will be discussed at length in the first part of this chapter.

If conversion is important to building international peace, it is also necessary for the establishment of economic justice. Many Third World nations have severe economic and social problems caused by the inability to meet the basic human needs of their people. A major factor in this situation is the excessive spending on armaments by the political leadership of these countries. Their leaders find ready suppliers of military hardware in the developed nations who are pleased to reduce their balance of payments problems by exporting arms to the Third World countries. The result is the inability to establish just societies in these nations. The first part of this chapter will also consider this problem.

Part II of the chapter will examine the process of economic conversion itself as a practical alternative to military spending particularly in the effort to create jobs. Successful examples of conversion will be cited and an analysis will be made of the steps necessary in the conversion process as well as the formidable obstacles that it faces. Finally, a brief survey will be presented of the major legislative proposals in the United States to encourage conversion among military firms.

Part I. Military Spending

Inflation

The most fundamental fact of military spending is that it creates inflationary pressures in the economy. It puts money into the hands of defense plant workers but does not expand the supply of goods available for purchase in the marketplace. As a result there are more dollars chasing fewer goods and prices are driven up. Moreover, military production uses a disproportionate number of skilled workers and pays them higher wages than are available in the civilian sector of the economy. The result is a shortage of skilled labor for the rest of the economy and an inflationary pressure on wages which in turn drives up the cost of products manufactured in civilian industry.

In addition, the military is the greatest single consumer of such vital resources as oil, coal and nuclear energy and a major consumer of steel, precious minerals and metals, water and land. The result is smaller–and therefore more expensive–quantities of these resources available for civilian production. Again, the effect is inflationary. The same is true for available credit. The federal government must borrow money in the open market to finance the military. This not only adds to the federal debt, it adds to the interest costs of servicing that debt and it bids up interest rates.[1] Credit is then more expensive for the producer of civilian goods–and everyone else as well–and that cost is inevitably passed on to the consumer.

Finally, owing to large–scale military spending abroad for various wars and for the maintenance of more than 300 bases on foreign soil, the U. S. has accumulated an immense balance of payments deficit that has additional inflationary consequences. Since 1970, the U. S. balance of payments has been in deficit because the U. S. has been putting more military money into the world economy than it gets back from foreign nations in trade of any sort. The result once again has been to bid up the cost of money in the united states, adding to the inflationary spiral.

Civilian Industry and Consumer Goods

Inflationary pressure is not the only serious drawback of massive military spending. Equally important is a negative impact on the competitive position of civilian industry in the world marketplace. Hence consumer goods are not available to people at a fair price. Nearly one–half of the American scientific and engineering work force works on military–related programs and over 60% of the entire federal research and development budget goes to the military.[2] As a result, this great pool of talent and money is unavailable to develop new civilian commercial designs. The effect is retardation in civilian manufacturing capabilities. While the U. S.

can produce the most sophisticated nuclear missiles on earth, it has fallen dramatically behind in the manufacture of electronic goods, radios, televisions, machine tools, shoes, clothing, automobiles and other manufactured items.[3]

Marion Anderson, an economist and author of numerous studies on this problem, puts the matter succinctly: "there is no mystery why the Germans, Japanese or Swedes have pulled equal to or ahead of us in steel, machine tools and electronics. Virtually all of their scientists and engineers are working on civilian technology".[4] In her annual *World Military and Social Expenditures*, Ruth Leger Sivard has pointed out that, "with a smaller research budget overall, the European countries nevertheless spent 45% more on civilian research than the U. S. did."[5] Sivard also argues this point in a broader comparative perspective:

> Among 10 developed countries for which historical data are available, the slowest growth in investment and manufacturing productivity has occurred in two countries (UK and US) where military expenditures are the highest in relation to GNP. The best investment and productivity record is in Japan, where the military to GNP ratio has been very low and productivity has grown at an amazing eight percent per year ... The poorest record may well be in the Soviet Union where the proportion of GNP devoted to military programs is higher than in the NATO countries, perhaps twice as high.[6]

The competitiveness of American goods is also adversely affected by the inflationary pressure on wages described earlier. Because there is a shortage of skilled workers in civilian industry due to their use in military production, wages must be increased for these workers in the civilian sector. This, of course, drives up the price of the country's products making them less competitive in the world marketplace.

Developing Nations

The impact of militarism is perhaps even greater on developing nations than on those responsible for military production. Because of their commitment to military manufacturing, the developed nations spend far less than they might on economic aid to the Third World. In 1982 the military expenditures of the developed countries (including the centrally planned) were 17 times larger than their extensions of aid to countries in need. [7]

Newly emerging nations often have large appetities for military hardware which the developed nations are only too ready to satisfy. This has had a significant impact on the ability of these young nations to meet their growing debts. As Sivard observes, "Among 25 countries which, since 1981 have had to negotiate to reschedule their debt, six had spent more than 1 billion U.S. Dollars each for arms imports in the five years preceding. All 25 rang up a bill of $ 11 billion for arms in that period." [8] Sivard goes on to point out that, "among 20 countries with the largest foreign debt, arms imports between 1976 and 1980 were equivalent to 20 percent of the increase in debt. In four of the 20 the value of arms imports was equal to 40 percent or more of the rise in debt in that period." [9]

The conclusion from these statistics should be obvious: many of the emerging nations are unable to meet the basic human needs of their citizens in part because of their purchases of military equipment. By investing so much in military hardware these countries cannot commit adequate funds to economic development including health, nutrition, education and other social resources. Without such development their citizens will not only fail to contribute social progress in their countries, but they will quickly become a danger rather than an asset to these societies.

The statistics on unmet human needs are truly staggering: 2,000,000,000 people live on incomes below 500 Dollars per year. Approximately 600,000,000 have no jobs or are less than fully employed. Moreover, 11,000,000 infants die before their first birthday; 450,000,000 people suffer from hunger and malnutrition and 120,000,000 children of school age have no school they can go to. While most sickness and disease in the Third World is attributed to unsafe water and poor sanitary conditions, 2,000,000,000 people do not have a dependable supply of safe water to drink. [10] The words of Pope Paul VI sum up the situation accurately: "the armaments race is an act of aggression which amounts to a crime for even when they are not used, by their cost alone, armaments kill the poor by causing them to starve." [11]

It is also important to remember the obvious fact that military exports to developing countries help to facilitate hostilities between these nations. American military exports have often been justified as necessary to redress military imbalances between rival developing nations. Yet rivals never synchronize their build–ups and perfect balances exist only on paper. Our assertive allies in the Third World often request weaponry that can overcome, and not merely match, the weapons of their rivals. This causes rivals to increase their arsenals still further, frequently by a request to the Soviet Union. The result is an increase in the likelihood of armed conflict between Third World nations and also a danger that actual hostilities might provoke a superpower confrontation.

Finally, it needs to be pointed out that military exports often go to repressive regimes in the Third World allowing them to continue their authoritarian and often violent rule. Fifty–six governments, or approximately one–half of the developing nations, are under military rule. Eighty percent of these 56 governments have used physical violence against their own citizens. [12] These are the countries most often cited by organizations like Amnesty International, The International Commission of Jurists, and the U. S. Commission on Human Rights for persistent reports of torture, assassination and arbitrary arrest. In many cases the continued existence of these regimes is made possible by military assistance from the developed nations.

Part II Economic Conversion

Conversion and Jobs

The previous pages have attempted to support the argument that military spending is bad for the economies of both developed and developing countries. It remains to consider the alternative to military production: economic conversion. This is particularly important because a substantial reduction in military spending could obviously put a considerable number of defense workers out of work in the developed countries. If these workers are not to be held hostage to the peace movement and the effort to establish new, more human priorities for the economy, then means must be found to provide them with employment that is appropriate to their skills and not dependent on military production. That is the fundamental purpose of economic conversion.

The strongest argument in favor of the conversion of military manufacturing to civilian industry is the weakness of defense production in providing jobs. A study by the U. S. Department of Labor's Bureau of Labor Statistics shows that for every billion spent in military contracting, that same billion, if spent in the commercial, civilian sector, would create 20,000 *more* jobs on the average. Specifically, the study indicates that a billion dollars spent in the defense sector creates approximately 75,000 jobs. In contrast, the same billion spent in state or local government employment would generate about 87,000 jobs; if spent in transportation, 92,000 jobs; in education, 187,000 jobs; in health and sanitation, 139,000 jobs. The study's conclusion makes the point clearly: "if the goal is to provide jobs and employment opportunities, then almost any category of civilian employment will produce more work for one billion dollars than does defense production."[13]

The major reason that military spending creates fewer jobs is that it is highly *capital intensive* rather than *labor intensive*. For the production of increasingly sophisticated weaponry, more complex and more expensive technology is required along with a greater concentration of highly skilled, highly paid engineers and technicians. Military production far exceeds civilian manufacturing in these high cost areas. In his thorough study of *The Defense Industry*, Jacques Gansler found that the ratio of production workers to the total work force in key defense industries is considerably less than in the U. S. industry as a whole.[14] On average, 90% of the jobs in U. S. industry are for production, but in the military sector, including such areas as guided missiles and electronic communication, only 30% of jobs go to production workers and in aircraft only 50%.[15]

A study done for the Machinists Union (IAM), one of the two major unions involved in military work, shows that in 30 states, IAM members suffer a net *loss* of job opportunities when military spending is high. There are today over 118,000 *fewer* jobs for IAM members in civilian industry because of the military budget. These are the civilian jobs foregone when people are heavily taxed to pay for the military and are unable to spend the money on their own needs. Machinists are overwhelmingly involved in the production of durable goods and services. These two categories are among the hardest hit when military spending is high.[16] Even IAM members who are currently employed on military projects suffer lessened job opportunities because, with fewer machinists' jobs available in the economy, a member who is dissatisfied with his present job, who wants to move or who wants to negotiate his wages upward, has just that much less opportunity to do so.

Moreover, military spending is particularly unhelpful to unskilled and semi–skilled workers. First, it employs few such workers. Secondly, it tends to discourage civilian industry, which makes greater use of these workers, from moving into an area dominated by military firms. The latter, using a large proportion of the educated and skilled workers, leave other industries without adequate supplies of these workers or require civilian industries to upgrade the salary scales to attract them. All of this has the effect of keeping civilian industry out of a defense–dependent region, thereby failing to diversify the regional economy. This lack of diversification severely restricts job possibilities for the unskilled and semi-skilled worker.

Conversion Possibilities

In light of the above it is hardly surprising that the IAM as well as the United Auto Workers (UAW), another union involved in defense work, have campaigned for a transfer of government funds from military production to the civilian budget. Some of the ways in which such a transfer could take place have been detailed in Philip Webre's study, *Jobs To People: Planning for Conversion to New Industries*. This study lists four key industries in need of upgrading or development. They are: railroads, mass transit, solid waste disposal and solar energy. Webre's research shows that investing $14.3 billion per year in these four industries would generate a total of 777,000 jobs per year. These would draw heavily on the skills which workers in military industries have developed and they would be working in a stable, expanding civilian market in contrast to the "boom and bust" cycle of military production.[17]

Webre's study is not the only one focusing on solar technology as a possibility for military conversion. The Centre for Economic Conversion, in its study *Creating Solar Jobs: Options for Military Workers and Communities*, has shown that highly defense – specific technicians and engineers, as well as machinists, craft workers and semi–skilled assembly workers, could be matched to jobs in the solar energy industry. This claim has been supported by the conversion of two California companies: Acurex Corporation and Varian Associates, located in Santa Clara County. These two firms, originally committed to a very high degree of military contracting, successfully converted to the production of solar and environmental technology.[18]

Two other California defense firms, Aerojet General in Sacramento and Lockheed Missiles and Space Co. in Sunnyvale, have also been the focus of a conversion study. In an analysis of 127 skilled technical and production jobs in these two firms, the Arms Control and Disarmament Agency arrived at the following conclusions: that "the vast majority of occupations surveyed could be matched with at least one non–defense occupation; more than 60% of all occupations were found to require no re–training at all ... and only about 5% were found to require more than three months of retraining." [19]

Perhaps the best known conversion effort is that by the workers of Lucas Aerospace in England, as documented in the book *The Lucas Plan*. The book tells the story of the workers' ten year struggle against management to save jobs by developing civilian products. Faced with the inability of military production to maintain employment levels, the Lucas workers designed and manufactured a series of civilian products including oceanic equipment, railroad buses and kidney machines which saved their jobs and set an important precedent in conversion planning.[20] Other types of conversion projects have succeeded recently in West Germany and Italy. In the United States the AVCO engine plant of South Carolina, previously a manufacturer of military helicopters, now makes truck engines and employs more workers than it did before converting.

Possibly the best evidence that conversion is possible is the fact that numerous defense contractors have already entered commercial fields related to their military work. Raytheon's military sonar and radar systems have been adapted for commercial ships and air traffic control systems. Litton's Ingalls shipyard has also been involved in oil rig construction. Another shipyard, Tenneco's facility at Newport News, provides a variety of design, construction and repair services for the commercial power generation industry. McDonnell Douglas, the aerospace contractor, has a computer subsidiary that provides computer services to health care institutions. Two other noted aerospace firms, Boeing and Grumman, have also taken commercial advantage of computer expertise developed initially for military purposes.[21]

This list makes it clear that it is possible to convert the technology of defense firms to civilian purposes. However, the corporate efforts listed above represent primarily *diversification* rather than *conversion*. Diversification is the adding of civilian items to a firm's production line without foregoing

military contracts. This process allows the company to participate in military contracting, often more profitable in the short
run, without being entirely tied to it. Unlike conversion,
however, diversification does not represent a reduction in a
firm's military production, only a reduction in the company's
dependence on that type of production.

Conversion Problems

The major obstacle to economic conversion is the simple
fact that corporations which depend on Pentagon contracts
for the greater part of their revenue are reluctant to undertake conversion. To do so would require them to leave the
relative safety of government contracting to enter the more
competitive and less secure environment of the civilian
marketplace. The latter demands flexibility as well as marketing and cost–cutting abilities to a high degree. These skills
are fundamentally different, as Seymour Melman has often
pointed out, than those required in the bureaucratic, one–
customer defense market.[22] Lloyd Dumas, a long–time student
of military procurement, has summed up the situation accurately:

> Rather than knowing how to run an effective
> electronic and print media advertising campaign,
> how to survey markets for public acceptance of a
> new product line, how to price a product for
> penetration into new markets or expansion of
> existing one, etc., it becomes critical (for defense
> managers and engineers) to know the minute
> detail of the Armed Forces Procurement Regulat-
> ions, to develop good working relationships with
> key government procurement personnel and to be
> able to lobby effectively with members of the
> Congress.[23]

In light of the above it is not surprising that some
conversion efforts have failed. Boeing–Vertol's rail vehicle,
Grumman Aerospace's solar panel and Rohr Industries' subway
car are all examples of conversion products that have not
succeeded. These products were not designed appropriately for

civilian use, nor were they manufactured and marketed according to the cost–minimizing and multi–consumer methods of the non–military marketplace. These failures demonstrate the fact that conversion must include a careful retraining of a firm's management and engineers/scientists if it is to be successful in the open market.[24]

If there are difficulties in the conversion process, they are less imposing when compared to the problems a firm can experience in military contract work itself. The most obvious of these is the lack of contract continuity. When a firm completes a major contract without a similar program to take its place the impact on the company can be drastic. Morcover, the current military buildup will not prevent the cancellation of individual contracts. The Pentagon itself has indicated that certain of its weapons systems will not be able to go forward if it is unable to extract more military dollars from the Congress. Finally, arms control agreements, however remote they might appear at a given moment, cannot be ignored entirely. The implementation of such agreements would mean the end of some contracts. All of these factors contribute to the "boom and bust" syndrome of military contracting which plays havoc with workers' lives and with the stability of a firm.

While it is important to preach the perils of military contracting, it is even more necessary to make conversion attractive to defense–related firms. The government must play an extensive role in meeting this need. Specifically, government *planning* for conversion can offer these firms the opportunity to undertake this process without risking their economic futures. Three tasks are required of government conversion planning:

1) enabling legislation which mandate:

    — prenotification of contract losses,

    — planning grants for alternate use production,

    — the formation of alternate–use committees or studies for factory re–use,

— worker income assistance and retraining monies either during the conversion process (3 months to 3 years) or as a result of permanent layoffs.

2)   planning at the national (and state) level to allocate R & D monies, tax incentives, and federal procurement monies for plant modernization, the conversion process of retraining and retooling, and the start–up of new product lines.

3)   local planning in particular industries and impacted communities through the formation of local alternate use committees made up of management, labor, local community and local government representatives. These committees would:

— inventory job skills and physical machinery in the plant,

— assess potential job skills and potential and compatible product ideas of what could be produced and marketed,

— define open and potential markets, discerned from local needs to what would sell in the international marketplace,

— set a timetable for retraining and secure funding for income support and start–up of the conversion process.[25]

The state of Connecticut has made a beginning toward accomplishing these tasks. Grass roots conversion efforts in 1978–80 spurred the state legislature to mandate an official study, "Defense–Dependency in Connecticut." The study resulted in the Defense Readjustment Act (PS 80–267) which established mechanisms to promote diversification and conversion. The legislation required the state's Product Development Corporation to give high priority in loans and tax breaks to military related firms wishing to diversify or convert. It also encouraged the coordination of defense–dependency planning with local and regional agencies.

Although a step forward, this legislation has serious shortcomings in light of the three major tasks enumerated above for conversion. The Connecticut law did not make real provision for pre–planning *before* a military contract expires. In addition, the legislation did not *mandate* many of the steps indicated above for conversion. As a result, Connecticut's legislation has been unable to overcome the traditional reluctance of these firms to move beyond military contracting and into the civilian marketplace.[26]

Some of the important shortcomings of the Connecticut act are remedied in federal legislation proposed by Representatives Ted Weiss (D–NY) and Nicholas Mavroules (D–Mass). These bills, particularly Weiss', are more extensive and would make substantial progress toward making economic conversion a reality. The Weiss measure (HR 425) has four basic features: 1) a national Defense Economic Adjustment Council, composed of cabinet level officers as well as industry and labour representatives, to encourage conversion planning by Federal agencies and private industry; 2) alternative use committees at every defense facility of 100 employees or more to develop concrete plans for the use of the plant, its equipment and the skills of the existing work force in civilian production; 3) one year pre–notification of military base closing or major defense contract cutback; 4) financial and re–training assistance for affected workers while conversion is taking place. In sum, the Weiss measure will set up a coordinated, federally mandated, and federally financed planning process at every large military facility in the country.[27]

The Mavroules bill (HR 4805) is similar to the Weiss measure in that it provides for prenotification of contract cutbacks and worker re–training and re–adjustment assistance. However, HR 4805 does not have a ''reserve fund'' similar to that proposed by Weiss and it makes alternative use planning dependent on local government. Finally, the Mavroules bill puts administration of conversion programs into the hands of an already existing agency chaired by the Secretary of Defense. Less comprehensive than the Weiss bill, the Mavroules measure is thought to have a better chance of success in Congress.[28]

Nevertheless, despite the virtues of both the Weiss and Mavroules bills there is no immediate prospect for the passage of either. While the American public has clearly embraced the concept of the Freeze and forced its Representatives to go on record in favor of it, that same public has not yet become aware of the parallel need for the economic conversion that should precede and accompany a Freeze. Conversion and minimizing a potentially negative effect of the Freeze, are unlikely without such an awareness. The fundamental ingredient in economic conversion is the political will to achieve it and this remains to be accomplished.

Notes

1. Marion Anderson, *Destructive Investment* (Lansing, M I: Employment Research Associates, 1983), p 8.
2. Marta Daniels, *Jobs, Security and Arms in Connecticut* (Boston: American Friends Service Committee, 1980), p. 14. See also Marion Anderson, *Destructive Investment*, p. 8 and Lester Thurow in the *New York Times*, May 31, 1981.
3. Marta Daniels, p. 14.
4. Marion Anderson, p. 8.
5. Ruth Leger Sivard, *World Military and Social Expenditures 1981* (Washington, D. C.: World Priorities, 1983), p. 17 and Sivard, *World Military and Social Expenditures* 1983, p. 12. Hereafter these works will be abbreviated as *WMSE '81* and *WMSE '83*.
6. Sivard, *WMSE '81*, p. 19.
7. Sivard, *WMSE '83*, p. 23.
8. *Ibid.*, p. 24.
9. *Ibid.*
10 *Ibid.*, p. 26.
11. Pope Paul VI, Statement of the Holy See to the United Nations on Disarmament, 1976; presented at the request of the UN Commission on Disarmament.
12. Sivard, *WMSE '83*, p. 11.
13. U. S. Department of Labor, Bureau of Labor Statistics Report, "Structure of the U. S. Economy in 1980 and 1985" (Washington: Government Printing Office, 1975) as quoted in Marta Daniels, p. 9. See also Marion Anderson, *The Empty Pork Barrel* (Lansing, MI: Employment Research Associates, 1982) and Marion Anderson, *Converting the Work Force: Where the Jobs Would Be* (Lansing, MI: Employment Research Associates, 1980).
14. Jacques Gansler, *The Defense Industry* (Cambridge, Mass.: MIT Press, 1982), p. 53.
15. Robert DeGrasse, Jr., *The Costs and Consequences of Reagan's*

Military Buildup (New York: Council on Economic Priorities, 1982), p. 26.

16. Marion Anderson, *Destructive Investment*, p. 6.

17. Philip Webre, *Jobs to People: Plannning for Conversion to New Industries* (Washington: Exploratory Project for Economic Alternatives, 1979).

18. Robert DeGrasse, Jr., et al., *Creating Solar Jobs: Options for Military Workers and Communities* (Mountain View, CA.: Center for Economic Conversion, 1978).

19. Arms Control and Disarmament Agency, "The Economic Impact of Reductions in Defense Spending" (Washington, Government Printing Office, 1972), p. 24 as quoted in *The Nuclear Weapons Industry* (Washington: Investor Responsibility Research Center, 1984), p. 110.

20. Hilary Wainwright and Dave Elliott, *The Lucas Plan: A New Trade Unionism in the Making?* London and New York: Alison and Busby, 1982).

21. *The Nuclear Weapons Industry*, p. 13.

22. See Seymour Melman's works: *Pentagon Capitalism* (New York: McGraw-Hill, 1970) and *The Permanent War Economy* (New York: Simon & Schuster, 1974).

23. Lloyd Dumas, "Conversion of the Military Economy: United States," *The Political Economy of Arms Reduction*, American Association for the Advancement of Science, p. 30 as quoted in *The Nuclear Weapons Industry*, p. 109.

24. These examples of failed conversion efforts are discussed in *The Nuclear Weapons Industry*, p. 109.

25. These points are taken from a number of studies referred to above including those by Marion Anderson, Robert DeGrasse, Jr., Philip Webre, Hilary Wainwright and the Arms Control and Disarmament Agency, as well as Seymour Melman, ed., *Conversion of Industry From Military to Civilian Economy* (six volumes, 1970).

26. On the Connecticut situation see especially Kevin Bean, "Challenging Defense Dependency in Connecticut," *Plowshare Press* (May/June, 1984).

27. William D. Hartung, *The Economic Consequences of a Nuclear Freeze* (New York: Council on Economic Priorities, 1984), pp. 91–93.

28. *Ibid.*, p. 112.

CHAPTER 5

Economic Injustice and Work Alienation: Equality Through Meaningful Work

RICHARD G. LYONS
University of Lowell

A common way to illustrate economic injustice is to compare similar numbers of people and show what percent of the world's wealth they consume. People in the Third World, for instance, have a high percent of the world's population but a low percent of the world's wealth. The United States, on the other hand, has a low percent of the world's population but an extremely high percent of the world's wealth. One obvious solution to the imbalance between population and consumption is to have the rich consume less and the poor to consume more of the world's wealth. Another way to look at economic injustice is to emphasize the amount of extreme poverty in the world. A solution is to raise the consumption level of the poor, as well as the rich, by producing more wealth. Thus, while the relative percent of wealth consumed by the United States and poorer nations remains unchanged, the actual consumption by all of the world's countries would increase. The rich get richer but the poor consume more. Both methods have been used to address the issue of economic injustice.

This chapter will argue that any concern with economic injustice should not only include a solution to the problem of poverty but also include a solution to the problem of work inequality and alienation. That is to say, even if we are to make significant progress toward the elimination of poverty, we must consider the working lives of people. A high level of consumption, widely sought in America, is capable of providing high levels of work inequality and alienation. By alienation I mean the divorce of our working lives from our intellectual, emotional, and moral capacities. I use the term inequality to mean the degrees of work alienation between people as well as the wide range of consumption in the world.

Nevertheless, I do not wish to imply that a consumption model to measure some aspect of economic injustice is unimportant. When people are suffering from famine and disease, we should confront these problems – even if some degree of work alienation and consumption inequality are evident. However, we should not assume that the reduction or elimination of difference in consumption levels eliminates work alienation and inequality.

Let me now examine a recent theory of work developed by the industrial psychologist Frederick Herzberg and examine its implications for the problem of economic injustice and inequality.[1]

Herzberg's work is confined to industrialized societies dominated by socialist or capitalist ideologies. His model to measure the quality of our lives, including our working lives, is simple and straightforward. We have two sets of motivations. The first he calls the maintenance of hygiene factors which can be derived from a scientific analysis of man. This set seeks to avoid pain and possible death and is directly linked to human scarcity. Thus the human needs for adequate food, safety, shelter, and other conditions for human survival. Clearly, much of the Third World is dominated by such motivations. After a basic threshhold is met, he suggests that other types of motivations are cultivated. Yet, he observes that people are dominated by consumerism. Clothing, housing, cars and food consumption continue to play a significant part in our lives well after we have avoided scarcity. Ironically, we find people willing to engage in meaningless work to increase these items. The modern pre–occupation with money and things, Herzberg argues, reflects only one aspect of personality – namely pain avoidance, whether psychological like safety or physical like hunger. One advantage to a low standard of living is that work responds to real and not fabricated scarcity.

Utopian thinkers such as B. F. Skinner suggest that if alienating work cannot be avoided, people with alienating jobs should work shorter hours but for the same compensation as people with interesting work. Furthermore, people with alienating work should change jobs and those with interesting work should assume some responsibility for the less attractive tasks in a community. Skinner's solution to economic injustice involves the sharing of distasteful tasks as well as a higher compensation level for those with alienating work. All of us must empty our garbage and compensate the collector with shorter hours. Unfortunately, we do exactly the opposite. Alienating work pays poor wages and involves longer working hours.

Economic injustice, i. e. the unfair and imbalanced distribution of wealth within a community is combined with inequality of job opportunity for minorities and women. In the twentieth century, some of the crafts became mechanized with the introduction of assembly line work. Further de–skilling of work was justified by Frederick Taylor and the scientific management movement with its rigid organizational network and over specialization of tasks. We could satisfy our animal needs or hygiene needs, to use Herzberg's term, by engaging in more dehumanizing work. Production increased with scientific management, but the relative consumption of wealth was still imbalanced.

While Taylorism favored increase of production at the expense of satisfying work, Frederick Herzberg argues that productivity will increase with more stimulating jobs. He warns, however, that when we are successful in meeting real scarcity and pain through alienating work, we may continue to work under the justification of artificial and fabricated scarcity. Since scarcity is never fully met, we can justify unsatisfying jobs. Consumption, not work, can be the motivation of people.

Herzberg insists that work must bring novelty. For example, our jobs should enable us to have new information, see new relationships between facts, and provide an opportunity to create. This intellectual standard should be combined with an emotional criteria. His emotional standard covers our motivations. Rather than being motivated only by salary, we should be motivated by ambigious situations which give us opportunity for problem solving. We should also be motivated to protect our integrity when it conflicts with management. Lastly, we must be motivated by real growth of personality rather than the symbols of success used to reward people. Money, titles, awards and any other sign of success must not be substituted for real growth.

Another facet of Herzberg's work is the study he conducted to determine the perceived factors which make work meaningful and unalienating. Working, like living, can be divided into two categories – pain avoidance and growth. What facets of work help us avoid pain? His study suggests that the hygiene factor or pain avoiders located on our jobs are the physical working environment, overall company policy toward workers, supervision, relationships with peers, and salary. When all or some of these factors were absent, the worker experienced job dissatisfaction. One would think that if the above factors were eliminated or improved job satisfaction would become evident. Herzberg's ingenious and creative study suggests, however, a different conclusion. When the hygiene factors are improved the long term effect is not job satisfaction but no job dissatisfaction. When we are not unhappy with our jobs, we are not necessarily happy with our jobs either. For instance, if a person is dissatisfied with his salary and the company raises pay, the long term result is not worker satisfaction. The reason, according to this analysis, is that salary and the other minimum standards only respond to our need to survive and maintain ourselves and not to personality development spelled out in intellectual and emotional criteria. Employers become confused when salary and other minimum factors are improved yet workers continue to complain. Their complaints, however, revolve around issues like boring routines and lack of novelty.

Workers maintain that work, like life, should be evaluated in terms of growth. Consequently work must provide us with an opportunity for achievement and accomplishments, recognition for our work, responsibility to see that our tasks are accomplished, promotion and a challenge to our abilities. The reader will notice that the rather simple illustrations of work providing us with a means to avoid pain and have food, shelter, and other necessities of life are given a modern context. For example, our relationship with our peers is included as part of the minimum standards.

What, we might wonder, is the explanation for people who are governed by pain avoidance or hygiene standards when these two conditions are met? What if people are motivated only by salary when they are paid very well? Herzberg has a straightforward reply. They are neurotic. The neurotic suffers from incorrect motivation endemic to our culture. On the other hand, people who do not have jobs conducive to their own growth, and are forced to settle for jobs which only respond to pain avoidance criteria, are regarded as healthy if they are motivated by growth formulation outside their work. But minorities and women are denied access to work which fulfills the growth standard and harbor a great deal of hostility.

A fascinating aspect of Herzberg's study is that workers decided what work experience gave rise to work satisfaction or no work dissatisfaction. Thus the worker claimed that salary was not as important as intellectual challenge. Herzberg, unlike Marx, derives the moral criteria for satisfying work from the workers themselves. Nevertheless, one has little doubt that if workers viewed salary as more important than the work itself, Herzberg, like Marx, would develop a less scientific and more moral analysis of what constitutes satisfying work.

The fact that a small percent of minorities have opportunities for jobs which have been closed is encouraging from the view of compensation and is a step toward equalization of wealth. Nevertheless, the issue of the degree of alienation in these same jobs should be addressed. People in Third World countries may register a high level of satisfaction if they are provided with work which helps defend against malnutrition and death. However, the real issue in living is not pain avoidance, but growth. If Herzberg is correct in his analysis, and we begin to realize a shift away from salary and working environment as the most significant aspect of our jobs, then we are in a position to de–value the life style of consumerism and divert more of our wealth to the Third World. What makes this so difficult, which Herzberg does not emphasize, is the fact that so much of our wealth goes toward national defense. The Soviet Union and the United States are engaged in the kind of competition that emphasizes avoidance of danger. An atmosphere of fabricated danger is used to overcompensate for our need for safety in the same way we use an atmosphere of fabricated scarcity to overcompensate for our need to consume. Safety is a hygiene need like food and housing and it is fairly easy to convince people that alienating work is not only productive in facing danger but also patriotic. Yet, the monies spent on defense should be seen as wealth that could be used to reduce real worldwide poverty. International competition, however, focuses our talents on avoiding danger.

Herzberg's analysis of working and living must also address two additional issues. The first concerns productivity and satisfying work. He seems confident that productivity will increase if we enlarge work to include intellectual and emotional growth. One notable exception is the Volvo automobile assembly plants in Sweden. Volvo employed the typical American auto assembly line which created a high level of worker alienation. Workers responded with wild cat strikes, job changing, and absenteeism. Workers and managers then restructured the manufacturing process. Instead of the assembly line, small groups emphasized cooperative planning and the development of high level skills. However, Volvo soon realized that they could be more productive if they returned to the conventional assembly line methods.[2] Nevertheless Volvo decided against reverting to the assembly line because workers and management insisted that productivity should not outweigh employees' satisfaction. In other words, tension exists between the need for higher productivity and job satisfaction. Contrary to Herzberg's analysis, jobs which have higher levels of satisfaction need not be justified on the grounds that productivity increases.

The picture in the United States is not bright. Studies have emphasized that union workers have been interested only in the traditional bread and butter issues such as pay, fringe benefits and safety.[3] American workers continue to emphasize what Herzberg calls the work dissatisfiers rather than the work satisfiers. A recent study confirms the tendency in American unions to emphasize compensation.[4] This combines with President Reagan's insistence that we should produce more in order to consume more. Job satisfaction appears irrelevant.

The second issue Herzberg's analysis fails to address is the relationship between ends and means. He views growth in the work place largely in economic and psychological terms rather than socio–political terms. We could, for instance, be engaged in very meaningful work but produce goods and services which are harmful. We must, therefore, appraise our work along two major dimensions. Work should not only extend the personality of the worker, but also extend the personality of the consumer. If my work fails the test of extending others it should not be judged meaningful, as Herzberg would have us believe. Herzberg rightly draws attention to the dreadful working conditions of our lives, but fails to emphasize that what we produce is also a moral consideration. We must go beyond Herzberg's account of satisfying work and emphasize that our relationship to the consumer cannot be measured only in terms of productivity criteria. Nevertheless, we should keep in mind Herzberg's basic argument: the elimination of scarcity should be a means toward growth, not an avenue to consumption. Job related growth, however, depends on what is produced and how it is produced.

Finally, the global elimination of economic injustice involves several interrelated ideas. One, the distribution of wealth should emphasize the demands of the poverty-stricken to maintain life and eventually produce wealth, which does not compromise their need for stimulating work. Second, one should keep in mind that the hideous inequality in consumption and working conditions is related to the distribution of power. If we maintain that power should be distributed equally, then we must insist that the jobs we have and contributions we make are irrelevant as a condition for democratic participation and consensus in a society committed to growth through work.

Notes

1. Frederick Herzberg, *Work and the Nature of Man*, (New York: Thomas Y. Crowell, 1966), Chapter 6.
2. Newsweek, "Manufacturing: The Assembly Team," *Newsweek* (August 21, 1972), p. 69.
3. Derek C. Bok and John T. Dunlop, *Labor and the American Community*, (New York: Simon and Schuster, 1970), p. 356.
4. Andrew Levison, *The Workingclass Majority*, (New York: Penguin Books, 1977), p. 269.

Bibliography

Braverman, Harry, *Labor and Monopoly Capital: The Degradation of Work in the Twentieth Century*. New York: Monthly Review Press, 1974.

Callahan, Raymond E., *Education and the Cult of Efficiency*. Chicago: University of Chicago Press, 1962.

Carnoy, Martin and Levin, Henry, *The Limits of Educational Reform*. New York: Longman, 1976.

Feinburg, Walter and Rosemont, Henry (ed.), *Work, Technology, and Education*. Urbana: University of Illinois Press, 1975.

Herzberg, Frederick, *Work and the Nature of Man*. New York: Thomas Y. Crowell, 1966.

Green, Thomas F., *Work, Leisure, and the American School*. New York: Random House, 1968.

Hackman, J. R. and Oldham, G.R., *Work Redesign*, Reading (MA): Addison-Wesley, 1977.

Levin, Henry, *Education and Work*. Stanford: Institute for Research on Educational Finance and Governance, December, 1982.

Report of a Special Task Force to the Secretary of Health, Education and Welfare, *Work in America*. Cambridge : The M. I. T. Press, 1973.

Sarason, Seymour, *Work, Ageing and Social Change*. New York : The Free Press, 1977.

Sarup, Madan, *Marxism and Education*, London: Routledge and Kegan Paul, 1978.

Skinner, B. F., *Walden Two*. New York : Macmillan, 1948.

Taylor, Frederick, *The Principles of Scientific Management*. New York: Harper, 1911.

Wirth, Arthur G., *Education in the Technological Society*, Washington : University Press of America, 1978.

— . *Productive Work – In Industry and Schools*. Washington: University Press of America, 1983.

Willis, Paul, *Learning to Labor*, New York : Columbia University Press, 1977.

CHAPTER 6

Nonviolent Civil Disobedience: The Winooski 44 Case Study

DAVID R. CONRAD
University of Vermont

In late March 1984, as the war in Central America grew hotter and ever more brutal, a group of citizens organized a demonstration outside United States Senator Robert Stafford's office in the small city of Winooski, Vermont. Stafford, a moderate Republican with a good record on issues affecting education and the environment, had been unresponsive on Central American issues. In fact, he consistently supported Reagan administration military aid to El Salvador and voted for funds for contras trying to overthrow the government of Nicaragua.

Most protesters who gathered outside the restored Champlain Mill on the edge of the Winooski River that cold Friday afternoon had attempted to communicate with Senator Stafford about their concerns. Some had written long letters expressing their anguish about the terror of death squads in El Salvador and U. S. efforts to destroy the revolution in Nicaragua, but had received cold form letters in response. Others had tried to meet with senior aides, but found this frustrating.

Many believed that the Senator was ill–informed about the tragedy unfolding daily in Central America and were angered to find this critical area low in priority. Everyone thought the Senator should hold a public forum to engage in dialogue with constituents. They knew that few Americans understood what was happening in their names in that part of the world where military intervention in the twentieth century was almost commonplace. And they felt that Senator Stafford was helping to perpetuate an illegal, immoral foreign policy which could only lead to more killing, maiming, suffering.

After demonstrating peacefully outside the Mill for more than an hour, about 100 people—most in affinity of a dozen or so—entered the building and walked up several flights of stairs to the Senator's office. There they discussed grievances with the staff and announced their intention to stay in the office until Senator Stafford agreed to reverse his support of administration policy and hold an open meeting with Vermonters. They reminded the staff that many Vermont Town Meetings voted strong opposition to military aid for El Salvador and Vermonters' indicated strong distaste for current Central American policies through a statewide petition as well.

Several hours later, when the Senator in Washington had still not responded, the group decided to remain in the office area. After the staff left in late afternoon, the building's owner invited the group to stay over the weekend as long as individuals respected property and did not interfere with business at the retail shops downstairs. Members of the group readily agreed to this request and their relationship with the owner remained cordial throughout the weekend.

Thus began the three day occupation of a United States Senator's office in a building that once served as workplace for hundreds of adults and children who toiled long hours at deafening looms. Now in this silent building on the bank of a still rushing river, individual protesters were free to come and go for several days, realizing that in all likelihood a showdown would not come until Monday when the office would reopen for business.

Frequent meetings were held over the weekend to discuss strategy, publicity and issues surrounding Central America. One very important concern centered on education for the participants themselves as well as for members of the community who were invited to visit the newly–named Archbishop Oscar Romero Memorial Peace Center. On Sunday morning, Quakers in the Burlington area joined interested participants in a Quaker meeting and several other worship services were held. In the afternoon, a nondenominational ceremony to clear the office of negative influence and a ritual planting of dried seeds which promised new life and hope took place. But most energy was concentrated on planning a series of workshops and seminars for Monday morning in the various spaces of the office complex.

By 8 : 00 on Monday, the office area had been vacuumed by the occupiers, sleeping bags and supplies removed and signs put up indicating specific spaces for educational activities. The woven web of life which symbolized interdependence of all peoples remained hanging from the high ceiling as it had since Friday when the yarn web was strung intricately from light fixture to desk to light fixture to chair. During the weekend, as someone brushed against one thread of the web, the whole web danced and everyone felt the symbolic interconnection of people and ideas. Now the web was pulled higher in order not to impede seminars progressing below. The U. S. military buildup in Honduras, history of intervention in Central America, the Sandinista revolution, liberation theology–all of these and more were subjects of study and discussion by over one hundred people that day.

In mid–morning, everyone was asked to leave Senator Stafford's office area because "they were informed, business as usual" could not be conducted. Spokespersons for each affinity group told the Senator's chief aide, Rey Post, that the group would leave if the Senator agreed to a public meeting on Central America. This request, which represented a willingness to negotiate on the part of the protesters, was transmitted to the Senator in Washington but was rejected. Police were called to arrest the occupiers for unlawful trespass. Workshops and seminars were halted, and those present not prepared by previous training for nonviolent civil disobedience left the office area and waited in a large space immediately adjacent.

City and state police then carried 44 individuals down a long hallway and several flights of stairs to waiting vans outside. No one resisted and police generally were courteous. Support members of affinity groups watched helplessly, but painfully, as their friends were handcuffed, loaded into vans and taken to a nearby state police barracks for fingerprinting and citations.

II

The Winooski 44 direct action was part of a long tradition of nonviolent civil disobedience in the United States. As early as 1657, banished members of the Society of Friends (Quakers) entered Puritan Massachusetts from safe Rhode Island to spread their teachings, even though punishment for defying banishment meant having an ear cropped or tongue bored with a hot iron. When this civil disobedience campaign of the Friends was brought to the attention of King Charles II in 1661, Massachusetts authorities defended their actions by calling Quakers unfit to inhabit the earth and "malignant promoters of doctrines tending to subvert both our church and state." Eventually, King Charles ordered the government of Massachusetts to stop its persecution of the Society of Friends. Imprisoned Quakers were released and in 1665 all Quakers in Massachusetts were permitted to conduct their business unmolested.[1]

In the early nineteenth century, the New England Non-Resistance Society committed itself to radical social change without violence. Abolitionist William Lloyd Garrison, women's rights advocate and abolitionist Lucretia Mott, early feminists Sarah and Angelina Grimke and Congregational minister and abolitionist Henry Clarke Wright challenged injustice and championed social change. In 1848, Henry David Thoreau lectured on civil disobedience at the Concord Lyceum under the title "On the Relation of the Individual to the State." Thoreau explained his refusal to pay a poll tax to the state of Massachusetts for six years and was put in jail as punishment. Though not opposed to all taxes, Thoreau believed that paying the state poll tax expressed allegiance to an unjust government which tolerated the practice of slavery in the South and warfare in Mexico.

In the twentieth century, nonviolent civil disobedience has been practiced widely since World War I when young men who refused noncombatant service under military authority were sentenced to years of suffering in military prisons. In 1917, members of the Congressional Union for Women Suffrage began what may have been the first demonstration at the White House in Washington. The silent vigil demanded that President Wilson keep his promise to work for a constitutional amendment granting women the right to vote, but after several months of vigiling police started arresting demonstrators for obstructing sidewalk traffic. Over two hundred women from 26 states were arrested and almost one hundred imprisoned. Most served sixty days, but a few served seven months. Non–cooperating with prison officials, many women organized a hunger strike and were painfully forcefed. But within a year's time President Wilson supported and Congress passed the Suffrage Amendment.

On October 16, 1940, the first day of registration under a new draft law, eight students at Union Theological Seminary in New York declared that they would refuse to register for the draft. Among those who were sentenced to a year in prison and later forced to serve a second term for this first act of resistance to the Second World War was David Dellinger, a defendant in the Winooski 44 trial 44 years later.[2]

Thousands of other pacifists spent time in prison during World War II or in Civilian Public Service (CPS) Camps where some organized a walk–out in 1942 to protest the camp system which they considered a hated form of conscription. The protesters were given prison sentences and received brutal treatment, but their 82 day long hunger strike inspired the pacifist community.

After the war, groups like Peacemakers and the Committee for Nonviolent Action were active in peaceful direct action against conscription, war taxes and militarism. In 1955, religious activist Dorothy Day, Ralph Di Gia of the War Resisters League, A. J. Muste of the Fellowship of Reconciliation and others organized a civil disobedience action against compulsory nationwide air raid drills. In 1958, several members of the Committee for Nonviolent Action sailed a 30 foot boat, *The Golden Rule*, into the hydrogen bomb testing area at Eniwetok in the Pacific. Albert S. Bigelow, a naval officer during World War II, explained his reasons for this act which ended with arrest and jailing of the crew in Honolulu:

> I am going because it is time to do something about peace, not just *talk* about peace. I am going because, like all men, in my heart I know *all* nuclear explosions are monstrous, evil, unworthy of human beings. I am going because war is no longer a feudal jousting match; it is an unthinkable catastrophe for all men.[3]

Certainly the most famous and influential theoretician and practitioner of nonviolent civil disobedience in twentieth century America was Martin Luther King, Jr. King provided leadership for the 1955 Montgomery bus boycott which led to the outlawing of bus segregation. The boycott began after Rosa Parks refused to give up her seat and move to the back of the bus as blacks were required by law to do at that time. King encouraged sit–ins at lunch counters and organized demonstrations across the South for integration, voting rights and fair housing. He wrote:

> The nonviolent resister must often express his protest through noncooperation or boycotts, but he realizes that these are not ends themselves; they are merely means to awaken a sense of moral shame in the opponent. The end is redemption and reconciliation. The aftermath of nonviolence is the creation of the beloved community, while the aftermath of violence is tragic bitterness.[4]

Civil disobedience was practiced widely during the sixties and early seventies to protest the war in Southeast Asia but in the mid 1970's the focus turned to nuclear power plants being built in spite of grave threats to health and safety. Organizations like the Clamshell Alliance sprouted and many direct actions resulted in crippling delays in construction and licensing. In the 1980's civil disobedience centered largely on nuclear weapons construction, transportation and deployment. Many were arrested in New York during the UN Second Special Session on Disarmament and many more around the nation at weapons labs, air force bases and submarine launching sites. "Nonviolent civil disobedience is one of our last, best hopes for freeing humanity from nuclear slavery and preventing global holocaust," wrote Pat Farren, editor of *Peacework*, a New England peace and social justice newsletter, in the introduction to an entire issue devoted to "Nonviolent Civil Disobedience: Gentle Strength in Action."[5] Farren pointed out that nonviolence is particularly active today among Catholic Left groups and in some radical feminist groups. But even U. S. Congressmen were arrested in late 1984 at the South African Embassy in Washington as they protested that nation's racist policies. Thus, the long history of nonviolent civil disobedience in America continues today and the Winooski 44 takes its appropriate place in that tradition.

III

The first trials of the Winooski 44 included only a few protesters. The judge ruled that the jury had to decide whether or not the defendants were trespassing, and that was all. What the protesters thought about the situation in Central America was irrelevant, the state's attorney argued. One defendant pointed out that she was arrested during regular office hours of her elected representative and that her deeply held moral beliefs *were* her defense – and they were certainly not irrelevant. Another defendant explained that their presence in the Senator's office was based on the most sacred laws of all times; their act was a witness aimed at saving the lives of neighbors in Central America. They had offered to end their vigil if an open forum were scheduled, but the Senator decided to order their arrest rather than hold a meeting, he

observed. After ten minutes of deliberation by the jury, the
first three defendants were declared guilty of unlawful trespass.
In two other trials with a single defendant, once again the
verdict was guilty.

Eight defense attorneys, volunteering their time, met
regularly with the remaining defendants to develop a plan of
action. Separate trials in groups of 3 or 4 defendants would be
very time consuming and expensive for the state. Besides,
it was clear that trials which focused exclusively on the
narrow issue of criminal trespass would probably end with the
same verdict. Finally, it was agreed by defense counsel and
Judge Frank Mahady, a strict follower of the First Amendment
and a judge known for his fairness, that the remaining 26 defendants[6] would be tried in a single trial and could make use
of the so-called "necessity defense." The defendants viewed
this argeement very favorably since they could then bring
into the trial the reasons behind their action; indeed, Reagan
administration policy in Central America would be put on
trial.

In a necessity defense, the harm taking place is deemed
greater than the crime to be committed. The harm is so
imminent that if a person does not do something right away
a greater harm may occur. There is no other reasonable thing
to do under the circumstances; a person seeing someone in
a burning house, for instance, would have no reasonable
alternative to committing trespass in order to save the threatened person. The situation, then, must be of sufficient seriousness to outweigh the criminal act.

Acceptance of the necessity defense meant that the
defendants and their lawyers would gather a number of witnesses to prove the occupation was a reasonable necessity to
stop the bloodshed in Central America. "We will show that
a state of emergency exists," defendant Jeanne Keller said
at a press conference before the trial began, "that our democracy is in jeopardy due to the disinformation campaign out
of the White House, that the lives of our brothers and
sisters in Central America are in danger, and that our alleged

criminal act was necessary to bring to light the illegal wars being waged in our names in El Salvador and Nicaragua." Another defendant, Philip Fiermonte, wrote in the local newspaper: "The action taken by the Winooski 44 was an act of conscience in solidarity with the oppressed people of Central America and in opposition of the policies of our government."[7]

The main trial of the Winooski 44 began with jury selection in Vermont District Court on November 13, 1984. Potential jurors were asked if they might feel prejudiced if strong evidence were shown that the President or the administration had not been telling the truth. Several individuals felt more comfortable being excused because they believed they might be so prejudiced. After other potential jurors were excused for various reasons, opening statements were made by the deputy state's attorney Karen Shingler and defense attorney William Dorsch.

Thus began an historic trial in a hot, stuffy courtroom in Burlington, Vermont exactly one week after President Reagan's landslide re–election. The trial would prove to be an education in civil disobedience and foreign policy for twelve members of the jury and an attentive audience which jammed the courtroom each day. The courtroom became a classroom of sorts as expert witnesses testified about U. S. intervention, Salvadoran refugees told chilling personal stories and defendants expressed outrage at the behavior of their government. Jurors listened intently, the judge probed deeper on occasion and the audience watched respectfully as the drama unfolded.

The defendants sat in three rows across the courtroom from the jury. One defendant with a small baby helped those present relate to the human side of war discussed by witnesses. Now and then a baby's cry would break the stillness of the courtroom. Other defendants included several city officials and university professors, a financial manager, workers in small businesses, longtime peace activists, a teacher and a real estate salesperson. Ages ranged from the twenties to the sixties. A few defendants had participated in the Witness for Peace program in Nicaragua and several others had travelled in Central America, but many had never visited the area. All held in common a strong desire to guarantee self–determination to the people of Central America.

Though lack of ventilation in the courtroom seemed suffocating at times, the trial itself was liberating. Prosecution witnesses, inculding Senator Stafford's aide, the Champlain Mill owner and two policemen, testified the first day about technical details of the arrest. Defense attorneys made a motion for dismissal on the grounds that neither the aide nor the building's owner were in lawful possession of the office rented by Senator Stafford, but the motion was denied. Soon the state rested its case, opening the way for an impressive string of witnesses to peel away layers of U. S. foreign policy.

The first defense witness, Philip Fiermonte, explained the significance of Senator Stafford's position. The Senator, he claimed, could have a deep impact on other Republicans if he challenged instead of supported the administration. Fiermonte had communicated about thirty times with the Senator through letters, phone calls and meetings with staff, but felt that his message was not getting across. The timing of the protest was critical, he said, since U. S. involvement was growing and votes were coming up in Congress. Asked by the state's attorney if he ever thought he was in the Senator's office without lawful authority, Fiermonte responded decisively: "No."[8]

The next witness, a 26 year old Salvadoran refugee named Sonja Hernandez, spoke through an interpreter about the murder of her father by the National Guard. At the time, she was studying to be a nurse in San Salvador. Later, her fiance, a student, was kidnapped and brutally murdered by the death squads, but neither she nor his family dared claim the body since they would then be marked for a similar fate. Soon afterwards, while living with a kind woman in the capital city, Hernandez received a telephoned death threat. The woman warned her not to return home. "They came and looked for me one night," she testified, but not finding her, they took the woman's 17 year old son "and murdered him—disembowelled him," she said. The woman "lost her mind" and Hernandez herself spent ten anguishing days looking for a place to stay, wandering from one house to another "knowing I was a curse to them." She continued: "On the verge of madness myself, I decided to leave my country."

Hernandez went to Guatemala, where the situation of fear and repression were similar, and finally to Mexico and the United States. During cross examination by the deputy state's attorney who seemed insensitive to the powerful emotions stirred by Hernandez' story, reference was made to El Salvador's "civil war." The witness firmly but politely responded that she and other Salvadorans see the war as "a conflict between the people and the State." With that, cross examination concluded and Hernandez stepped down. The courtroom suddenly had become a focus for the ongoing human tragedy in El Salvador.[9]

The education of the jury–and of everyone present in the crowded courtroom–continued with testimony by Phillipe Bourgois, a doctoral degree candidate in anthropology at Stanford University. Earlier in the morning, Bourgois had appeared on a local radio talk show to discuss his harrowing experience in Honduras and El Salvador. Most callers were critical of his serious reservations about U. S. policy in the area, prompting him after the program to wonder if everyone in the listening area had a similar attitude. He must have wondered further as he related his experience to twelve local jurors in the courtroom.

Bourgois went to Honduras to study Salvadoran refugees in a camp bordering El Salvador. The refugees suggested he cross over the border for a short time to experience El Salvador for himself and visit people in their homeland. Bourgois' visit became a 14 day nightmare when Salvadoran helicopters and armed troops attacked the farming community he was visiting. He and about 1000 villagers were constantly under fire as they tried to flee. One night the villagers tried a diversionary tactic with young people going in one direction with guns to draw attention away and old people, women and children going in another to escape. But "babies cried a lot and gave away our position," Bourgois related sadly, and the troops changed the direction of their machine guns, aiming them directly at the sound of screaming babies. Using Green Beret–type tactics during these terrifying two weeks, "troops killed every living creature they could get their hands on," he charged.

Finally, after hiding in caves during the daylight and running each night, about half of the villagers made it to the river dividing El Salvador from Honduras. Honduran troops were stationed along the river preparing to shoot anyone who tried to cross. But an NBC television crew happened to be doing a story on the refuge camp at the time, heard the raging warfare across the river and rushed to the scene. Not wanting millions of U. S. citizens to see a massacre occur on home television sets, however, the Honduran army was called off and Bourgois and others escaped. Asked if he had shared this horrifying story with the media upon his return to this country, Bourgois replied that NBC said his story "wasn't dramatic enough," the New York Times said it "didn't need any more stories" and National Public Radio took six weeks before listening to him. But the CIA did an investigation of Bourgois which backfired; they called him a liar and a propagandist before a Congressional committee which eventually cleared him, he added with satisfaction.[10]

A professor of political science at nearby Middlebury College, David Rosenberg, took the stand to share his research on insurgency and counterinsurgency in Third World countries. Rosenberg did consulting for many U. S. government agencies, including the CIA, and was recently visiting lecturer at the Foreign Service Institute in Washington. He was intrigued to find that people formerly working on the Philippines and Vietnam were now working on Central America. The controversial CIA manuals, which demonstrate how to use terror selectively, were seen before in Vietnam and before that in the Philippines, Rosenberg claimed.

Reviewing the recent history of U. S. intervention in Nicaragua, Rosenberg noted that the National Security Council (NSC) first approved a destabilizing plan for that country in December of 1981. It included an economic boycott and direct military actions with CIA support. The CIA–backed raids over the borders began in March 1982 and covert, overt, economic and psychological pressure continue, he stated. Rosenberg found considerable reluctance to use U. S. combat troops unless there is widespread support, but he also found the "Pegasus" war games in the region close to intervention. Opposition to covert action exists in Congress, but Rosenberg discovered that the CIA has often not disclosed plans it thinks Congress may find objectionable. In conclusion, he asserted that the U. S. is violating international law with the boycott and U. S. law with funding of covert CIA operations, a theme developed further by later witnesses.[11]

Defendant Lea Terhune gave testimony about her experience as a member of the Witness for Peace delegation from New England which visited Nicaragua a month before the demonstration. Terhune said she was very impressed by the Nicagaruans she met and the ongoing revolutionary life which holds so much promise for all the people. Several attempts to visit Senator Stafford's aides in his Winooski office were rebuffed, she noted, and the Senator himself refused to meet with more than one well–respected member of the Witness for Peace delegation. Terhune observed, however, that Stafford's position on Central America had changed since the sit–in. Perhaps he had begun to learn from the protest since he voted four times since March against covert aid to the contras. Terhune's voice filled the courtroom as she spoke with firmness and deep feeling.[12]

Some members of the jury sat on the edge of their seats while two former CIA operatives testified about work of the secret intelligence agency. John Stockwell, once a high-ranking CIA official until he quit in disgust in 1979, testified that during his 13 years with the agency he helped prepare false news reports for newspapers and radio stations in order to fool the American people. "An entire department of the CIA is devoted to producing misinformation which is designed to support United States policy," he charged. "One third of the men under my supervision were propagandists." But the CIA can be brought under control by citizens, Stockwell added: "It's absolutely essential that they make themselves heard, by speaking out and by demonstrating, so that public knowledge and concern can override the agency's ability to distort for its own purposes."[13]

David McMichael, a senior staff member of the CIA from 1974–1983, said he was hired by the CIA because of his familiarity with insurgent and counterinsurgent movements. McMichael could find no credible evidence that Nicaragua has been sending arms to Salvadoran guerillas, even though the U. S. government continues to use this excuse to justify its actions against Nicaragua. When asked directly about the purpose of our involvement by a defense attorney, McMichael responded unequivocally: "The real reason has been to cause the overthrow of the Nicaraguan government."[14]

The last day of the trial featured several expert witnesses on civil disobedience and international law as well as testimony by a final defendant. The courtroom was as stuffy as ever physically, but invigorating intellectually. Every seat was taken and the aisles were packed with fascinated spectators. As always, Judge Mahady was gentlemanly and presided over a court profoundly respectful of law and justice. "Please stand for the jury," the audience was told and the courtroom fell silent. Shortly, Judge Mahady appeared. No sooner had he entered than he said kindly: "Please be seated." Within seconds, court was in session and the next witness called. It had been this way all week as the courtroom was transformed into a special place for learning, observing, questioning, challenging. Disturbing words were uttered, probing questions hurled, intense feelings displayed as the trial progressed at a steady pace.

Howard Zinn, professor of history at Boston University and author of many books including *A Peoples History of the United States*, began the final day with discussion of the history of civil disobedience. From early protests against the Stamp Act to the antiwar movement during the Vietnam war and into the present, nonviolent resistance and civil disobedience have been – and continue to be – legitimate forms of protest in the United States, Zinn argued.[15]

Richard Falk, Milbank Professor of International Law at Princeton University, affirmed that direct action has played an enormous part in the shaping of Congressional and Presidential behavior. "Our government relies on citizens and their initiatives to be sure that government doesn't exceed legal boundaries," Falk stated. In the past, the U. S. demobilized in times of peace, but since World War II has built a permanently strong military. Early American leaders felt it was risky to have standing armies, but now Americans have become so accustomed to a vast military presence – with an ensuing erosion of civil liberties–"that we are no longer aware of the way the military dominates policy." Continuing, Falk declared: "In this setting, direct action plays a vital role in checking abuse of governmental power."

Had the peace movement not existed during the Vietnam era, according to Falk, United States planes would have bombed dikes in South Vietnam killing two or three million people. In regards to South Africa, most likely the U. S. government would not have banned weapons exports without forms of direct action. Falk maintained that pressure at home could have a significant effect on the media, elected representatives and the courts. It is extremely important to provide every opportunity for people to express reservations about what their government is doing, he insisted. The U. S. has a rich tradition of possible initiatives, one of the most important being civil disobedience "in order to promote visions of justice which appear to be jeopardized," Falk stated. "Our country is admired for this tradition of civil disobedience as much as anything else ... In a given context of urgency where people are getting killed," he concluded, "civil disobedience is extremely appropriate, perhaps the only effective alternative."[16]

Richard Falk's testimony not only strengthened the defense, but Judge Mahady called him before the bench later in the day to clarify questions about international law. It was ironic that Falk's testimony proved so helpful since it seemed likely, early in the morning when he arrived at the Burlington airport, that he would not have an opportunity to testify after all. Defense counsel hoped to conclude testimony on this last busy day by noon or so and have closing arguments in the afternoon. Soon after arriving, Falk was interviewed on the same radio talk show Philippe Bourgois had appeared on several days earlier. Like Bourgois, he drew considerable hostility to his ideas. One caller recommended angrily that he be properly "indoctrinated" in patriotism by "the Army, the Marine Corps or the CIA." On second thought, she felt the CIA should have nothing to do with this misguided professor's traitorous notions. Falk responded with patience and rational argument based on years of research, teaching and scholarship in the area of world law. Immediately after the program, word came from District Court that he was indeed needed to testify.

The best known authority to testify, and one most stalked by the media, was former Attorney General of the United States Ramsey Clark. Clark spoke only a short time, much to the chagrin of some defendants and many of the audience, because the defense wanted to wind up its case. Though brief, everyone listened with great interest as Clark asserted that the constitutional right to petition takes many forms. Representative government cannot function without the right to petition and civil disobedience is certainly a form of petition, he noted. Asked by a defense attorney if citizens should be allowed to participate in foreign policy decisions, Clark retorted: "It's their children who go off to war and get killed." Does the right of petition have an impact, the lawyer queried: "Yes," Clark commented in his usual pithy way, "an enormous impact." Noting that he had travelled to El Salvador and Nicaragua numerous times in the last two years and had seen for himself the grim situation there, Clark concluded: "If people want peace–if they don't want their government committing crimes in their names–they have to speak out."[17]

Closing arguments began with state's attorney Kevin Bradley admitting that over the weekend of March 23–26 "it was a peaceful protest...nothing happened." But when Monday came, he continued, "the time had come to get back to business." Bradley urged the jury to focus on the trespassing charge and not be drawn in by a "smoke screen of what's going on in Central America." The necessity defense does have a valid place in Vermont history, he granted, but this was not a situation where it applied. Then, after outlining the four basic elements of a necessity defense, Bradley showed why he believed none of them applied in this case.

The war had been going on for many years and no real emergency exists because it will probably go on for many more regardless of U. S. involvement, Bradley claimed. The defendants' action was not likely to have an immediate effect, either, because it was too far removed and many alternatives– from hiring lobbyists to going to Washington–could have been tried. Bradley looked directly at the jurors as he made a persuasive plea to forget the necessity defense and concentrate on the issue of whether or not the defendants were guilty of trespassing. Then he pointed to the map of Central America that had been taped to a blackboard during most of the trial and dramatically pulled it up, revealing a diagram of the Senator's office underneath. "It's not what's happening here (Central America) that's improtant," he insisted, "...it's what happened here (Stafford's office)."[18]

Joan Bauer, an attorney offering one part of the closing argument for the defense, disagreed strongly with Bradley. "I think the issue is very much what's going on in Central America," she declared, pulling the map of Central America down again where it remained for the rest of the trial. Bauer asserted that her clients were not involved in a simple tres- pass action, but were putting their bodies between killers and victims.[19] Bauer continued by pointing to a distinction bet- ween disruption and inconvenience. The sit–in may have been an inconvenience, but it pales in light of the terrible disruption caused by thirty bombs a day being dropped on the civilian population of El Salvador. That deadly disruption and "disruption" of Senator Stafford's office are impossible to equate, she asserted.

A second defense attorney, William Dorsch, completed the closing argument by reviewing the necessity defense and discussing why indeed it did apply in this case. The state must prove there was *not* a necessity for the defendants to do what they did and clearly the state did not do this, he argued. Then, in a moment of deep emotion, Dorsch asked each defendant to stand as he introduced them one by one to the jury.[20]

In Judge Mahady's charge to the jury, he explored the legal principles that applied. In terms of the necessity defense, the judge said the act of necessity is clearly recognized in Vermont and *may* be justified. Was it seen as a reasonable necessity by the defendants, the jury was asked to consider. It was appropriate to consider whether or not the U. S. government was violating U. S. law, he affirmed. Resolutions in the United Nations and the Geneva agreements, of which the U. S. is a signatory, maintain that no state or group of states has the right to intervene in the affairs of any other state and acts of terror against civilians are violations of international law, the judge told the jury. It was appropriate to consider all of these principles. Before excusing the jury to begin deliberations, Judge Mahady reminded them that the burden of proof of guilt rested with the state and that each verdict must be unanimous.[21]

After deliberating a little over an hour, the jury arrived at a verdict and filed back into the courtroom. Judge Mahady asked the defendants to rise and face the jury. When the jury foreman responded "Not Guilty" to the first defendant's name, pandemonium broke out in the courtroom. "Defendants and supporters gasped," the local newspaper reported, as all 26 defendants were found innocent of unlawful trespass "in a surprise verdict that was hailed as an important turning point in citizen action against U. S. intervention in Central America."[22] The verdicts shocked many people in the community, but not the defendants, defense lawyers or supporters who believed that the trial had raised the consciousness of the jury during those incredibly intense days.

This opinion was confirmed by jury members who spoke about the experience after the verdicts were reached. The foreman, an IBM employee and mother of two, said she was surprised that so many others were surprised about the verdict. "Basically," she stated, "what it did for me is to give me an education about Central America."[23] Another juror said she was moved by the trial. "It was an inspiring experience," she commented, noting that it brought out the best in the American system. [24] Still another exclaimed: "I was honored to be on that jury ... I felt a part of history. [25] Most jurors had compliments for the prosecution, defense lawyers and Judge Mahady.

State's attorney Bradley was naturally not pleased with the verdicts, predicting that even though it was only a District Court decision it could promote civil disobedience in Vermont. "That's the truly unfortunate upshot of this case," he lamented. [26] Bradley decided not to appeal because he felt all necessary evidence had been presented. Defendant Jeanne Keller, insurance administrator for the City of Burlington, called the trial "a lesson for the people in Vermont on the necessity defense and how it works." Nationally, she saw it as a "people's precedent" which might inspire similar actions by others. [27] When receiving inquiries about use of the necessity defense from people around the country, Keller commented: "I tell them that the most important thing is sincerity ... I tell them that civil disobedience is not to be taken lightly." [28]

Five randomly selected individuals, asked by the local newspaper how they felt about the outcome of the Winooski 44 trial, said they viewed it positively. One man said: "The jurors balanced what they heard and came up with what I thought was a good common-sense decision." Another commented: "I think, frankly, the action taken by the Winooski 44 was justifiable ... we always assume the government knows best but it's apparent that's not always so. I think we need this type of offbeat action to wake people up." And a third remarked: "I was impressed by the energy and devotion of the defendants and by the independence of the jurors. I was happy the jurors acted independently rather than merely rubber-stamping the opinion of the state's attorney's office." [29]

The trial of the Winooski 44 helped educate the entire community about nonviolent civil disobedience and the deepening U. S. involvement in war in Central America. The necessity defense which had seldom been used successfully, was now debated hotly in newspapers and on radio and television. *The Burlington Free Press*, Vermont's largest and most influential newspaper, editorialized that courtrooms were not the place for foreign policy debates and worried about the precedent set. Many letters to the editor and several longer articles, both attacking and defending the trial, appeared. One critical article by a former aide to President Reagan living in Vermont examined mournfully the future dire consequences of the verdict on the entire state.

For their part, the defendants and some jurors jointly planned a celebration of their victory. And plans were drawn to raise money to purchase the trial transcript. Filming a re–creation of the trial and staging a reader's theatre were seriously contemplated. The trial seemed to spark renewed energy and commitment to peace on the part of everyone involved. Many lives were transformed – and perhaps in the long run some literally saved in Central America–by events taking place during those four November days in that stuffy courtroom. It had surely been an education in peaceful civil disobedience and its rich potential.

Notes

1.   Robert Cooney and Helen Michalowski, ed., *The Power of the People:Active Nonviolence in the United States* (Culver City, California: Peace Press, 1977), pp. 16–17.
2.   *Ibid.*, p. 98.
3.   Albert S. Bigelow, "Why I am Sailing into the Pacific–Test Area," *Liberation* (February, 1958), pp. 4–6. Reprinted in Staughton Lynd, *Nonviolence in America: A Documentary History* (Indianapolis: Bobbs Merrill, 1966), p. 346.
4.   Martin Luther King, Jr., quoted in *The Power of the People*, p. 167.
5.   Pat Farren, "Nonviolent Civil Disobedience: Gentle Strength in Action," *Peacework* (November, 1984), p. 1.
6.   Some protesters refused to give their names at the time of the arrest and subsequently were not pursued by the state's attorney and others had separate trials, leaving 26 for the main trial.
7.   Philip Fiermonte, "Trial a Unique Opportunity to Examine Latin America," *Burlington Free Press* (November 15, 1984), p. 8 A.
8.   Testimony, Philip Fiermonte, November 14, 1984.
9.   Testimony, Sonja Hernandez, November 14, 1984.
10.   Testimony, Phillipe Bourgois November 14, 1984.
11.   Testimony, David Rosenberg, November 15, 1984.
12.   Testimony, Lea Terhune, November 15, 1984.
13.   John Stockwell, quoted in Tom Slayton, "Witness Says U. S. Planned an Invasion," *Rutland Herald* (November 16, 1984), pp. 1 and 4.

NONVIOLENT CIVIL DISOBEDIENCE 103

14. David McMichael, quoted in Ted Tedford, "Sit-In Witness Deplore Central American Policy," *Burlington Free Press* (November 16, 1984) p. 1 B.
15. Testimony, Howard Zinn, November 16, 1984.
16. Testimony, Richard Falk, November 16, 1984.
17. Testimony, Ramsey Clark, November 16, 1984.
18. Closing Argument, Kevin Bradley, November 16, 1984.
19. Joan Bauer, quoted in Deborah Schoch, "Protesters' Trial a Lesson in Law and Map Reading," *Burlington Free Press* (November 18, 1984), pp. 1 B and 4 B.
20. Closing Argument, William Dorsch, November 16, 1984.
21. Charge to the Jury, Judge Frank Mahady, November, 16, 1984.
22. Deborah Schoch, "Stafford Sit-In Defendants Cleared," *Burlington Free Press* (November 17, 1984), p. 1 A and 4 A.
23. Patricia Bedard, quoted in Schoch, "Protesters' Trial a Lesson," p. 4 B.
24. Sylvia Knight, quoted in Schoch, "Protesters' Trial a Lesson", p. 4 B.
25. Rob Borger, quoted in Susan Green, "Criminals to Patriots," *Vanguard Press* (November 25, December 2, 1984), p. 5.
26. Kevin Bradley, quoted in Schoch, "Protesters' Trial a Lesson," p. 4 B.
27. Jeanne Keller, quoted in Schoch, "Protesters' Trial a Lesson," p. 4 B.
28. Jeanne Keller, quoted in "Protesters' Unusual Defense Ends in Controversial Victory," *The New York Times* (December 4, 1984), p. A 28.
29. "Your View," *Burlington Free Press* (November 25, 1984), p. 9 B.

PART II

EDUCATING FOR GLOBAL CONSCIOUSNESS

Introduction

Though global justice and peace remain elusive goals, they must be kept in the forefront if we as a species hope to survive. No longer can we isolate ourselves, pretending that guarded national borders or devastating weapons of war will somehow protect us from the rest of the world. In the age of nuclear proliferation, every nation is vulnerable, every person stands on the front line. There can be no winners; we all stand to lose.

The once–comforting division between "conventional war" and "nuclear war" becomes more and more blurred, even dangerously deceptive. Tomahawk missiles being installed on U. S. warships around the world, for instance, may carry a conventional warhead or a nuclear warhead, no one outside the Pentagon will ever be quite sure. A "small" war between several Third World countries could easily escalate into a superpower confrontation with horrendous consequences. As long as people suffer from lack of food or employment, adequate health care or decent housing, and continue to be exploited by the rich and powerful, armed struggle will remain an option for the oppressed. But what does armed resistance or warfare achieve, we might ask? Perhaps not much that is positive, but what alternatives are open to those struggling for freedom? How can we, in highly industrialized countries, respond more effectively, more equitably, more humanely to the needs of our brothers and sisters around the globe? These are difficult – but important – questions to confront.

What we must do is acknowledge that all of us today live on a single fragile planet which seems to be growing smaller as communications and transportation grow more sophisticated. We seem more bound together than ever. Severe hunger on one continent affects the well–being of all – and we sometimes face the ugly fact that our own national policies may be causing the suffering we deplore. We are beginning to see that the luxurious lifestyle of many Americans and other Westerners is having a negative impact on the poor in Third World countries. The demand for certain foods in highly developed countries encourages developing nations to produce these goods as much-needed cash crops, thereby neglecting the nutritional needs of their own people. More and more Americans are finally realizing that popular struggles in Central America, the Philippines, the Middle East and South Korea are basically struggles for human needs and human rights.

In spite of right-wing propaganda which bombards Americans daily, many now believe that the nuclear arms race between the United States and the Soviet Union is not only counterproductive but exceedingly treacherous. They know about the so-called "bomber gap" and "missile gap" which were used some years ago — and are still being used — to frighten Americans into supporting heavily inflated military budgets. In the mid 1980's, they see the President promoting a "Star Wars" scheme which further intensifies the genocidal arms race and costs tens of billions of dollars which could be used to satisfy human needs. The obscenity of this gimmick is even greater when distinguished scientists confirm that "Star Wars" won't work and will, in fact, act as further stimulus for a First Strike nuclear attack. Many Americans are beginning to grasp the meaning of this deadly hoax, but many others remain gullible.

Global consciousness is growing inside educational institutions as well as outside schools and universities. Global studies or global education is now a respectable field of study. Young people are confronting the issue of nuclear weapons and disarmament more than ever before, too. Even a recent poll of college freshmen, who turn out to be more interested in making money than any previous group polled, also indicates that more freshmen than before consider nuclear disarmament a major concern. Groups such as Educators for Social Responsibility have developed excellent curricula on nuclear issues and certainly deserve credit for expanding awareness. Thousands of teachers at all levels are making nuclear and peace education a focus of study. Nuclear education has come of age and will never go away. However, it also must be enlarged to include more controversial dimensions, like the role of militarism in society and the deadly connection between nuclear arms development and intervention in Third World countries.

Part II addresses a variety of ways of educating for global consciousness. The first chapter concentrates on education for peaceful and just relations in teaching and learning. The second chapter examines a statewide effort to help young people analyze the bilateral nuclear arms freeze proposal and subsequently make an intelligent decision on this issue. In the next chapter, many creative examples of use of the arts to further a global perspective are presented. The following chapter concentrates on educating about genocide, its terrible consequences in the global community and ways it can be prevented. A critical study of the textbook portrayal of America as champion of freedom and protector of peace in Third World countries is next. The broad concept of "worldmindedness" and education for "worldmindedness" as a path to peace and justice is examined in the following chapter. The educational challenge and promise of "mutual aid," a term originally developed by Peter Kropotkin to suggest social cooperation, is offered as a way of promoting greater equality and freedom in education in the concluding chapter of Part II.

Both formal and informal education can focus on the movement from a war system to justice and peace. In this section, many suggestions are made to expand global consciousness in schools and colleges. Clearly, educational institutions have a critical role to play in the effort to develop and interpret a global perspective. In addition, education for global consciousness requires cooperative understanding and action from informal educators. Citizens learn from active involvement in local and regional issues which directly affect their lives. The process of educating for an emerging world of justice and peace is lifelong and takes many forms. The most important thing, as the following chapters suggest, is that we must work with activists to raise global awareness and fulfill our hope for peace.

CHAPTER 7

Educating for Peaceful and Just Relations:
Confluence and Context in Teaching and Learning

MARY – LOU BREITBORDE SHERR,
Curry College

Ideals of peace and justice must be taught and practiced by teachers and students, not as a separate curriculum "package" but as an integral part of the experience of schools. Strategies for making explicit the social context of learning and the confluence of ideas in a social group must be available. So, too, must strategies be available for making explicit the historical and social context of curriculum content and the connections between, or the confluence, of knowledge and value, thought and action.

The goals of effective teaching and learning require an infusing of the ideas of context and confluence throughout the content and process of education. While life and work are essentially social, so too is learning. For Dewey,[1] learning is experiencing: educative experience is experience mediated by others and thus is inherently social. For Buber,[2] the quality of educational experience depends upon the strength of human relationships. To the extent that school experience consists solely of didactic instruction by teachers and quiet acquiescence by students, children will be prevented from the full potential of learning in groups. Learning is not always solitary, nor is it always quiet. Certainly it is not always stimulated by one adult alone. If Dewey was correct in saying that the "interest" of the student must be engaged before full understanding can occur and if Piaget was correct in saying that there is something qualitatively different about human beings at various ages and levels of experience, then students may be more responsive and understand better when they learn in collaboration with their peers.

What follows is a description of some strategies for changes in process and curriculum content to reflect greater social awareness and to educate toward peace. Process strategies include group learning techniques, peer tutoring, ways to build community in the classroom and peaceful conflict resolution. Proposed curricular revisions include multicultural and interdisciplinary education, the contexting of "facts" in their social and political frameworks, the teaching of skills in context and connection and the confluence of cognitive affective and behavioral dimensions of experience.

What unites these proposed changes is the idea that knowledge is confluent and contexted. It is not bounded by "disciplines" nor limited to lists of skills and information to be "mastered". Neither does it reside with one person in total authority, nor exist separate from the varied conditions of human life. Knowledge is created from the flowing together of experience and meaning derived from several sources of many types in a social and historical context. Schools ought to be collaborative environments which make that creative process explicit.

To depend on a curriculum "package" to teach communication and cooperation skills, separate from both stated and hidden curricula, is risky. Too often the lessons learned in these isolated times will be contradicted by the experience of the rest of school day. I think it far more powerful to infuse education for peace and justice into all areas of the curriculum and the processes through which the curriculum is conveyed. The next several pages will describe first some ideas for change in the teaching–learning process, then ways in which many curriculum areas need revision.

Relational Strategies

Structured collaborative learning provides students and teachers with new and peaceful relationships with each other and with knowledge. Peer tutoring, as one example, benefits the learner, whose experience, interests and language more closely match his or her tutor. Peer tutoring also benefits the tutor, who takes on a more active, empowered relationship with the material presented. Other forms of collaborative learning, such as group projects, learning teams, and group investigations, place students in new relationships with each other, with a group and with knowledge.

Collaborative learning may simply entail having study groups work on teacher–presented material. It may be a "jigsaw" method, wherein each member of a group researches an essential piece of the group's topic and conveys that information to the group. [3] In group–investigation techniques, the group may determine the specific subject of study, perhaps within a larger unit presented by the teacher, and also determines the division of research tasks among members and the format of presentation.

Research into the cognitive effects of collaborative learning yields positive results for all kinds of students in all areas of study where the technique requires the contribution of all members and where there is a clear reason for helping others. [4] There is some evidence that different collaborative techniques may improve different kinds of learning and thinking; group–investigation, for example, may develop students' higher–order problem–solving skills. [5] But students must be given specific responsibilities and each member's contribution must be needed by the whole group. In addition, students must receive whatever help they might need to accomplish their tasks, whether from the teacher, from other students, or from another resource person. There is no reason, for example, why a student with a reading disability cannot receive help from the resource room teacher on his or her part of a group project, thereby practicing skills in the context of meaningful content.

It is important to note that collaborative learning challenges some of the usual assumptions about authority and about knowledge. That teachers sometimes avoid group projects and peer tutoring for fear that student learning will be unevenly distributed and unobservable, reveals the teacher's need to control the distribution of knowledge. Further, it reveals their assumption that knowledge is something finite which they possess and their students do not. Freire called this the "banking concept of education."[6] But if knowledge is confluent, in the sense that it advances from exchanges of meaning and experience, the best teachers will be open to learning from their students. Any differences among students and teachers in the amount, the kinds and the quality of knowledge they can contribute should be valued in collaborative exchange. Some students can easily master and remember written facts; others can contribute an analytical dimension; still others learn and convey concepts best through graphic, experiental, or creative means. A student who seriously studies the arts and crafts of a Native American tribe and who can discuss cultural form and symbolism has a different, not lesser, knowledge of tribal life than another student who has read about and reported on tribal beliefs and ways of life. These two students have much to teach each other. Alone, each has a less complete, more fragmented knowledge. The literature on the complementary nature of left and right brains, as well as on educating "the whole child", is relevant here.

Exchanges of knowledge will also allow participants to realize that knowledge is always contexted in the social and personal background of the "knower". Students presented with the same information will differ slightly in their focus and understanding; another interpretation may modify, expand or refute one's initial perception. Two children studying Sacajawea's role in the Lewis and Clark expedition may "know" differently if one is a white child who reads "facts" from an encyclopedia and the other is a Shoshone.

Similarly to collaborative learning, collaborative teaching offers students models of adult cooperation. As long as teachers are presumed to know everything that their students need to know, then it will be difficult for them to admit to themselves and each other that there are   areas better left to another teacher. If knowledge is understood to be the product of ongoing social exchange, and the excitement of learning understood to be the discovery or creation of that knowledge, then teachers might happily collaborate with other adults in finding ways to create that experience for themselves and their students.

The "in–between" times during a school day are important opportunities to restructure learning processes. A child refuses to do his work, or fights with another child over a book or recess ball, or insults another's physical appearance or ethnicity. The ways these problems are resolved convey messages about power, control and relationship. The wealth of literature on humanistic education, moral education, classroom–as–community, conflict resolution and peace–making skills can be taken together to make the learning of those aspects of classroom life called "hidden curricula" more peaceful and more socially responsible.

Many resources in the tradition of "humanistic education" are available to teachers who want to teach tolerance, acceptance, trust and communication skills. Two of these are Stanford's *Developing Effective Classroom Groups*[8] and Simon et al, *Values Clarification.*[9] Happily, the nuclear arms control movement has spawned a host of educational materials aiming to teach conflict resolution and peacemaking skills. These are easily obtained through organizations like the Children's Creative Response to Conflict Program in Nyack, New York; Educators for Social Responsibility in Cambridge, Massachusetts; and the Wilmington College Peace Resource Center in Wilmington, Ohio. Among the best of these materials are William Kreidler's book, *Creative Conflict Resolution;*[10] the handbook by Priscilla Prutzman et al. *The Friendly Classroom for a Small Planet;*[11] and the K–12 curriculum developed by Educators for Social Responsibility, entitled *Perspectives.*[12]

Lawrence Kohlberg's method of teaching ethical problem-solving skills through discussion of moral dilemmas[13] can be modified to draw upon naturalistic problems that occur in an average schoolchild's day. Decision–making concerning the child who is always selected last for sports teams, the child who suspects another of stealing her lunch money, the child who cheated on a test because home problems prohibited her studying, are some of many scenarios which can be used to resolve problems which come up during the week. This can be done in a way that involves students in a sharing of decision–making responsibility and an awareness of the points of view of others. Carol Gilligan, however, has pointed out the limitations of Kohlberg's theory of moral development which has not taken enough account of the differences between girls' and boys' moral decision–making. In fact, she says, girls have typically been more sensitive to the needs and viewpoints of others, a sensitivity oftentimes interpreted as weakness and dependence.[14]

It is a central tenet of this chapter, however, that skills-building even in human relations will not necessarily become habits of behavior or mind. The authors of *The Friendly Classroom* themselves admit in their introduction that "skills are not enough," that "even very young children learn very quickly the kinds of answers that teachers like." When asked to consider actual conflicts that might arise in their own homes, children's responses were more honest and quite different, to wit: "I'd punch him in the nose." These authors correctly point out that children learn through experiencing.[15] But experiences arranged for the purpose of learning to relate peacefully and justly ought to be meaningful to children and reinforced consistently throughout a compatible school environment. William Glasser's model of institutionalizing classroom meetings as contexts for addressing a variety of class issues helps to create such an environment.[16]

This kind of problem–solving approach to social relations cannot be divorced from the whole matter of classroom rules. The context of expectations for behavior should be open to negotiation and input from students, without, however, sacrificing the ultimate responsibility and wider perspective that is the teacher's alone. William Kreidler offers ideas for "effective rule–making" in his valuable book,[17] where he attempts to balance democratic decision–making with teacher responsibility and authority. In brief, this technique asks the teacher to list 10 or 15 rules important to her, then to present this list to the class and discuss the reasons behind each rule. Students may object to some rules, add to them, agree on consequences for infractions, and, in general, negotiate with the teacher, who has to temper students' ideas (often too punitive) with her own perspective and philosophy.

Similarly, among their excellent contributions to the area of teacher–student interaction, Thomas Good and Jere Brophy offer their views on enhancing student participation in classroom management, well presented in their book *Looking in Classrooms*:

> Ideally, rules should be elicited in guided discussion, not presented as laws. When teachers [and students] clearly define problems that need solution, students are capable of developing rules that will do the job. Participation in the establishment of rules helps students see the reasonableness of the rules and accept responsibility for keeping them. Also, helping to make the rules guides students in learning to plan their lives rationally and to see themselves as actively controlling their destinies rather than just responding to external pressures[18].

As students help to create, test out, refine and eliminate rules, they practice cooperation and negotiation which are essential to problem–solving and decision–making in a social context.

One last word is needed about contexting the teaching-learning process in peaceful and just social relations: a word concerning the impact of computerized instruction. Laying aside for the moment arguments about the value of interaction between teacher and student to teaching and learning arithmetic operations or sound-symbol relationships in phonics, I question the computer's ability to teach the kind of analysis, problem-solving and evaluating which takes into account the thoughts and concerns of other people. Educational software which confronts children with economic problems such as how to maximize sales profits may present "factual" reports of the concerns of several parties, but has nothing to say about how to communicate, negotiate or evaluate those conflicting concerns or how to adjudge different ways of communicating or negotiating. The concepts of need, trust and value go unexamined in computer software. Computers are "revolutionizing" problem-solving no more than the old dittoed sheets did; they are simply making the same processes more complex and more efficient.

Curriculum Changes

Ideas and information exist in relation to each other, and are contexted in personal, historical and social frameworks. Curricular content — both information and skills — cannot be artificially parsed, but should be presented as interdisciplinary, multicultural, and multisensory. Curriculum should address affect and behavior along with cognition. It should also concern itself with intrapersonal, interpersonal, and intergroup circles of influence, as well as consider right – and left – brain capabilities. All those components of learning comprise what George Isaac Brown and others call "confluent education".[19] Taken further, this broader conceptualization of curriculum implies that one's own experience — that is, one's interpretation of fact or event — is but one among many. It implies as well that one cannot separate thought from feeling or action, or self from others, in the quest for knowledge.

While the originators of confluent education had in mind as learning goals the development of creativity, personal awareness, communication skills, and personal development in general, confluent education has much to offer education for peaceful and just relations. Learning to be sensitive to the viewpoints and feelings of self and others, learning to recognize how personal acts are linked to their social backgrounds, learning to take responsibility for one's own actions and learning to question value and feeling along with understanding are necessary to educating for peace.

Confluent education would eliminate the practice of confining the curriculum within strictly bound disciplines and rigid time schedules so that a subject might be studied through its literature, language and scientific basis. It is not difficult, however, to infuse the traditional disciplines with the idea of confluence. History, for example, should be taught from a multigroup perspective, the "dark side" taught alongside more sanguine interpretations. Westward expansion in America ought to be presented from the various viewpoints of white settlers, federal and state governments, Native American tribes and entrepreneurial trappers and railroad builders. This great change in the face of our country was contexted in a particular set of personal biographies, social and technological changes, international developments and the clash of very different cultures. Students can research the frames of references of different parties to the same series of events and try taking on alternative perspectives through techniques such as puppetry, role play and guided fantasy. By examining the literature of the time — autobiographies, documents, fiction, diaries and logs — and by creating their own fictitious accounts, staging debates, enacting Congressional inquiries and the like, students can examine their own feelings and values as they link cognitive with affective learning.

The study of war, to take another example from history, is a study of tensions and conflicts among many parties in particular contexts of time and space, tensions and conflicts which possibly could have been resolved nonviolently. One need only look at how very different are prevailing American and Soviet interpretations of World War II for evidence that context determines "fact" and that two parties may see conflicts and their resolutions differently. Again, students can be encouraged to put themselves in the place of the American president, a Japanese–American or German–American citizen, a European Jew, a Russian peasant, a German soldier or a pacifist. These "personal" experiences coupled with "expert" historical accounts, government documents, paintings and literature of the era will more fully inform students of the issues and alternatives than does the typical one–textbook, one–filmstrip approach.

In literature, children can study the conflict which is essential to well–written and interesting stories from the viewpoints of several characters, and discuss constructive and destructive ways of resolution. There are currently available listings of children's books which serve as models of positive, nonviolent conflict resolution. Both UNICEF and the organizations mentioned previously in this chapter make such lists available to the public. [20] Among these books, Shel Silverstein's *The Giving Tree* [21] describes the changing relationship of a growing boy and his favorite tree. Tomie de Paolo's *The Knight and the Dragon* [22] would really rather not fight, despite public pressure. Bruce and Katherine Coville's *The Foolish Giant* [23] teaches the local townspeople about altruism and looking beyond appearances and the latest Dr. Seuss book, *The Butter Battle Book*, [24] explores the folly of the notion that building bigger weapons will ensure one's survival.

Science offers examples of group behavior and conflicts in animal life, of the difficulty of balancing progress with pollution, of ethics and the positive and negative effects of technological innovation. C. A. Bowers, for example, offers a model unit plan on technology from an existential–phenomenological perspective in his book *Cultural Literacy for Freedom*. [25] In his unit, students look at the history of technology and the relationship of technological to historical–political development and critically examine the impact of technology on their own lives, their community, America and the world. Social studies can include comparative looks at cultural behavior and cultural conflict, as well as patterns of human adaptation to physical and social conditions. How fortunate if the classroom or the community offers a mix of people of different cultural backgrounds: if not, students must still be exposed to the fact of our multicultural society and world.

Finally, to make education confluent and contexted, the teaching of "basic skills" needs modification. Instead of the present method of linking skills solely by their presumed sequence, which in itself is debatable, we must teach skills holistically and within the context of their usefulness. We must be concerned with more than the "how" in skills teaching; we must consider also the "what." It is far more meaningful to children, and far more important to the educational goals expressed in this essay, to teach reading skills in the context of good literature than to present skills practice as a series of worksheets or workbook pages with little apparent connection or application, as if they were ends in themselves.

Similarly, math practice must move from pages of "problems," which are merely rote operations, to the solving of actual problems using these operations. Students might, for example, practice math skills by helping the building principal budget for paper supplies. They might exercise their questioning and outlining skills by finding out and presenting the issues and concerns behind a local referendum and practice computational skills using the results on voting day. Ultimately, if teachers begin to care more about what their students are reading and what problems they are solving and to depend less on the limited materials offered by educational publishers, the connection between skills and content will be easy to make. We must move beyond the idea that knowledge is having a number of facts at our disposal, that the knowledgeable person scores highest in "Trival Pursuit."

The idea of world citizenship ought to inform all areas of the curriculum. To express Dewey's theory that "interest" precedes any real learning, we must move beyond the present and immediate interests of children to issues which are *in* their interest. Dewey never meant to limit interest to fleeting passions; decorating worksheets and bulletin boards with Michael Jackson, Smurfs and Care Bears does not satisfy the kind of interest Dewey had in mind. Rather, the themes of confluence and context would dictate a conception of student interest which links personal experience to the world community, with each affecting the other.

It is no longer sufficient to educate for personal development or personal survival. Human development is not merely personal, nor is survival possible without peace in the world. Both these goals hinge on a critical understanding of social issues, an ability to negotiate one's needs in peaceful ways, and a recognition that responsibility to self is contexted in and confluent with responsibility to the social world. The ideas and suggestions offered in this essay are one part of the effort to educate our youngsters and our teachers toward these ends.

Notes

1. J. Dewey, *Experience and Education*. (New York: Macmillan, 1938).
2. M. Buber, *I and Thou* (translated by Walter Kaufmann). (New York: Charles Scribner's Sons, 1970).
3. E. Aronson, *The Jigsaw Classroom*. (Beverly Hills, CA: Sage Publications, 1978).
4. R. E. Slavin, "Synthesis of Research on Cooperative Learning." *Educational Leadership*, 38, (May, 1981), pp. 655–660.
5. *Ibid*.
6. P. Freire, *Pedagogy of the Oppressed*. (New York: Seabury Press, 1974).
7. K. Benne, "Authority in Education," *Harvard Educational Review*, 40 (1970) pp. 385–410.
8. G. Stanford, *Developing Effective Classroom Groups*. (New York: Hart, 1977).
9. S. B. Simon, L. Howe & H. Kirschenbaum, *Values Clarification: A Handbook of Practical Strategies for Teachers and Students*. (New York: Hart, 1972).
10. W. J. Kreidler, *Creative Conflict Resolution*. (Glenview, IL: Scott, Foresman, 1984).
11. P. Prutzman, M. L. Burger, G. Bodenhamer & L. Stern, *The Friendly Classroom for a Small Planet*. (Wayne, NJ: Avery Publishing Group, 1978).
12. *Perspectives: A Teaching Guide to Concepts of Peace*. (Cambridge, MA: Educators for Social Responsibility, 1983).
13. L. Kohlberg, "The Cognitive–Developmental Approach to Moral Education" and "The Moral Atmosphere of the School." In D. Purpel & K. Ryan, eds., *Moral Education: It Comes with the Territory* (Berkeley: McCutchan, 1976).
14. C. Gilligan, "Woman's Place in Man's Life Cycle," *Harvard Educational Review*, 49, (November, 1979), pp. 431–446.
15. Prutzman, et al, *op. cit.*, p. 6.

16.   W. Glasser, *Schools Without Failure*. (New York: Harper & Row, 1969).

17.   Kreidler, *op. cit.* See chapter 3.

18.   T. L. Good, and J. Brophy. *Looking in Classrooms*. (New York: Harper & Row, 1978) p. 171.

19.   G. I. Brown, *Human Teaching for Human Learning: An Introduction to Confluent Education*. (New York: Viking Press, 1971).

20.   A. Pellowski, "A Personal, Selective Bibliography of 50 Books That Generally Bring Out Peaceful and Understanding Feelings in Children." (New York: Information Center on Children's Cultures, United States Committee for UNICEF, 1975).

21.   S. Silverstein, *The Giving Tree*. (New York: Harper & Row, 1964).

22.   T. dePaolo, *The Knight and the Dragon*. (New York: G. Putnam & Sons, 1980).

23.   B. Coville, and K. Coville, *The Foolish Giant*. (New York: Lippincott, 1978).

24.   A. S. Geisel, (Dr. Seuss), *The Butter Battle Book*. (New York: Random House, 1984).

25.   C. A. Bowers, *Cultural Literacy for Freedom*. (Eugene, OR: Elan Publishers, 1974).

CHAPTER 8

The Nuclear Freeze in Schools: Educational Reconstruction in Action

DAVID R. CONRAD

University of Vermont

For a decade the philosophy of educational reconstruction has struggled to stay alive as teachers and administrators grow more cautious, students concentrate on future careers and educational institutions confront retrenchment. A small number of educators have continued to stress education for social change–for transformation of self and society from exploitation, greed and nihilism to sharing, empowerment, and justice–but their quiet voice has been muffled by the roar of others. The situation is changing, however, as the demand for a more provocative, more globally conscious education grows. Ironically, this is occurring at a time when government and corporate officials are promulgating a narrower, "back to the basics" education in an effort to ensure a high tech future.

Progressive forces are gathering strength and educational reconstruction is rising to bring controversial issues like the nuclear freeze and disarmament into the mainstream of schools across the United States. Few teachers and students realize the nuclear education being introduced has close ties to the philosophy of educational reconstruction. But the fact is that for many years reconstructionists have considered it their obligation to deal thoroughly and critically with such critical issues as peace, disarmament and the creation of a democratic world community of nations.

In 1932, George Counts challenged educators to "face squarely and courageously every social issue, to come to grips with life in all of its stark reality"[1] in his powerful speech entitled "Dare Progressive Education Be Progressive?" Theodore Brameld, "the leading reconstructionist since mid–century"[2] according to Maurice P. Hunt, urged in 1970 that curriculum be redesigned and that controversial issues become the focus. Brameld called for a curriculum "focused on the pressing concrete problems of mankind and subjected to the most searching questions and criticisms that can be raised in the adventure of teaching and learning".[3] Twenty years earlier in *Ends and Means in Education: A Midcentury Appraisal* Brameld urged that American schools be transformed . into "powerful institutions of cultural change toward the goal of a planet-wide democratic order".[4]

Today, thousands of educators at all levels are taking Counts' and Brameld's words seriously in their exploration of issues dealing with peace and disarmament. Respected journals like *The Teachers College Record*, *Phi Delta Kappan* and *Educational Leadership* have devoted all or most of recent issues to this theme. Nuclear curriculum materials are hotly debated and even attacked by the President of the United States. A fast-growing organization, Educators for Social Responsibility, has sponsored several "Days of Dialogue" on the nuclear arms race and chapters around the country have organized educational activities. From workshops in Palo Alto, California on "Children and the Effects of the Nuclear Threat" and "How Can Educators Influence the Political Process?" to establishment of a network of adult educators involved in nuclear issues in Syracuse, New York, this group is working actively to make education respond to our crisis times.[5]

Scholars representing a variety of disciplines have urged recently that education deal with disarmament problems in the curriculum. Richard J. Barnet, author of *Real Security*, claims that "the teaching profession has failed to prepare young people to live in the nuclear age"[6] and Michael Nagler, author of *America Without Violence*, deplores the "American student's and American public's illiteracy with regard to peace." "Of all illiteracies to be identified in recent years," Nagler argues, "this should be most distressing, for why Johnny cannot conceive of peace is ultimately more dangerous than why he cannot read".[7] Educational philosopher Maxine Greene maintains that peace education should "lead to a critique of technical talk and control" and that young people should "be empowered to ponder new possibilities, alternatives to destruction and war".[8] And Jonathan Schell believes that education is "our only hope for the long term...education for new ways of thinking," according to Stanley Elam.[9] "Educators," Schell told Elam, "are the front line".[10]

Schell may be correct, but it is certainly not clear that the school as an institution dedicated to transmitting cultural values has the freedom to deal openly and incisively with controversial issues like nuclear disarmament. Jonathan Kozol, for instance, expresses a dim view of what schools can accomplish: "School does not exist to foster ethics or upheaval. It exists to stabilize the status quo ... It exists to get its citizens prepared for moral compromise".[11] And Nobuo Shimahara, an educational anthropologist, shares pessimism with others that schools have failed to "become a frontier of social change," but he asserts that "education (which is not always schooling) will be able to play a more active role, *if* it is infused with galvanized enthusiasm for renewal, if it helps to fulfill social self–realization and if it demonstrates a bold commitment to the alteration of our course of action".[12] Educational reconstructionists support this active role suggested by Shimahara, though they know well the barriers Kozol identifies. Contemporary reconstructionists agree with Brameld that the choice for the future is clear: "...whether to take sides with the forces of global annihilation or with the forces of global transformation".[13]

In recent years several psychiatrists have become identified with the "forces of global transformation" in their profound concern about the effects of the nuclear weapons buildup on the human psyche. William Beardslee and John Mack distributed a questionnaire to 1000 elementary and high school students between 1978 and 1980, with more detailed responses requested from 100 students in grades 10–12 in the Boston area. The results indicated that adolescents are deeply disturbed about the possibility of nuclear war and have serious doubts about their future survival. Cynicism, sadness, bitterness and a feeling of helplessness were expressed. To overcome these negative feelings, Mack maintains, "at the very least these young people need an opportunity to learn about and participate in decisions on matters which affect their lives so critically".[14] Robert Jay Lifton also reports on the deep sense of hopelessness expressed by adolescents during workshops he conducted. "Questions arise among the young about adults' capacity to keep them, and the world, alive," Lifton observes, noting that "In different but parallel ways the young and old become frightened, angry, confused. And we begin to see the truth of the contention that nothing in our lives is unaffected by these demonic technological entities".[15]

Tony Wagner, Executive Director of Educators for Social Responsibility, quotes a letter from a thirteen year old girl who wrote to ESR. She speaks about her fear of nuclear war and observes that her teachers will not teach about nuclear weapons because this subject is not part of American history or biology, mathematics or English. Her principal said she should ask her parents or learn about nuclear issues in church. "Please help us quick," she implores. "Next year we'll be in high school and it's about time we got educated."[16] Wagner has found in working with young people on nuclear issues that listening carefully and exploring concerns without imposing a particular viewpoint helps students share deep feelings so that they "... no longer feel alone and powerless in a solitary world of unshared fears."[17]

The Town Meeting Project

In order to help high school age students become more hopeful about the future and address the kinds of concerns outlined by Beardslee and Mack, Lifton, and Wagner, the Center for World Education at the University of Vermont and the American Friends Service Committee in Vermont teamed up to initiate the Vermont High School Town Meeting on the Nuclear Weapons Freeze project in the Spring of 1983. The project began in December 1982 when staff members of the two organizations and several interested high school teachers met to discuss possible ways to help students deal with the nuclear issue which troubled them greatly. Recalling the previous two Vermont Town Meeting Day votes on the nuclear freeze in 1981 and 1982 when a total of 184 towns voted for the freeze, the organizers believed that young people would be interested in voting on the same issue their parents had considered. Moreover, the 1982 vote became important national news because so many towns in a traditionally conservative state voted overwhelmingly for the bilateral freeze. As the Town Meeting votes inspired people around the country, perhaps a statewide project focusing on the same issue in high schools would inspire educators in other states to make a similar effort. Most important, however, was the need to explore, analyze and debate the issue so that students would gain a deeper understanding of the nuclear arms race and feel more competent in dealing with it.

At a January meeting, some twenty high schools in different parts of the state were represented by students, faculty and / or administrators. It was quickly agreed that students and faculty would work cooperatively in the schools, with student councils often taking major responsibility. The wording of the resolution was discussed and the group agreed to accept essentially the same wording for the high school vote as for the earlier adult vote. The day of the vote and a commitment to balance and diversity in educational work preceding the vote was agreed upon. A policy of multiple perspectives was accepted as good educational pedagogy, but the group also knew that such a controversial issue would only be accepted by public school authorities if a "balanced" presentation was made and, even then, some antagonism could be anticipated.

A statewide coordinating committee was established to make further policy decisions. Several participants volunteered to prepare a bibliography of print and media materials available on the subject and several others offered to look into development of a poster for statewide distribution. Each school would design its own activities and seek its own resources, but the coordinating committee and sponsoring organizations would provide films, articles, resource lists, ballots, and background material. Both pro and anti–freeze films were obtained and a list of local resource people and materials presenting different perspectives was sent to participating schools. Multiple copies of statements on the Freeze by the U. S. State Department (against) and the Center for Defense Information (for) were mailed to each cooperating teacher.

The structure of the project varied from school to school. Though the voting day and text of the resolution were agreed in common, little else was identical. True to reconstructionist principles, democratic decision – making and a grass – roots effort were emphasized. In some schools, debate took place in large assemblies as well as individual classrooms. In others, students participated only in English and social studies classes. In several schools an entire day was devoted to exploration of peace and disarmament issues. One of these, Champlain Valley Union High School, offered students numerous options during its "Defense and Disarmament" day – long program. Sixteen concurrent events each period featured lectures on a stronger defense, student presentations on various nuclear issues, films like "Dr. Strangelove" and "The Atomic Cafe," debates between community peace activists and defense advocates, slide programs followed by discussion, panel discussions featuring students from nine different countries and a videotape of a conference call between students and U. S. Senator Patrick Leahy. Harry Chaucer, an experienced science teacher who organized events at this school and had a chance to observe various sessions, commented:

> "I can state with pride that I have never seen this degree of sustained intense learning displayed by any large group of students in any program in my teaching career. These adolescents struggled with the most difficult issues of our times. They

wrestled with inconsistencies between speakers, strove to accumulate information and meticulously built arguments."[18]

With Chaucer's help the Vermont–NEA (National Education Association) Board of Directors voted unanimously to endorse the statewide high school project and later this organization was awarded the NEA's Dorros Peace Trophy for its support of the project.

Another high school, Bellows Free Academy in St. Albans, devoted the week before the vote to "Global Awareness and Peace Education Week." Professors from local colleges and universities addressed peace issues for several days, followed by an entire day of activities at the end of the week. As guest speakers arrived in the morning, they were ushered to seats at one end of the gymnasium. Soon the high school band began a stirring number and students filed briskly to the bleachers. After a few comments and brief introductions of the guests, the program began. The lights grew dim, a John Denver song wafted through the hall and a tiny 3 or 4 year old girl with a lighted candle walked slowly to the center of the gymnasium where she passed the flame to a circle of high school students gathered there. Before long each person in the circle had a lighted candle and the group started singing peace songs. Most remarkable was the attentiveness of hundreds of students sitting in the bleachers of the darkened gymnasium. The mood created in this American high school in the 1980s was one of seriousness and concern, respect and caring.

When the assembly ended, students and guests adjourned to various rooms where more didactic presentations were scheduled: the medical effects of nuclear war, the lessons of Hiroshima, links between environmental concerns and global peace, the Gandhis of history, the role of the military in society and a variety of war / peace films. In the afternoon, the Bread and Puppet Theatre led a peace parade of students and faculty to a local park. Throughout the day, students made choices whether or not to participate in the peace activities. They could either remain in their regularly scheduled classes or select one of a half dozen seminars or presentations.

Attendance was good at most peace events, with films filling viewing rooms for second and third showings. Not as many students as expected participated in the Bread and Puppet parade down Main Street, however. The teacher organizing the parade speculated that a lack of information may have contributed to the participation of only 250 out of a possible 975 students. She received good support from city officials, the police and the school administration and would attempt a parade again but next time have students organize it themselves. A more successful artistic expression of peace was a series of art exhibits on display in a local bank and in a florist's window. Prepared by commercial art students, the art work was a collection of original designs and illustrations.

Imaginative and creative ways of exploring peace and the freeze issue prevailed during the high school project. Certainly aesthetic approaches played a prominent role. A poster contest with both pro and anti-freeze themes was organized in one school and in another a poster workshop was held. Student–made posters covered the walls of many schools. Writing classes concentrated on the nuclear theme and an essay contest was held; a committee judged the contest and the winning essays were posted. Some teachers asked students to write about their feelings, stressing that no easy answers were needed just a willingness to struggle with questions. In several schools the school newspaper was devoted to poems and articles about nuclear war. Films were a central feature of many programs, too, with the Center for Defense Information's "War Without Winners II" and the American Security Council's "Countdown for America" receiving most attention. Films on civil defense like "No Place to Hide" and on citizen responses to the nuclear threat like "Washington to Moscow (Vt.): The Road to Global Sanity" were shown in a few schools. Literally dozens of other films were screened and discussed.

Peace scholar Johan Galtung argues that "students in a school do not have more control over their own situation than do workers in a factory." [9] Though Galtung's observations about the limits of student control in general may have merit, students participating in the high school project certainly exercised considerable control. In several cases, students were the primary organizers and represented their school at planning meetings. In one of the largest high schools in the state, two interested teachers decided that students should do almost everything themselves. "It was to be their project or it wasn't worth doing," a teacher commented. "We would advise on how to get organized, insure a balanced approach, go with them when they asked permission, and tell them how to get information out. The actual doing was up to them," she continued.[20] At first nothing happened. The two teachers wondered if they should take charge. Then, students got serious and started organizing a program. A teacher who asked her writing classes to do essays on the subject, and did one herself, comments on the process:

> "Within three days they had decided to go for it, gotten permission, held a bake sale, and gotten most of the speakers rounded up...Kids made posters, stuffed mailboxes, registered voters, wrote a computer program for alphabetizing names for the checklist, thought of having a real town meeting assembly the day before the vote, and prepared for their role on the student panel... They used all of their skills – math, English, history, art, logic, listening, social, economic – and did an amazing job. I relaxed after the first day. They did what they said they would do – no reminders were needed ... I couldn't have planned a better learning activity for them and for me."[21]

In a different school, a social studies teacher became involved in the project as a result of two seniors asking her to help. Students and teachers met together for a month and a half and at the end, the teacher declared: "This was clearly the *most* meaningful thing I did as a teacher this year." And this in spite of the fact that at this school administrators were terribly fearful. Though the school board gave the go-ahead, not a single word about 400 students and faculty investigating the dilemma of the arms race reached the local press. The teacher's report and "thank you" to the board never reached them; the prevailing attitude, this teacher reports, was "'Phew, we got away with that one.''

Many teachers and guest presenters were impressed by the quality of dialogue taking place in schools across the state. The project seemed to raise more questions than were answered but neither teachers nor students seemed dismayed by this. One enthusiastic teacher commented: "I think I was a bit in awe of the intelligence shown by the students. Their questions and comments were articulate and insightful. They did the preparation for the project, the research, and carried the day. Quite frankly, they conducted themselves with more dignity and intelligence than their parents do at Town Meetings !'' Many agreed that as a result of the analysis and debate taking place, students voting were probably better prepared and more knowledgeable about the implications of nuclear weaponry and arms control than their parents had been when they voted on the freeze during Town Meeting days.

Of course, not all activities or aspects of the project were equally successful. In a few situations, it was not possible to involve a large segment of the faculty. In one, science and English faculty were generally supportive but social studies faculty were uncooperative. More often, social studies teachers exerted leadership. In some cases, invited speakers were boring or spoke over the heads of students. Sometimes not enough outside information or resources were allowed into the school, though one teacher reported that in–house talent was superior to imported speakers anyway. In spite of vigorous efforts on the part of the coordinating committee and individual schools to obtain speakers opposed to the freeze, including contacts with the American Legion, a few teachers reported that they would have liked more anti–freeze speakers. In several schools the administration was skeptical from the beginning, but in most the administration was supportive even enthusiastic. A few parents called one school to say they thought the program was not balanced, but their objections disappeared once they observed the program. After the vote, another parent said the presentations were biased because the final vote was so lopsided. An occasional teacher and parent commented that the issue was not appropriate in a high school.

But, on the whole, parents, students, teachers and administrators were pleased by the educational nature of the project. "Outstanding" was the usual student response, a teacher organizer noted, while another observed that students "were wildly enthusiastic and felt like they experienced something worthwhile. All those teachers and students who participated had little but praise for the project." In one school, teachers thanked the local organizers for being the "conscience" of the department.

Participating teachers grew personally and professionally from immersion in this project. Many were delighted by the ability of high school students to understand and internalize material on this complex subject. "I have seen kids go from despair to empowerment and that is exciting," an experienced teacher commented, continuing: "They have become more politically aware and politically active and that, to me, is the heart of what social studies is all about." Others noticed that students became comfortable expressing diverse, sometimes unpopular, viewpoints in public. Teachers took satisfaction in seeing young people learn the value of researching and becoming knowledgeable in a current issue of worldwide importance.

For themselves, teachers spoke of a renewed sense of involvement, a growing awareness of the critical nature and intricacies of nuclear concerns. One teacher said she finally faced the issue squarely after avoiding it for years and another was stimulated to do more reading on the subject. Some school organizers gained a great deal from the experience of coordinating a schoolwide activity. And a teacher who had been an 18 year old member of the occupation force in Japan and had seen Hiroshima concluded: "I got great satisfaction in that people were finally beginning to listen to arguments I have used since the 1940's. The kids, for the first time in my educational experience, were concerned and taking political action."

From a student point of view, the project was successful because students deeply cared about the issue. One student wrote in a school newspaper: "For the first time in at least three years, the entire student body is being given the chance to cast their vote on an issue of national importance."[22] In a different school, a student organizer enjoyed talking in front of different classes and feeling that he was working actively for peace. "Instead of always talking with people who agree totally with my view, I spoke to those who were uninformed and hungry for information," he noted, adding: "Many students told me they wanted to learn more." A school administrator reported that some students surprised themselves by their own courage in speaking their minds in a large group. Incredibly, one ninth grade honors student remarked: "I never knew that an atomic bomb was dropped on Hiroshima. My parents never told me."

Continuing to explore problems fostered by the growth of nuclear weapons is a major concern of organizers and participants in the high school town meeting. The culminating vote of 28 schools with 72% of students voting for the freeze and 2 schools with 28% of students voting against the freeze was interesting since it paralleled state and national results, but organizers knew that follow-up and further educational work was necessary. A plan for student representatives from each school to meet with all members of the Congressional delegation in the State House to debate the question of "What is national security?" was suggested. Individual schools came up with their own designs as well. Teachers in some schools planned to design units on nuclear war and others to organize a "day of dialogue" patterned after the model designed by Educators for Social Responsibility. A student club called "Peace Seekers" was formed in one school to provide an outlet for students working on peace-related issues and STOP (Student / Teacher Organization to Prevent Nuclear War) groups have been started in several others. Some schools intended to have annual town meetings and debate other controversial issues as well. One high school decided that students would be recognized for their world peace efforts through the Mohandas Gandhi Peace Award awarded each year at graduation. As a result of media coverage, including a brief debate on network television by four students and the awarding of the National Education Association's 1983 Dorros Peace Trophy, coordinators hoped that educators in other states would be encouraged to try similar programs. Television viewers in West Germany and newspaper readers in Japan who heard about the project might also be heartened by the debate occurring in Vermont high schools, the coordinators believed.

Beyond the Freeze Debate

In spite of the success of the high school town meeting, questions remain about the impact on students' attitudes and behavior. Was debate on the freeze issue comprehensive enough? Were links made to other issues like military vs. social expenditures? Will students translate their new knowledge into constructive action? Will they be more critical voters and more active, questioning citizens generally? Did schools permit teachers and students to examine the freeze issue primarily because it was a relatively narrow question on a relatively acceptable issue? Would school authorities set up roadblocks if the focus became broader, like the impact of militarism on American society? These are central questions which demand serious consideration.

What should the next steps be? How would reconstructionists proceed beyond the high school town meeting project? Zacharias, Gordon, and Davis suggest that basic questions need asking, questions which could well form the core of a reconstructed curriculum: "What are the costs and benefits of a policy of deterrence in a nuclear age? How does our national security policy affect our foreign policy and our domestic economy? With a trillion dollars, how can the security of the United States and its allies be best guaranteed?"[23]

Analysis of war itself, not nuclear weapons in isolation, must become the focus of instruction in the future, a number of scholars agree. More than ten years ago, educational reconstructionist William Boyer argued that militarism or "war education" which teaches Americans to accept war as a necessity in dealing with human problems must be examined critically. "The military outlook pervades every dimension of our American system," Boyer asserts.[24] He suggests that "reconstructive" planning which means planning of the future, exploring a variety of possible peaceful futures, should replace "expansive" planning which emphasizes quantitative, technological, militaristic solutions.[25] Boyer sees war as a cultural institution which, like other institutions established by humans, can be disestablished. Education can and must turn its attention to nonviolent ways of resolving conflicts, especially conflicts between nations, as well as explore alternative forms of world organization which will make war obsolete.

Of course it will not be easy for schools to address the problems of war and militarism with boldness and openness. As international law authority Richard Falk maintains, "...the roots of militarism are deeply embedded in the huge, implacable structures of governmental bureaucracy and reach out to encompass powerful, privileged sectors of the economy, including parts of the media."[26] But the difficulty will not deter educational reconstructionists who believe that human survival depends upon the willingness – and the commitment – of educators to confront this issue head-on. Nothing less in this volatile world is sufficient. Everything that is beautiful and unique about human creativity and the natural world depends upon a reversal of present modes of thought and action. Falk speaks of the need for a "holistic vision," a new type of world order to substitute for the present war-dominated system. Like reconstructionists, he argues that "We require a politics, as well as an imagery, of transformation."[27] Is it too much to ask that this become the central concern of education? Reconstructionists do not think so.

Disarmament educator Betty Reardon writes of the role of education in achieving a demilitarized world. The underlying values of militarization must be examined, she argues, and educators in churches as well as schools must become involved. Reardon sees social violence (when human needs are unmet) and warfare (when physical violence is fomented) as forms of pathology.[28] Are social violence and warfare indeed forms of pathology, reconstructionists would inquire? If so, how can educators develop a sustained study of these problems? Why is war used so frequently to settle disputes and what are the consequences of war? What links can be found between oppression in Third World countries and a comfortable life for many in the West and Japan? Can connections be made between U. S. interventionist foreign policy and the nuclear arms race? Can peace ever be achieved without social justice?

These and many other questions lead the debate beyond the nuclear freeze issue so well explored in the High School Town Meeting project. More vigorous opposition to such broader questions may occur, but a commitment to diversity of viewpoints and openness of discussion as practiced in the high school project may lessen antagonism. Educational reconstructionists insist upon diversity and open dialogue, but do not deny a value orientation toward peace and social justice. Theodore Brameld notes that "...education neither is nor should be neutral in the wider cultural struggles of our time."[29] Contemporary reconstructionists accept this challenge, urging educators to become engaged in the struggle. The town meeting project was a significant beginning. With its success and important learnings behind, educators can choose to move toward debate, analysis and action on the broadest and deepest problems confronting humanity.

Notes

1. George Counts, quoted in *The Transformation of the School* by Lawrence A. Cremin (New York: Vintage Books, 1964), p. 259.
2. Maurice P. Hunt, *Foundations of Education: Social and Cultural Perspectives* (New York: Holt, Rinehart and Winston, 1975), p. 100.
3. Theodore Brameld, *The Climactic Decades: Mandate to Education* (New York: Praeger, 1970), p. 70.
4. Theodore Brameld, *Education for the Emerging Age* (New York: Harper and Row, 1961), p. 1.
5. See *Forum*, Newsletter of Educators for Social Responsibility, Vol. 2, (Summer 1983).
6. Richard J. Barnet, "Teaching Peace" Teachers College Record, 84, no. 1 (Fall 1982), p. 30.
7. Michael J. Nagler, "Education as a Five-Letter Word," *Teachers College Record*, 84, no. 1 (Fall 1982), p. 109.
8. Maxine Greene, "Education and Disarmament," *Teachers College Record*, 84, no. 1 (Fall 1982), p. 135.
9. Stanley Elam, "Trying to Change One's Mode of Thought: A Personal Testament," *Phi Delta Kappan*, 64, no. 8 (April 1983), p. 537.

10. Jonathan Schell, quoted in "Trying to Change One's Mode of Thought" by Stanley Elam, p. 537.

11. Jonathan Kozol, *The Night is Dark and I am Far From Home* (Boston: Houghton Mifflin, 1975), p. 183.

12. Nobuo Shimahara, "Introduction: Toward A Transformative Psycho-cultural Orientation" in *Educational Reconstruction: Promise and Challenge* (Columbus: Charles E. Merrill, 1973), p. 14.

13. Theodore Brameld, "Social Frontiers, Retrospective and Prospective" *Phi Delta Kappan*, 59, no. 2 (October 1977), p. 119.

14. John Mack, "Psychosocial Trauma" in *The Final Epidemic: Physicians and Scientists on Nuclear War* edited by Ruth Adams and Susan Cullen (Chicago: Educational Foundation for Nuclear Science, 1981), p. 26.

15. Robert Jay Lifton and Richard Falk, *Indefensible Weapons* (New York: Basic Books, 1982), p. 56–57.

16. Tony Wagner, "Why Nuclear Education?" *Educational Leadership*, 40 (May 1983), p. 40.

17. *Ibid.*, p. 41.

18. Harry Chaucer, quoted in "Vermont–NEA Wins Peace Trophy for Support of High School Nuclear Arms Freeze Vote" by Laurie B. Huse, *Vermont–NEA Today*, 49, no. 8 (May / June 1983), p. 1.

19. Johan Galtung, "Schooling and Future Society," *School Review* (August 1975), p. 545.

20. Joanne Calhoun, "The Evolution of a Student Town Meeting Day," unpublished manuscript, 1983.

21. *Ibid.*

22. Mark Gundel, "To Freeze or Not to Freeze," *S'Newsweek*, Essex Junction Education Center, April 8, 1983 p. 1.

23. Jerrald R. Zacharias, Myles Gordon and Saville Davis, "Common Sense and Nuclear Peace," *Bulletin of the Atomic Scientists*, 39, no. 4 (April 1983), p. 11S.

24. William Boyer, *Education for Annihilation* (Honolulu: Hogarth Press, 1972), p. viv.

25. *Ibid.*, pp. 127–28.

26. Lifton and Flak, *Indefensible Weapons*, p. 247.

27. *Ibid.*, p. 256.

28. Betty Reardon, *Militarization, Security and Peace Education* (Valley Forge, Pa: United Ministries in Education, 1982), p. 16.

29. Theodore Brameld, *The Climactic Decades*, p. 197.

CHAPTER 9

Toward a New Human Community: Using the Arts in Teacher Education

GERTRUDE LANGSAM
Adelphi University

Prologue

> The artist has often been the visionary
> who sees or intuits a pattern in the
> chaos and attempts to make sense of history.[1]

Several years ago I witnessed a performance of *Henry V* at the American Shakespeare Theatre in Stratford, Connecticut that has stayed with me and has implications that I would like to share.

As we walked into the theatre that day, we faced a large, open stage where the actors were dressed in informal, modern clothing and were engaged in a lively game of basketball. The energy of the players was tremendous and the spirit of the game quickly caught our attention. Before we knew it, we were involved in watching the ball as it was passed from person to person and the stage, without any props, magically caught our attention.

What connection did all of this have to do with Henry V, the Battle of Agincourt or the history of the Kings of England? We could not make a reasonable association until we remembered the lines of Shakespeare's "Prologue" to *Henry V*. Here, he apologizes to the reader (or audience) for the inadequacy of his stage and implores us all to bring our imaginary powers to the foreground. In this way, he is saying, all the parts of the drama (writer, actor, audience) can work together and make the scene come alive. Shakespeare wrote:

> Piece out our imperfections with your thoughts;
> Into a thousand parts divide one man,
> And make imaginary puissance; (armies)
> Think, when we talk of horses, that you see them...[2]

The art of teaching is, in many ways, a cooperative act. We, together with our students, must stretch our imagination across the proscenium, close the space and discover new ways of "seeing" and "hearing" the other. At the same time, we are involved in teaching courses such as history, drama, English, politics, science, economics and psychology – as well as philosophy of education, methods and ethics. How can we do all of this within the limitations of our craft ? How do we overcome the "imperfections" of our place ?

Shakespeare's "Prologue," and the improvisation offered that day at Stratford, can give us a sense of proportion – and hope. In spite of all our difficulties, the teacher must continue to believe in the possibilities of her profession. She must lift the aesthetic vision of her students, enlarge their aspirations for themselves and their community and encourage their feelings of self-worth and self-respect.

Introduction

In the emerging world community, the artist, dramatist and teacher will help to design new patterns for looking at the world of the past – and the world yet to be born. As we struggle to build this better world, we know that individual growth is central and that is what we mean by the goal of self-transformation. At the same time, we must be aware of our responsibilities toward the larger needs of humanity and look toward the goal of social-transformation.

In this two-fold commitment towards personal awareness and communal fulfillment, the arts play a significant and dramatic role. Art and artists help us to know what society is thinking. Artists reflect to a great degree the values, joys, emotions and crises of the outer world and to a great degree art is an omen of the future. Artists have an uncanny sense of the direction towards which the world is moving. From the point of view of the teacher who is trying to ally herself with the arts, art is important because it keeps us in touch with certain emotional and spiritual patterns, and, ultimately, gives the classroom a more universal and transcending quality.

In my experiences as a teacher-educator for many years, I have taught a wide variety of courses: Introduction to Education, Philosophy of Education, Philosophical Problems of Education, School and Society, Child Development, Child Guidance, Educational Research, Educational Psychology and History of Education. I have taught these courses in both the undergraduate and graduate divisions of C. W. Post Center of Long Island University, Dowling College and Adelphi University.

It is my intention in this chapter to present a variety of art experiences which occurred in some of the courses I have taught. By presenting the specific experience against the backdrop of the course itself, I hope that you, the reader, will be able to relate positively to some of the art experiences discussed and see their connection to the goals of each course.

History of Education

In the summer of 1971, I had a unique opportunity to link my "History of Education" class with an art exhibition that had just opened at the Museum of Modern Art in New York City. The exhibit was entitled "The Artist as Adversary" and the textbook that I had adopted for one of the required readings was *Models of Man: Explorations in the Western Educational Tradition*.[3] The author, Dr. Paul Nash, had compiled a collection of readings by great teachers moving in time from Plato and Aristotle up to the 20th century with such diverse exemplars as Dewey, Skinner and Buber. In his "Introduction," Nash said that the history of education could be examined in at least two ways, and proceeded to explain his point of view in teaching history through the writings of "the educated man." Nash's idea was that a "model" could be studied either as a source of "prescribed" behavior or as a "clue" to what man could become. He hoped that through these readings both kinds of activities would be stimulated.

I felt that Nash's plan of opening up the history of education through such models fit well with my own ideas of "doing history and philosophy," and I looked forward to this biographical approach to the course. Moreover, I felt that the "models of man" selected by Nash were appropriate since they were men who had confronted challenge and change in their lifetime, and represented a quality of personal courage. Through these models, we could help our students widen their horizons, deepen their sensitivities and enhance their appreciation for intellectual diversity.

Thus, when the Museum of Modern Art announced its exhibit consisting of more than 140 pieces of socially conscious art representing 21 countries and covering the period from 1863 to 1971, I felt this would be an excellent opportunity for students to relate the history of "challenge" to the history of education. We went as a group to New York City and one of my students, who was also a high school art teacher, volunteered to act as our tour guide for the day.

The results of our experience were tremendous. For many of the people in the class it was their first encounter with Picasso's "Guernica," and the shock was overwhelming! Many students were almost moved to tears at photographs taken by Jacob Riis and Lewis Hine of slums in our American cities. Photographs of early child labor by these artists were graphic and heartrending. Other students were saddened by their confrontation with examples of rural poverty, family displacement and the desperate plight of depression victims. The experience of poverty in the 1930's was "connected" with present–day examples of poverty in some areas of the United States. Students who came from the eastern end of Long Island compared the conditions seen in art works to some of the problems faced by migrant workers not far from their homes in Riverhead.

While "The Artist as Adversary" was by no means a complete historical survey, members of the class were able to make dramatic and personal "connections" between "models of man" and the exhibit before them. The artists in the collection, especially Ben Shahn, Jose Orozco and George Grosz, were recognized as men of their century who saw the inequities of their society and responded to the need for change in ways they knew best. The "tools" might have been different, but the artist and the teacher were representative of the "educated man" who accepted challenge and responded in appropriate modes. In the larger framework of human history, the artist and the teacher were both "models of man" – and models of change.

The analogy was effective and it was interesting to hear some of the reactions when we returned to the classroom. One of the students said that perhaps the hemlock, not the apple, should be the symbol of the teacher–and the educated man. She saw "The Artist as Adversary" as the enlargement of the Socratic principle– "the unexamined life is not worth living." Another student said that it was not knowledge that was the distinctive characteristic of the "model," but rather his attitude towards his right to learn and his willingness to defend this right. It was especially interesting to observe the comments of teachers who came from communities where censorship and book–banning had become major issues in the schools and public libraries. They saw real and viable connections between "intellectual freedom" and the "artist as adversary."

The visit to the Museum of Modern Art stands out in my mind whenever I think about using art as the foundation of teacher education, since we referred to that visit over and over again during the course. The work of Ben Shahn, for example, enabled our students to "see" elements of conscience and protest in ways they had never witnessed before. The concept of the "moral dilemma" became alive, and our students were involved in thinking about *sharing* moral responsibilities with men and women from all disciplines. It was a growth experience from many points of view. When we reached the 20th century and our encounter with Martin Buber, one of the students recalled the "Artist as Adversary" exhibit and said that the "real person" stands on a sacred precipice always ready to make free choices. By teaching history through the arts, I found that the teacher can help her students explore his or her own fears, responsibilities and commitments in ways that are intuitive, non–authoritative and creative.

Philosophy of Education

One semester, while teaching "Philosophy of Education," I discovered that one of my students was a high school music teacher. I searched through our Fine Arts Library at Adelphi University, determined to make a "connection" between the books we would be using in the course and music. I discovered a recording of Leonard Bernstein's "Serenade After Plato's Symposium" directed by Bernstein and performed by the Israeli Philharmonic Orchestra. I suggested to my student that he study the piece and then try to relate it to the class in terms of his own musical understanding. He did that, and after giving us a brief analysis of the music itself, he opened up discussion for the total "impressions and reflections" concerning the *Symposium*. It was a wonderful experience for all of us and the class related warmly to Plato, Bernstein and this young music teacher.

Inspired by this adventure, another student returned to the Fine Arts Library and came back with an oration by Edith Hamilton. This was the oration delivered by Edith Hamilton herself when she received a special tribute from the city of Athens. We felt that "we were there!" The Greek spirit took wings that semester and we were constantly brought back to Socrates and Plato! One student came in with his "prize," which turned out to be a recording of *The Apology* delivered by Sir Ralph Richardson, and someone else turned up with a record by Scott Buchanan called "How to Read a Platonic Dialogue." Buchanan was a "model" of the Greek spirit in many ways and he is remembered in Santa Barbara, California, for his rigorous contribution to American scholarship.

I call "Philosophy of Education" my "zig–zag" course because of the enthusiasm of students who kept returning to our Greek scholars throughout the semester. We could be in the middle of Skinner's *Walden II* when someone would appear with another Greek record, piece of sculpture or vase! At a Period in our educational history when the world seemed to deplore lack of good language in our schools and a loss of respect for the classics, it was pure delight for us to "zig–zag" from Idealism to Behaviorism. The best way to support teachers in their desire to inculcate a love of learning, a taste for good tooks and a respect for the spoken arts is to create a classroom where these elements are respected, nurtured and demonstrated. This was such a class! The contagious spirit resulted in the whole class participating in a musical play as a surprise for the instructor. It warmed our hearts and lifted our spirits. The class felt that through a variety of aesthetic experiences they became a special human community. Buber's existentialism came alive through the exchange of musical experiences, dramatic monologues and romantic poetry.

Introduction to Education:
Philosophical, Psychological, Social and Historical Foundations

This is a beginning course in teacher education and I try to introduce students to education by emphasizing the quality of *diversity* – diversity among students and diversity in methods of teaching. I have used the metaphor of the "garden" developed by Arthur Combs quite effectively, and my students respond very well to the idea of different problems in the garden requiring different implements–the tool, the rake, the shovel and so forth. One semester, while I was trying to teach the concept of "patterns of educational philosophy," I tried using the metaphor of the orchestra to explain crucial differences among the respective philosophies and how teachers adapt different patterns for different situations without losing sight of their own intrinsic commitment.

One of the students facilitated the musical metaphor by going to the blackboard and drawing a large diagram of the various positions of different musical instruments. She described for us the respective sections of the orchestra and showed that each section had its own particular strength, tone and quality. She related the sections of the orchestra to the "patterns of philosophy" and we were able to discuss the insights of the individual "patterns of thinking" to the brasses, horns, woodwinds and percussion. The students responded to the beauty of the metaphor and continued to "do philosophy" by "hearing" the different sounds that each section made. We spoke about the importance of the individual instruments and the responsibility of the individual musician to the total sound. Later on, we spoke about different "sounds" and different "children" and the importance of diversity in the orchestra from that point of view. Once, I brought my record player to class and we played part of a major concerto. The students talked about the music they heard–and the patterns of philosophy–in ways that were exciting and uniquely comprehensible. The diagram on the blackboard was a good teaching device because it helped to outline the various positions of the instruments and show the "connections" among individual musicians and the orchestra as a whole. Later, when we discussed the history of philosophy, we found our class returning to the musical metaphor. We spoke about old forms of music, such as Baroque music, and more modern music produced by Charles Ives, John Cage and Samuel Barber. We spoke about our own love of the Baroque and yet our full appreciation of the symphonies of Charles Ives. One of the students related the metaphor to teaching, arguing, for preserving some of the "basics," as well as having the courage to move out to free, more open ways of teaching. When students went back to a drawing, mood or model that was used earlier in the semester, I felt that we were able not only to "reinforce" learning (a healthy principle), but also give students an opportunity to see the larger implications of what they had already studied.

When we used the analogy of the orchestra, we asked the students: How do you see the maestro in this configuration? What is his role in the classroom/orchestra? He knows the sounds of each section and learns how to orchestrate their respective characteristics. How does the conductor / teacher do this? What else must he know? If a musician is not fulfilling his responsibility, how does the conductor approach this musician and help him become aware of his role in total symphony or concerto? What is the relationship between the classroom "dialogue" and the musical rendition? What is the connection between the individual and the whole?

We had used the analogy of the orchestra in "doing philosophy," and one day after a major public television program that featured such "stars" as Pavarotti and Marilyn Horne, one of my students said, "We're not all Pavarottis or Marilyn Hornes in this class, but I think we 'play together' very well, and I think we make a great sound." I think the entire class was touched by the remarks of this student, and we all knew what she was trying to convey. In teaching "Introduction to Education," I try to create a feeling of community in the classroom so that the prospective teachers become aware of their own sensitivity and respectful of the feelings of others. It is a *great* orchestra, we decided as a class, when each musician knows his or her part of the score and "tunes in" to the music of the whole. We learn to "do philosophy" by becoming conscious of ourselves and really listening to the "other."

One of my favorite experiences regarding music and philosophy goes back to a summer visit I had at the Marlboro School of Music in Marlboro, Vermont. I had gone there one week-end to hear Rudolph Serkin, one of the master pianists and teachers of the twentieth century. During the day, I watched Mr. Serkin in class as he turned the pages for his beginning piano students. The quiet, respectful and patient image of Mr. Serkin as he turned the pages for his young students stayed with me long after that summer experience had passed. Some time afterward, I read an interview with a *New York Times* reporter regarding Serkin's philosophy of teaching music. Mr. Serkin said to the *Times* reporter that he regarded the Marlboro School as a "community of equals." I sensed what he meant by that phrase and the feeling he was trying to convey. By "turning the pages," he was fulfilling his role in the "community of equals," for it was in the mutual commitment to music that the relationship between teacher and student was "equal."

When I discuss existentialism as a "pattern of educational philosophy," I talk about Martin Buber, the importance of the "I and Thou" relationship in the classroom and the meaning of freedom. I point out that Buber used the word "community" to describe the quality of dialogue and the importance of the free and open communication that should exist among equal human beings in contrast to the harsh, authoritarian and restrictive nature of a collective society. After talking to my students about the existential philosophy of Martin Buber, Carl Rogers and other exponents of this "pattern" of thought, I try to raise the level of the dialogue so that we begin to explore some of the more transcending qualities of thought and action that exist in the human community. We begin to move into the larger, more spiritual goals of education when we as individual teachers and citizens respond more fully, and knowingly, to our share of the true interpersonal relationship. There is a joy and beauty in participating in the real community, and I try to make this goal alive to my students.

Teaching Human Development Through Literature

There are many reasons why I believe that fiction (short stories, drama, novels) offers an exciting and perceptive way of understanding and teaching human development. I taught a course in human development one semester with two "required" textbooks. One was a good, solid text by Robert Biehler entitled *Psychology Applied to Teaching*[4] and the other was a more non–traditional approach called *Child Development Through Literature*[5] edited by Landau, Epstein and Stone. We used the literature text to amplify some of the concerns of the course, such as personality development, the problems of being "different," motivation, communication and so forth. We went back and forth between the two approaches, discovering that the world of "fiction" helped to sharpen the student's vision and make students willing to discuss problems of growing up that he or she faced as a child and that his or her future students might be confronting some day. We saw that writer's tools could be more penetrating than the data presented in the textbook and could open up doors and windows never dreamed of before! In addition to the stories in the Landau text, we read a Saul Bellow short story called *Leaving the Yellow House* because it gave us insights into "identity problems" which were sharp and dramatic. We also read a short novel by Edward Lewis

Wallant, *The Human Season*, to understand more clearly the grief and pain suffered by a man after the death of his wife. Many of the students chose to re–read Robert Frost's poem *The Road Less Travelled* and shared with us some of their *new* feelings regarding choice and freedom. It was interesting to see how some of the "familiar" poets (Frost, for one) became points of reference when students spoke about the problems of human development. This process of re–reading poems and novels from the perspective of "psychology and teaching" proved to be an exciting adventure in using the arts creatively in higher education.

I would like to state that I find a particular use for literature and films in classes where I have older and more mature students. At the university today, we have many "blended" classrooms where we have 18 year old sophomores in education courses, as well as mature men and women (40 to 60 years of age). Many of these older students are returning to college after a long period of active work in other fields. I find that many of our returning scholars are serious readers of fiction: people who remember well their Shakespeare plays and are serious followers of the new cinema, as well as the "revivals." Therefore, in teaching courses in human development or child development, I try to find as many identifiable references as I possibly can. Thus, when we discuss "identity," "parent–child relationship" or the problems of "old age," I find that *King Lear* is an excellent "cue"–the curtain rises and the discussion begins to flow. When we talk about "family relationships," I can talk about Willy Loman and the tragic figure of Arthur Miller's play takes on real form. Why did Loman's wife say: "Attention must be paid"? Who had failed Willy Loman? What was the cause of his downfall? I find in such discussions that, of all the art forms that I try to use as a point of common reference, drama is the most "democratic" of all the forms. It appeals to the widest number of students and, for the most part, it is the form of art that is most readily enjoyed and understood. Through means of drama (current theatre, plays of Shakespeare and plays of the 1940's, 1950's and 1960's,) I am able to reach my "older" students, as well as the younger students, and reflect with them on the problems of human development and child development as these problems are perceived by playwrights.

The discussion of psychological problems through the vehicle of drama and film offers common concerns to both generations. We talk together about such problems as "alienation," "adjustment," "man's inhumanity to man" and a myriad of daily crises that face all of us as parents, teachers, sons, daughters–and prospective teachers. Drama offers an opportunity for honest, open communication for the more mature "guest scholars" on campus as well as for the young college freshmen. Once we had a very exciting semester when educational television produced the short stories of Ring Lardner, Ernest Hemingway, John Updike and Irwin Shaw. The adjustment of the American soldier "coming home" in the Hemingway drama, for example, was a problem to which our students could all relate, especially if they had friends or family who had "come home" after World War II, Korea or Vietnam.

In addition to literature and drama, we have used the cinema as a means of amplifying concepts in human development. The film, "Loneliness of the Long Distance Runner," is a poignant illustration of the existential "hero" who chooses his own way to self–fulfillment. "Lacombe, Lucien," the French film directed by Louis Malle, is an excellent portrayal of an adolescent boy with no feeling for his own identity. Through the film, we could see how Lacombe was able to become a member of the Nazi party and regard the "uniform" as a badge of "manhood." "Being There" proved a dramatic way of studying the effects of television on national politics, human relationships and political leadership. "Being There" has been called a "modern fable," and it certainly proved to have moral implications as we discussed its full meaning with our students.

Philosophical Problems in Education

Through this graduate course I try to emphasize the problem–solving responsibilities for teachers in John Dewey's progressive philosophy of education and Theodore Brameld's reconstructionist philosophy. As a member of the John Dewey

Society, as well as the Society for Educational Reconstruction, I am concerned with the teacher's role in social change. I try to bring this spirit into the classroom by encouraging teachers to examine educational and social problems in their communities and become part of the "change system." At the same time, because I believe in using the arts wherever possible, I welcome "projects" from my students instead of more traditional "term papers."

At Dowling College, a few years ago, two of my students decided to make an ecological study of the area surrounding Oakdale, Long Island, and to put their research into two distinct forms. One was a *Manual on Ecology* which outlined resources on Long Island involved with problems and solutions regarding conservation and environment. It was a thorough project and would be useful to community organizations and village governments. Their second project was a "Media Happening" which utilized two projectors, two screens and a sound-track. On one screen, they projected examples of abuse and destruction of the environment (human, social and physical); on the other screen, they showed examples of positive cooperation, progressive attitudes, change and hope. The media project was shown to many groups at the college and in the local communities. Later, the students sent a copy of their *Manual on Ecology* to Professor William Boyer whose book was on the "recommended reading list" for the course and whose work had inspired their efforts.

In another section of "Philosophical Problems," one of my students, and a colleague in her school who was not in the class, did a conference project on "Using the Arts to Teach Reading." During the semester, we had done a good deal of reading in the area of open education. We read authors who had visited both British and American schools where they had seen active examples of free, informal and open education. The student wanted to approach the problem of reading through the arts and was convinced that through color, shape and size she would be able to help some of her pupils overcome their resistance to reading. The project became a teaching tool not only for her school, but for her district as well. She and her colleague created a workbook that was a continuous exercise in teaching and learning through color, imagery and artistic stimulation. The entire thrust of their project was to reach the child in an atmosphere of joy and play. By emphasizing the positive aspects of teaching, they were able to reach and touch the students in new ways. The student felt that her approach was an additional window in the movement towards more open education.

Another semester, a student was moved by her reading of *The Crisis in Education Is Outside the Classroom* by Professor James J. Shields, Jr. In this monograph, Dr. Shields suggested that the crisis in society consists of "sexism, racism, and ageism." This student wanted to do something about "ageism." She taught in a local high school not far from a nursing home and decided to involve her English classes in a "values" project that she could connect with her topic. She felt that by taking small groups of her students to the nursing home and providing for meaningful, warm encounters that she would help the "elderly" and the "young" learn more about themselves – and the other. The project worked out very well. The students visited several times with short books of verse, crayons and sketch pads. In a few weeks, many of the patients were writing poems of their own and doing lovely art-work. The results were heartwarming. In addition, her students learned about their own powers of communication and their ability to relate to older people. At the end of the experience, many of the students not only recorded the poetry of their new friends, but included original poetry that they themselves wrote after their visits to the elderly. The project made a difference to many people and showed the value of art and poetry in releasing the imaginative powers of all who became involved in such activity.

Education for Peace

I have been involved in Peace and justice education for many years. I am a founding member of the Society for Educational Reconstruction, a member of COPRED, Educators for Social Responsibility and other kin organizations. Recently I participated in the two-week summer institute on "Education for Peace" at Teachers College, Columbia University, that was led by Professors Betty Reardon, Douglas Sloan and Willard Jacobson.

My commitment to education derives much of its strength and conviction from my belief that education must be based on understanding what it means to be fully human, and to the responsibilities of living fully and equally in the human community. I am in agreement with the philosophy expressed by Douglas Sloan in the preface of his new book, *Education for Peace and Disarmament: Toward A Living World*:

> This attempt also grows out of the twofold conviction that the peace movement in general and education for peace in particular must not allow themselves to be impelled solely by fear, but must be grounded in a primary and positive vision of the fully human; and that, so grounded, education for peace is not a peripheral matter but lies at the heart of the educational venture.[6]

I concur wholeheartedly with Dr. Sloan's premise and believe that education for peace is not only at the "heart of the educational venture," but it is the common understanding through which we can reach all students in teacher education, regardless of their particular area or level of teaching. We facilitate our moving from self-understanding to world-understanding through awakening our students to what it means to be "fully human" and finding ways and means of expressing this conviction in our daily classroom teaching. The question that teachers ask, "What do I do on Monday ?" is crucial. How do we find the means of putting "education for the human community" at the center of our activities?

While I do not teach a course in "Education for Peace" in the framework that I see peace studies, irenology and other such courses in college offerings, I try to universalize this concept by placing it, as Professor Sloan suggests, "at the heart of the educational venture." However, a year ago I participated in the National Week of Dialogue sponsored by the Educators for Social Responsibility and other like-minded groups. These groups included a specific unit in the curriculum that centered on the issue of peace education. I participated in this process through an undergraduate class in philosophical, psychological, social and historical foundations of education.

My unit was a two–week group project that was tied in with the nation–wide observance and showing of the film, "The Day After." In this way, students on Long Island were involved, and connected, with students in different parts of the country. I announced the group projects after the class had met about 5 times, and explained that we would be doing "group activities" focusing upon three themes: (a) Using children's literature as a way of teaching peace; (b) Using the classroom to teach cultural diversity as a way of educating for peace; and (c) Using art forms and music for teaching children to think about a peaceful world. As the term progressed, students formed three groups based on these special interests. They met before class, after class, on campus at different places and sometimes during class–time. As a result, students became closer to each other and more aware of group needs and group responsibilities. The "Week of Dialogue" and the following week were devoted to dramatizing these projects– and the results were warm, positive and exciting. Among the books used to express feelings of self–acceptance as a bridge to understanding the feelings of others were *A Train for Jane*, *Ferdinand the Bull* and *The Story of the Churkendoose*. The story of *William's Doll* was read, acted out and sung! The second group examined the principle of "diversity" through exploring cultural differences in schools and in the celebration of holidays. Students covered the walls with the pictures of school–rooms in different parts of the world, while others spoke about Thanksgiving and how this holiday is highlighted in the United States, England, Norway, Germany and Hungary. This group concentrated on diversity and the responsibilities of school and home. The third group used music and art to show how feelings of peace can be taught in the classroom. One of the students, a professional musician and very adept at handling tapes and cassettes, made a tape–recording for us by "splicing" together about twenty peace songs. Another student, who hopes to be an art teacher, used construction paper of different colors to help us "imagine peace."

We combined the projects with class discussion about what it meant to "become a person" in the Carl Rogers sense of the word, and what it was that they learned about themselves in doing this project and what was involved in working with others. Although teaching is a group process, I do not believe we provide sufficient opportunity for students to learn and practice the arts of cooperation. The various "peace projects" afforded real possibilities for sharing and working together in small communities. We related the concept of "real words," such as peace, war, death, destruction and "the day after," to Sylvia Ashton–Warner's concept of "organic words" and spoke about her experiences in New Zealand and how she used the children's "Organic Words" to teach language.

Later, when the motion picture "The Day After" was shown on national television, we discussed the impact of the film. What did it tell us? Some of the students said that "compared to the horror and violence that they see on 'normal' television, it wasn't that bad!" We discussed the deeper implications of this comment. What was it telling us about human values? We showed the documentary film, "In the Nuclear Shadow: What Can the Children Tell Us?", during class–time, and invited students and faculty to join us. One of the university chaplains came and joined us in a post–film discussion.

The students were touched by the chaplain's visit and his presence helped the class to see more fully that teaching is a moral activity. I think that the "Week of Dialogue" and the group projects moved our students to "connect" education with what Albert Schweitzer calls "reverence for life" and Erich Fromm refers to as "the heart of man."

Conclusion

I think it is appropriate that we conclude with Schweitzer's plea for "reverence for life" and Fromm's feeling for "the heart of man." If we are to respond to the urgency of the 20th century and heed the message of men such as Albert Einstein, Rene Dubos and Jonathan Schell, we must realize

that the *real* deficiency in education is not our lack of knowledge or information, but rather our failure to teach attitude–
an attitude that can help our students become more concerned
with their own identity and self–fulfillment in a just and
peaceful society. If we, as a society, are not sufficiently concerned with the fate of the earth, how can we move men and
women to become more concerned with their destiny, the future
of this planet and the health and well-being of generations
yet unborn?

I believe that, through the arts, we can arouse the
consciousness of our students and become connected to people
everywhere. The arts–music, drama, graphics, literature–can
become the touchstone for reaching people of all cultures
and helping them become aware of needed reforms. I think
that the arts can be agents of personal and social change
through which we can universalize our teaching.

I am reminded of the following quotation by Dr. Lewis
Thomas, eminent scientist and scholar. Thomas said this about
hearing Mahler's Ninth Symphony and his message projects
the bridge we are seeking:

> I cannot listen to that last movement without
> the door–smashing intrusion of a huge new thought:
> death everywhere, the dying of everything, the
> end of humanity.
>
> All through the last fading notes my mind
> swarms with images of a world in which the
> thermonuclear bombs have begun to explode...[7]

Because I, too, cannot listen to Mahler's Ninth Symphony or witness an exhibition of art such as "The Artist as
Adversary" without thinking of images of destruction, I believe that we, as members of the world community, have a
great responsibility to share with one another. Whatever
strength and hope I have as a teacher is the support I feel
when I work and study with world–minded individuals. It is
the strength that comes with common goals, common longings
and combined hope. I find that using the tools of the arts
gives me a feeling of comradeship–a tie with human beings

whose specific area of study I may not know, whose particular language I may not speak, whose local customs I may not share. But through music and art we can reach out and touch a sensitive, loving chord.

The arts are a useful teaching device because they are free, flexible and non-coercive. When we use the arts as a "touching stone" for education, we are able to open new windows and breathe new air. If one idea, device or technique does not work, I open another door or window and try another approach. My students expect this and often display a similar kind of improvisation or excitement in their projects.

The beauty, joy and spontaneity of teaching through the arts is the opportunity it gives me to turn myself around. I find that in my longing to make my classroom a more human community, one in which students and teacher can live together in mutual freedom, I as a teacher must be open to change, challenge and response. A teacher must be willing to "turn herself around" so that she is able to build a positive sense of diversity and wholeness in her classroom. Perhaps it is our faith in improvisation that enables us to try new patterns.

In this centering on the needs of the human community, I firmly believe that teachers can work creatively with other world citizens to create a living, hopeful world.

Notes

1. Steve Kemper, "The Rush of Power," *New Haven Advocate* (December 12, 1984), p. 42.
2. William Shakespeare, *King Henry V* (New York: Greenwich House, 1983), p. 813.
3. Paul Nash, *Models of Man: Explorations in the Western Educational Tradition* (New York: Wiley and Sons, 1968).
4. Robert Biehler, *Psychology Applied to Teaching*, 2nd Edition (Boston: Houghton Mifflin, 1974).
5. Elliott Landau, Sherrie Epstein and Ann Stone, *Child Development Through Literature* (New Jersey: Prentice-Hall, 1972).
6. Douglas Sloan, *Education for Peace and Disarmament: Toward A Living World* (New York: Teachers College Press, 1983), p. 1.
7. Lewis Thomas, *Late Night Thoughts on Listening to Mahler's Ninth Symphony* (New York: Bantam Books, 1984), p. 164.

Bibliography

Brameld, Theodore, *Education for the Emerging Age*. (NY: Harper & Row, 1965). *Education as Power.* (NY: Holt, Rinehart & Winston, 1965). *Patterns of Educational Philosophy in Cultural Perspective.* (NY: Holt, Rinehart & Winston, 1971).

Combs, Arthur W., *The Professional Education of Teachers: A Perceptual View of Teacher Preparation.* (Boston: Allyn and Bacon, 1965).

Dewey, John, *A Common Faith.* (New Haven: Yale University Press, 1934).

Drews, Elizabeth M. and Leslie Lipson, *Values and Humanity.* (NY: St. Martin's Press, 1971).

Eiseley, Loren, *The Night Country.* (NY: Scribner, 1971).

Fromm, Erich, *The Heart of Man.* (NY: Harper and Row, 1980).

Greene, Maxine, *Landscapes of Learning.* (NY: Teachers College Press, 1978). *Teacher as Stranger.* (Belmont, Calif.: Wadsworth, 1973).

Maslow, Abraham H., *Toward A Psychology of Being.* (NY: Van Nostrand, 1968).

Mische, Gerald and Patricia, *Towards A Human World Order.* (NY: Paulist Press, 1977).

Mumford, Lewis, *My Work and Days: A Personal Chronicle.* (NY: Harcourt Brace Jovanovich, 1979).

Nash, Paul, *Models of Man. Explorations in the Western Educational Experience.* (NY: John Wiley & Sons, 1968).

Purpel, David and Kevin Ryan, Editors, *Moral Education ... It Comes With The Territory.* (Berkeley: McCutchan Publishing Corp., 1976).

Schell, Jonathan, *The Fate of the Earth.* (NY: Knopf, 1982).

Sloan, Douglas, Ed., *Education and Values.* (NY: Teachers College Press, 1980).

Sloan, Douglas, Ed., *Education for Peace and Disarmament: Toward A Living World.* (NY: Teachers College Press, 1983).

Stoff, Sheldon and Herbert Schwartzberg, *The Human Encounter: Readings In Education,* Second Edition. (NY: Harper & Row, 1973).

Thomas, Lewis, *Late Night Thoughts on Listening to Mahler's Ninth Symphony.* (NY: Viking, 1983).

Ulich, Robert, *Education and the Idea of Mankind.* (Chicago, University of Chicago Press, 1968).

CHAPTER 10

Genocide Prevention: Awareness and Beyond

FRANK ANDREWS STONE
University of Connecticut

The human tendency to seek to annihilate groups that are regarded as enemies has a long history. Ancient accounts abound with examples, such as the Roman conquest of Carthage where the soil was salted in order to prevent it from ever again being productive. During the sack of Rome by the Vandals, in turn, the city's edifices and population were put to the torch. Modern technologies, however, have given human beings new destructive capabilities. Biological warfare and nuclear weapons make it now possible to wipe out an entire people and end their way of life forever. Humanity itself could well be terminated and higher forms of life on planet earth come to an end. Even so–called "conventional" technologies give an awesome power to those who use them destructively.

No part of the world has been free of the tragedies caused by violence. Millions of people were slaughtered in Kampuchea (Cambodia) and their civilization was leveled. At least half a million Communists were massacred in Indonesia in 1965. Systematic efforts have been made in Iran, Iraq and Turkey to eliminate the Kurdish minorities in these countries. Minority groups like the Crimean Turks and the Volga

Germans were decimated in the Soviet Union, not to mention the planned murder of over four million land owners by the regime that Stalin headed. During 1972 and 1973 100,000 Hutus, a tribal group in the Republic of Burundi in Central Africa, were killed by the ruling Tutsis. Thousands of other Hutus were forced to flee from their homeland and have become permanent refugees. Similarly, the policies of many American nations – including our own – toward their native populations have virtually destroyed the aboriginal peoples. One tragic example is the way that Paraguay has dealt with the Ache Indians. Kept from their own way of life, they have been forced onto unproductive reservations where idleness and disease have undermined a once healthy population. All of this evidence indicates that official inhumanity still exists and will probably continue to exist unless vigorous efforts are made to counter it and bring it to an end.

Although officially sanctioned mass violence has existed for a long time in various forms, only recently has a term been coined to designate it. The word "genocide" originally meant the total destruction of a national group as the result of some intentional policy. The meaning of the term has now been broadened to include all official actions to harm, in whole or in part, various types of human groups. Although the word had not been invented at the time, the widespread massacres of the Armenian minority in the Ottoman Empire between 1895 and 1915 were this type of tragedy. Similar vindictiveness was waged on Gypsies, Jews and Poles during the Holocaust perpetrated by the Nazis in Europe between 1933 and 1945. Sadly, recent history contains other examples of genocide. But these two terrible instances demonstrate what can happen again unless firm steps are taken to prevent any recurrence.

A U. N. Convention to Prevent Genocide

Global attention was drawn to the problem of genocide when in 1946 the General Assembly of the United Nations declared it to be "a crime under international law, contrary to the spirit and aims of the United Nations and condemned by the civilized world."[1] Then on December 9, 1948 the U. N.

General Assembly unanimously adopted a Convention that became effective in 1950, after it was ratified by twenty nations.

The sad fact, however, is that this international agreement has been frequently ignored. Although terrible government policies have caused the loss of life on a vast scale among hated minorities in many parts of the world in the last thirty years, no regime has ever been brought before a world tribunal on this account. During the same period of time, too, genocide awareness education has certainly not become a component of the basic learning experienced by children, youth and adults. In part this reflects the relative dirth of global studies and peace education courses everywhere. It is also a reflection of the professional preparation that most teachers receive, which lacks objective data or any instructional methodologies for teaching in this controversial area. Perhaps the biggest cause of neglect is the policy of military/political regimes everywhere to regard genocide awareness education as dangerous and threatening to their continued power. In the United States a major reason we are little concerned with fostering genocide awareness is the failure of the United States Senate to ever ratify the U. N. Genocide Convention.

According to article two of the document, genocide is defined in these words:

> In the present Convention, genocide means any of the following acts committed with intent to destroy, in whole or in part, a national, ethnic, racial or religious group, such as:
>
> a. Killing members of the group;
>
> b. Causing serious bodily or mental harm to members of the group;
>
> c. Deliberately inflicting on the group conditions of life calculated to bring about its physical destruction in whole or in part;
>
> d. Imposing measures intended to prevent births within the group;
>
> e. Forcibly transferring children of the group to another group.[2]

It is important for us to realize that the basic concept of genocide awareness is to help people recognize that it is a criminal act to deliberately assault the integrity of any legitimate group. The size or status of the victim population makes no difference. Whenever a group of people ceases to exist, the creative diversity of humanity is diminished and impoverished. Once they have been annihilated, the same style and conditions of life can never be revived. Like an endangered species, they are permanently lost.

Raphael Lemkin, the individual who more than any other labored to bring about the U. N. Convention against genocide, wrote this explanation of it:

> Generally speaking, genocide does not necessarily mean the immediate destruction of a nation, except when accomplished by mass killings of all members of a nation. It is intended rather to signify a coordinated plan of different actions aiming at the destruction of essential foundations of the life of national groups, with the aim of annihilating the groups themselves. The objectives of such a plan would be disintegration of the political and social institutions, of culture, language, national feelings, religion and the economic existence of national groups; and the destruction of the personal security, liberty, health, dignity and even the lives of individuals belonging to such groups.[3]

There are two main phases in a genocide. The first syndrome is destruction of the target group's national structure. In other words, the leaders, organizations and institutions of that minority or nation are threatened and terminated. This procedure is followed by a second syndrome of terror. Here, the hostility of the oppressor is vented on the individuals who are identified with the target population. They become the victims of violence regardless of whether they are powerful or weak, innocent or guilty.

It is clear, then, that the term "genocide" represents an inclusive concept that covers a spectrum of policies. The process of deculturation is the least physically violent option. A group is being deculturized when its language, beliefs, patriotism, personal security, health, dignity and economic survival are being threatened. Next in their degrees of violence come lynching, terrorism, massacres and pogrom. A lynching is an extra–legal execution of a minority person. Terrorism is a pattern of planned acts of violence toward an enemy. It may be directed toward selected individuals or groups, or it may be indiscriminant. Part of the fear that terrorism engenders is its unpredictable irrationality. It tends to be the tool of the weak who may be frustrated because they lack the power to act in more open ways. Hence the clandestine aspect of terrorist attacks. Massacres entail the wanton murder of groups of people at a particular place and time. They are victims of a general hatred and are killed because they belong to the group, not because of their own personal misdeeds. Finally in this grim list of genocidal acts comes pogroms. A pogrom entails implementing a policy of property damage and destruction, together with mayhem and murder, over a district or region. A massacre involves the loss of life for a good number of the target group who are at a particular location at one point in time. A pogrom is more varied in the types of violence used and it spreads out over a wider area for a longer time period.

Beyond the levels of genocide that have so far been identified are a galaxy of types of mass destruction. They include defoliation, biological and chemical warfare and deliberate starvation. At their ultimate, they entail mass bombing of helpless civilian populations and holocaust.

Genocide in all of these degrees and forms is what the U. N. Convention is supposed to outlaw. As mentioned earlier, however, since the document was ratified its provisions have never been invoked. National governments and hate groups can pursue genocidal policies without much fear of being exposed or held accountable for their evil deeds. No international force has ever intervened to try to save the victims when a genocide was taking place.

Faced with these sad facts, it is critical that the young people of the world be made aware of genocide. They will soon become members of the "command generation" in their societies and be the decision makers of tomorrow. If they recognize the dangers of genocidal policies and have been taught to regard these types of behaviour as crimes against humanity, genocides will become things of the dark past. Only in this way will they finally come to an end.

A Basic Genocide Awareness Glossary

Words have to be used in order to communicate human experiences and be the vehicles of people's interpretations. When something is nameless and unutterable, it is secret and mysterious. The vocabulary that is connected with genocide must be brought out into the open. When we can recognize and recall these symbols, we also gain some control over them. Here are a half dozen of the key terms that young people everywhere must be able to understand.

CATASTROPHE (from Greek, "to overturn") This word signifies a momentous tragedy or sudden evil event that is marked by effects that range from extreme misfortune to complete overthrow and ruin. This is a euphemism that is now often employed to express the plight of the European Jews under the Nazi regime.

DEPORTATION (from Latin, de – "away, off" + portare – "to carry") Banishment from one's homeland is the meaning of this term, especially the expulsion of a minority or of undesirable aliens without legal recourse. Armenians under the "young Turk" rule and Jews and other minorities under the Nazis were summarily deported. The tragic "long march" of the Cherokee Nation from North Carolina to Oklahoma in the United States is another example of deportation.

GHETTO (Believed to have come from Italian as it was used in Venice in 1516). A ghetto was the section or quarter of a European city to which Jews were restricted. Thus, it also came to mean a slum area in an American city occupied predominantly by members of a minority who felt forced to live there due to economic or social pressure. In the early decades of the twentieth century Armenians belonged to one "millet" or religious nation within the Ottoman Empire and inhabited segregated quarters of towns and cities. Similarly, the Jews of eastern Europe in the 1930's were still restricted to living in set parts of the communities. In 1939 Adolph Hitler made this declaration concerning German Jews:

> Out with them from all the professions and into the ghetto with them; fence them in somewhere where they can perish as they deserve.[4]

HOLOCAUST (Greek, "a burnt whole sacrificial offering") This term refers to a total or thorough sacrificial destruction, especially when it takes place by fire. The word has come to indicate the death of six million Jews who were exterminated by the Nazi regime in the incinerators of concentration camps such as Auschwitz, Dachau and Majdanek.

MASSACRE (Old French) The act or an incident of the killing of a large number of human beings under circumstances of atrocity or cruelty; a wholesale slaughter of human beings. Massacres are often accompanied by mangling and mutilation of both the victims and any survivors.

POGROM (Yiddish from the Russian for "destruction, devastation") The organized looting and massacre of helpless people, usually with the encouragement and connivance of government officials.

Seven Approaches to Genocide Awareness Education

There are a variety of ways in which students of different ages, backgrounds and levels of maturity can learn to be aware of genocidal policies and acts in the world. Sometimes it may be most effective to combine several of the formats suggested here. There will doubtless be some other good approaches to becoming conscious of genocides that will not be described here.

1. An International Law and World Order Theme

Transnational relations and international regulations are the focus of this type of teaching. Students discover what has occurred in the past and then project scenarios where better behavioral systems would have prevailed in order to have prevented the disasters. The work of the League of Nations and the United Nations is studied. Events aimed at punishing genocide, such as the Nuremberg Trials, are investigated. Alternative concepts of global security to prevent genocides are explored.

2. *Socio–Economic Inquiries concerning the Causes of Genocides*

When a radical intergroup conflict occurs that leads to mass violence in a society, it is often linked to people's perceptions that the members of the minority are unfairly advantaged or are exploiting the majority in some way. The Young Turk rulers claimed that their Armenian population was supporting the Allied cause (the enemy) because they had a religious affinity to the British, French and Russians as Christians. Allegedly this developed through commercial and trading relationships because many Armenians had learned western languages and made their living as import and export agents. The Nazis asserted that the Jews of Europe controlled banking and commerce. It was claimed that there was an international Zionist conspiracy to undermine Germany. Such thinking is widely used in order to justify genocides.

This second approach to genocide attempts to explore the real conditions that pertained at the time when violence took place. Its rationale is that when people are informed about true minority and majority relationships, confrontation can be reduced and the possibility of a "final" solution to the conflict based on intergroup hatred and frustrations of wartime and defeat will be averted.

3. *Historical Studies of Genocides*

Ample scholarly data exists for conducting in–depth historical investigations of tragic events such as the Ottoman Genocide of the Armenians in 1915, the Jewish Holocaust under the Nazis during the 1930's, and 1940's, the 3,224 lynchings of blacks that took place in the United States from 1889 to 1918 and the Mai Lai Massacre perpetrated by American troops in Vietnam in the 1970's.[5] Based on the evidence of these case studies, students can try to ascertain what leads to genocidal policies and their implementation. What are the signs, as indicated by these past disasters, that a genocide may be imminent? How could these past catastrophes have been prevented?

4. *Affective Interpretations based on First Hand Accounts*

There is a tendency for us to want to reduce genocides to statistics and treat their carnage asepticly. We will hear debates about how many people actually lost their lives. Other types of death and destruction that went on simultaneously will be compared with the genocide in order to argue that it really wasn't excessive. A genocide, however, destroys real living human beings. Men, women and children are its victims. Even the aged and infirm are not spared. The target group has its homes wiped out. Its places of business are destroyed. Entire communities are obliterated, never to rise again.

Individuals who actually experienced these conditions have produced literary accounts or documentary films about them. Through their eyes we can come to comprehend what a genocide does to both perpetrators and victims. The entire way of life that once existed in the ghettos of eastern Europe is no more. The form of life that functioned in the Armenian "raya" villages and town neighborhoods of the Ottoman Empire was wiped out forever. These and similar living groups of the past are extinct in these forms today. Only the few survivors who are willing and able to talk about what happened to them can communicate the pathos of a genocide.

5. *Human Rights Activism*

While it is necessary that they be able to study about the causes, processes and effects of genocides, most students are going to be frustrated if they cannot do anything about them. For this reason, it is important that genocide awareness programs include practical, contemporary human rights activities.

These include becoming involved with efforts to overcome hunger and starvation. Such activity can lead the students to assist political refugees, especially people who have had to flee from Central America or Indochina because they have been threatened with extermination by their governments. Armenian Americans and Jewish Americans have told the author that the genocides of their people are past and over. "Why can't these old tragedies be forgotten as the twentieth century draws to a close?" they ask. But, unfortunately, the bigotry and anti–Semitism that fed the flames of these genocides have not ended. Minorities are still being defamed. Victims are still denied elemental justice. Thousands of people are unjustly imprisoned. Brutalizing political prisoners and prisoners of conscience is the order of the day under many current regimes.

Nobody enjoys facing these sad facts. Strangely enough, we have a tendency to blame the victims and to resent having to find out what actually happened to them. Unless people do become aware, and get active as opponents of the genocides of the 1980's, humanity will continue to have massacres in Lebanon, Northern Ireland and Sri Lanka – and many other parts of the world where intergroup hatred is allowed to grow and fester.

6. *Recognition of the "Righteous Few"*

During every tragedy of genocide there are always a few non–conformists who refuse to take part in the destruction. They often have risked, and lost, their own lives trying to save the victims. Some were citizens of the victimizing countries, while others were the nationals of other states. Both men and women have bravely intervened in this way.

We need to study what this "righteous few" did in order to discover what influences motivate people to act humanely in the midst of mayhem. It is then possible to try to inculcate similar values in students or give them parallel experiences, so that more people are likely to act affirmatively to oppose any genocidal policies they may encounter.

7. *Developing Theoretical Models of Genocide Prevention*

Through devices such as role playing and scenario planning, the radical disjunctures that can lead to genocides can be simulated. Students can come to recognize the types of incidents that produce confrontations and the escalation of violence that always precedes the final crisis. They can then try to conceive of alternative chains of events which reduce the friction and relieve the hatred. These non-violent strategies can then be used to replace genocides as the means of resolving conflicts.

Some Constraints on Genocide Awareness Education

Genocide has been declared illegal by a United Nations Convention, yet there have been tragic instances in recent years where it has occurred. Faced with such a pressing problem, we may ask why so little instruction in schools and colleges addresses this issue. At least four considerations militate against our teaching genocide awareness studies.

First and foremost, it is always uncomfortable and unpopular to teach children and young people about death and destruction. While admittedly human existence does include these tragic aspects, we say, must we dwell on them? There is a strong taboo in American society against realistic treatments of thanatos – human mortality. It is even more so when the deaths being studied were unnatural and caused by the ill will of others. Yet people cannot become aware of the grim facts of genocide in our world without encountering its brutality. Rather than accept this eventuality, many teachers, curriculum writers and boards of education expunge this domain from their instruction.

Second, teaching for genocide awareness is politically controversial. A few vocal individuals and militant groups in most communities will oppose bitterly any teaching in this area. Educators who venture into the field will be attacked. For example, when the television film "Holocaust" portraying the experiences of millions of Jews in the Nazi concentration camps during World War II was re-broadcast in September, 1979 by NBC, the local channel in West Hartford, Connecticut was picketed by about thirty protesters. They were members of the Polish American community of New Britain who were angered because they claimed that the screen play made it appear that Poles had all collaborated with the Nazis. The film failed to convey, they argued, that Poles were also victims of the German regime that killed three million Christian Poles as well as a like number of Polish Jews. In other words, representatives of a nation that perceives itself to have been a victim of genocide found themselves portrayed as accomplices to the crime. Intergroup confrontations of this type are not unusual.[5]

Representatives of the Turkish Embassy in Washington, D. C. have regularly protested whenever any curriculum has made reference to genocide of the Armenian minority living in the Ottoman Empire in 1915. The claim is made that this was only a relocation of a disloyal population during war-time in order to remove them from the scene of the struggle. The Turkish authorities assert that claims about the loss of life and property are greatly exaggerated, and that as many or more Muslim Turks lost their lives in the Balkans or on the battlefields. These counter-arguments have to be taken into consideration because public opposition to the programs is aroused due to them. Also, court cases have been initiated using these allegations to prevent genocide awareness from being taught.

The third constraint that hampers providing genocide awareness education in this country is our own ambivalence about United States government policies toward minorities–past and present. Who can deny that the treatment accorded many native Americans in the past was genocidal? Ours was a country that long tolerated and protected slavery as the "peculiar institution," as it was once termed by one of its advocates. The United States Senate refused to accept the League of Nations mandate for a free Armenia after World War I. Our government would not agree to accept non-quota Jewish refugees from Nazi occupied Europe in 1939. We used vast amounts of explosives and toxic defoliants in Vietnam, yet United States authorities have never repudiated any of these past actions. Any educators who decide to initiate geno-cide awareness education in their classrooms and schools must be sensitive to the moral quandry about our nation's policies that still divides our society.

Finally, the fourth constraint to initiating genocide awareness studies is the problem of finding a manageable way of teaching this domain. It will not be just to make instruc-tion in this field a "tack on" to what we are already teaching.

A "Band-Aid" approach, where a very superficial reference to genocide is considered sufficient, should also be avoided. There are hundreds of books concerning the Armenian Genocide of 1915, for instance, and thousands about the Jewish Holocaust. Unless we are careful, we can become mired in the complex accounts of past intergroup relations, government policies and official actions. Much of what has been written is protest literature. Although protest is justified, that kind of treatment contains few clues about how future genocides can be prevented. It is possible just to focus on the horror of what happened in the past, without ever teaching ways we can prevent these tragedies from happening again.

The goal of genocide awareness education, therefore, must be firmly oriented to the present and the future. The purpose of this kind of instruction is not to defame any nation. Teachers must be sure their students recognize that genocides are the result of evil official policies. In many cases, ordinary citizens of the society had no voice in their government's policy formation. Some of them may bravely have expressed their disapproval of it. Care must be taken that we do not unfairly generalize or stereotype an entire nationality.

Yet, at the same time, a degree of personal and group responsibility for genocides must be acknowledged. National leaders who decide to implement "final solutions" on minority groups in their societies are certainly culpable for what ensues. Military commanders who knowingly decimate helpless civilian populations are carrying out genocidal policies. And organizations that disseminate bigoted and prejudiced accounts of minorities, well designed to inflame passions and lead to violence, are certainly the agents of genocide. It is a legitimate function of education to expose these types of social malignancies and teach methods of countering and controlling them.

Why Genocide Awareness?

In the face of these four formidable hindrances, we may well ask why genocide awareness education should be developed at all. The main justification is that genocide is a crime against humanity. The basic purpose of all moral education is supporting and sustaining humankind. Educators thus have a mandate to help their students become sensitive to, able to recognize and committed to opposing acts of official inhumanity.

Another vital reason for teaching genocide awareness is the fact of cultural pluralism in American and many other societies. More than eighty identifiable ethnic groups live in southern New England, for instance, and many of them have been victims of genocides. Many children and young people will learn about holocausts and massacres at home or within their own cultural communities. However, they need an opportunity to achieve a more inclusive understanding of this problem. They must come to realize that this type of tragedy is not limited to any one group, place or time.

If individuals are to exercise their rights and responsibilities as the citizens of a constitutional democracy who participate in deciding and executing national policies, they must know how genocides were perpetrated in the past. It is imperative that they be aware of what a genocide does to the victimizers as well as the victims, bystanders as well as those directly involved. The horror of what happens when genocides occur cannot be hidden. We must be able to recognize the possibility that diabolical decisions can rule over human affairs in order for us not to become callous and brutalized ourselves. This is a matter of consciousness and conscience.

Genocide awareness education, however, cannot be separated from other fields and disciplines. It is clearly a vital dimension of all learning about human rights. It should be a component of general social justice education. Human beings need to learn non-violent ways of resolving interpersonal and intergroup conflicts, and genocide awareness is certainly a valid aspect of this type of instruction. It is hard to conceive of a worthwhile moral development education or values clarification program that excludes the topic of genocide awareness. Multicultural and international studies require inquiries into the tragic capacity of societies to foster alienation and discord that culminates in holocausts. This realm must also be a part of scientific studies because in many instances it is scientific discoveries and technological innovations which are used for destructive purposes. Genocide awareness education is equally relevant to the humanities, especially art, history, literature and music. Profound feelings about genocidal experiences can be expressed in dramas and poetry. In short, genocide awareness education does not belong on a single day or week in April. It must not be segregated as a special topic taught by a single teacher, or offered in a lone instructional department. On the contrary, genocide awareness education must become an integral part of curricula at all levels everywhere.

Notes

1. *Yearbook of the United Nations,* 1947–48 (New York: The United Nations, 1949), pp. 595–599.
2. *Yearbook of the United Nations,* 1948–1949 (New York: The United Nations, 1950), p. 959.
3. Raphael Lemkin, *Axis Rule in Occupied Europe* (New York: Carnegie Endowment for International Peace, 1944), p. 79.
4. *Websters' Third New International Dictionary of the English Language,* Unabridged (Springfield, MA: G. & C. Merriam Company, 1979), p. 555. The other definitions are also based on material in this standard reference.
5. *Thirty Years of Lynching in the United States, 1889–1918* (New York: National Association for the Advancement of Colored People, 1919), p. 7.

A Selected Bibliography

ARTICLES

Bennett, A. D. "Toward a Holocaust Curriculum," *Jewish Education,* 43, (Spring, 1974), 22–26.
Chorbajian, Leon A. "Massacre or Genocide: An Essay in Personal Biography and Objective Experience," *The Armenian Review,* 32, (June, 1979), 163–71.
Dadrian, Vahakn N. "A Theoretical Model of Genocide, with Particular Reference to the Armenian Case," *The Armenian Review,* 31, (February, 1979), 115–36.
Dyer, Gwynne "Turkish 'Falsifiers' and Armenian 'Deceivers': Historiography and the Armenian Massacres," *The Armenian Review* 31, (Spring, 1978), 70–78. Reprinted from *Middle Eastern Studies,* 12 (January, 1975), London.
Friedlander, H. "Toward a Methodology of Teaching about the Holocaust," *Teachers College Record,* 80, (February, 1979), 519–42.

Joseloff, S. H. "A Course on Holocaust Literature," *Journal of General Education*, 26 (Winter, 1975), 301-308.

Marran, J. F. "Approaching the Holocaust through Fiction," *Curriculum Review*, 17 (October, 1978), 342-344.

Papaleo, R. J. "Teaching the Philosophical Concepts of the Holocaust Issue," *Social Studies*, 70 (March/April, 1979), 90-92.

Robinson, Jacob. "Holocaust", in *Encyclopedia Judaica*, Volume Eight. (Jerusalem, Israel: Kater Publishing House, Ltd., 1972), 828-889.

Strom, M. S. "Facing History and Ourselves: The Study of the Holocaust and Human Behavior," *Media and Methods*, 14 (May/June, 1978), 16-20.

"Teaching about the Holocaust," (A Symposium), *Social Education*, 42 (April, 1978), 263-293. A bibliography is also included.

Wolowelsky, J. B. "Teaching the Holocaust: An Interdisciplinary Approach" *Jewish Education*, 45 (Fall/Winter, 1976), 44-45.

BOOKS

Arens, Richard, ed. *Genocide in Paraguay*. Philadelphia: Temple University Press, 1976.

Davidowicz, Lucy S., ed. *A Holocaust Reader*. New York: Behrman House, Inc., 1976.

Davidowicz, Lucy S. *The War against the Jews: 1933-1945*. New York: Holt, Rinehart and Winston, 1975.

Gutman, Yisrael and Livia Rithkirchen, eds. *The Catastrophe of European Jewry: Antecedents, History, Reflections*. Jerusalem, Israel: Yad Vashem, 1976.

The Holocaust. Jerusalem, Israel: Yad Vashem — Martyrs' and Heroes' Remembrance Authority, 1975.

Kuper, Leo *Genocide: Its Political Use in the Twentieth Century*. New Haven: Yale University Press, 1981.

Roskies, Dinae K. *Teaching the Holocaust to Children: A Review and Bibliography*. New York: KTAV Publishing House, Inc., 1975.

Strom, Margot Stern and William S. Parsons *Facing History and Ourselves: Holocaust and Human Behavior*. Watertown, MA: Intentional Educations, Inc., 1982.

Weisbord, Robert G. *Genocide? Birth Control and the Black American*. New York: Two Continents Publishing Group, Inc., and Westport, CT: Greenwood Press, 1975.

Wolf-Wasserman, Miriam and Linda Hutchinson *Teaching Human Dignity*: Social Change Lessons for Everyteacher. Minneapolis, MN: Education Exploration Center, 1978.

CHAPTER 11

U. S. in the Third World: Challenging the Textbook Myth

DAVID A. SHIMAN
University of Vermont
and
JAMES W. LOEWEN
University of Vermont

Civil strife in Lebanon, El Salvador, and Chad. Coups d'etat in Guatemala, Ghana, and Nigeria. Terrorist raids in Angola, Botswana, and Columbia. Warfare between Iran and Iraq and on the Nicaraguan border. Where are these countries? Who are these people? How did these crises come about? Is the United States somehow involved? Should we become involved? Is there a danger we will be drawn into another Vietnam? These and other questions race through the minds of Americans as they try to make sense of events transpiring in the Third World and determine what role, if any, the United States should play.

The world has become a very confusing place. Our confidence in America's* capacity to dominate and dictate the course of global events has been shaken and our understanding blurred by the proliferation of crises in Third World nations about which we know little. The Vietnam experience shattered the myth of a Pax Americana. The 1974 OPEC oil embargo, the massive increase in Arab investments in our

---

* We use the words 'America' and 'United States' interchangeably in this paper although we recognize the ethnocentric and imprecise nature of the former term.

economy, the Iranian hostage–taking, our continued involvement in the Middle East quagmire, and the emerging pattern
of revolution and counter–revolution in our Central American
'backyard' have reinforced our sense of vulnerability and
anxiety. Even little Third World nations seem capable of
affecting our lives and ruffling the fabric of our country.

Obviously, our public schools do not have the responsibility to solve Third World problems. They do have a duty
to help our youth to develop a more sophisticated and deeper
understanding of the ways in which the United States in-
teracts with these nations. In this increasingly interdependent
world, our citizens must be internationally literate if they
are to make informed judgments about the proper role of
their government in global affairs.[1]

For the past few decades authors of American history
textbooks have been describing the expansion of our nation's
international participation in the post-war world. They have
recorded the enlarged and changing nature of U. S. involvement in the Third World. Because almost all youth take
courses in American history during their high school years,
and because less than one quarter ever take another such
course, these high school texts provide the bulk of the knowledge adult Americans ever get from school on the role of
their country in this Third World.

What information and perspectives do these textbooks
provide about U. S. Third World relations?

We examined ten popular American history high school
textbooks.[2] We have drawn our examples principally from U.S.
relations with Latin America because of our longstanding involvement in this international arena and the several crises
presently before us.[3] We have selected textbooks as the object
of our study because they are the dominant instructional aid
in the public schools.[4] Teachers rely on their textbooks and
believe they are a source of authoritative knowledge,[5] particularly for topics where they have limited expertise of their
own. Over 75% of student time is devoted to textbook related

activities.[6] These books are therefore instrumental in determining what children learn about our nation's actions in the Third World.

Unfortunately, in textbook after textbook we find not the substance for student understanding and analysis but the perpetuation of a nationalistic myth. We find the United States portrayed as International Good Guy in the third World– the champion of freedom and protector of peace in a world threatened by Communist aggression and subversion. To be sure, the international America portrayed in textbooks does not possess the purity of the archetypal hero of the Old West who gallops bravely into the fray, rescues the maiden, re-establishes law and order, and rides off into the sunset. No depiction of America's role is so naive.[7] Nevertheless, with broad strokes our textbooks paint a picture of a reluctant giant assuming after World War II the mantle of political and moral leadership for nations yearning to breathe free. Text-book examination of our actions is shallow and unidimensional and therefore fails to provide students with either sufficient information to make sense out of the past forty years of U. S. involvement in the Third World or the intellectual tools to make intelligent judgments about American actions in the decade ahead. Our textbooks appear more concerned with having their readers approve our role in the world than helping them understand it.

On the following pages we seek to challenge the myth of the International Good Guy in the Third World and offer educators ways to engage students in examining this distorted description of the United States.

International Good Guy in the Third World

The textbook portrayal of America as champion of free-dom and protector of the peace is no longer couched in the language of virulent anti–communism found in earlier publi-cations. There is no "Red Menace" or "International Com-munist Conspiracy." Nevertheless, the overall tone or flavor of the textbooks remains essentially the same. Framed in softened Cold War language, our textbooks tell us that

America, confronted by the Soviet challenge, has been pursuing a foreign policy in the Third World aimed at promoting justice and a lasting peace for all people. The United States has therefore been helping poor nations to develop economically and establish democratic institutions. American policy is best for everyone, we are told, rich and poor alike.

Rather than having high school students examine the complex realities and contradictions of American foreign policy, high school textbooks offer a simplistic and therefore distorted depiction of U. S. motives and actions in the postwar world. One text states:

> The United States would help free nations to create new jobs, to protect themselves with American arms from attack by the Soviet Union, and to preserve the freedom to vote and to hold property. [8]

Another adds:

> ...Americans believe that people everywhere should be free to choose their own form of government. [9]

One text even cites unnamed Oxford scholars who praise the "unprecedented virtuousness of the U. S. foreign policy and... its good sense. [10]

As champions of freedom and protectors of peace, America, our texts tell us, is engaged in a "struggle for the minds of people," [11] a "war of ideas." [12] We compete with the Communists to "buy allies with gifts ranging from food to steel mills." [13] Our Peace Corps, mentioned in almost every text, symbolizes "America's desire to provide humane assistance as well as economic and military leadership in the non-communist world." [14] When U. S. development assistance is described, Americans are portrayed as generous people who, as one textbook states, have "always helped the starving people of other nations." [15] When Third World nations "face hard going, our government is there to help." [16]

Our textbooks never let the reader lose sight of the fact that U. S. actions in the Third World are part of a global struggle between the Evil Empire, as President Reagan has portrayed the Soviet Union, [17] and the International Good Guy. The responsibility for dividing the world into these competing camps lies with the Soviet Union; they, not the United States, want to dominate the world. For example, One textbook states that after World War II,

> The rise of communism threatened the entire
> free world. American leaders would have to deal
> with this new threat. [18]

Another adds that our government recognized the Soviets would "test the strength of the free world," [19] so we formed alliances with non–communist countries to meet this challenge. [20] The forces of Good were mobilized in the post–war policy of containment to thwart communist aggression and protect the free world.

Indeed, "Good" is often equated with "non–communist." Although one book forthrightly states that "many of these free nations were not so free after all, [21] most texts make little effort to differentiate between "free nations" and "non–communist" ones. Authors glide back and forth between these two phrases, leaving the distinct though generally unstated impression that they can be used interchangeably. The equation, free equals non–communist, therefore insinuates itself into the reader's consciousness.

Subtleties of language used to describe U. S. and Soviet interaction with the Third World perpetuate the image of Good Guy confronting the Evil Empire. Although America's opposition to free elections in Vietnam, systematic destruction of Allende's socialist experiment in Chile, and training of the Shah's Savak police in torture techniques are disturbingly similar to Soviet brutality in Eastern Europe, its invasion of Afganistan, and its attempts to dominate various Third World nations, the parallel is hidden by the language our textbooks employ. The Soviets 'impose,' 'spy,' 'subvert,' 'sabotage,' 'oppress' and 'crush.' When revolutionaries are described as Marxist, readers are left with the impression that professing a Marxist ideology is equivalent to becoming a Soviet vassal. American actions, on the other hand, are portrayed in less provocative language. The United States 'provides aid,' 'supports,' 'intervenes,' and 'has a hand in overthrowing.' The sharp edges are removed from the language and a much more benign America is portrayed.

However, we are talking about more than the biased use of language in textbooks to frame and justify American actions. The selection of facts and manner in which they are presented makes it exceedingly difficult for students to interpret our policies in other than favorable terms. In one of the better textbook treatments of American relations with Cuba in the postwar years, students learn that after having supported the dictator Fulgencio Batista for many years the United States government grew disenchanted with him and initially viewed the Castro revolution in a positive light. [22] Reporting that we supported Batista is true and helpful to readers, but the book does not go far enough. Like all others surveyed, it fails to mention that during the Batista years our trade relations had kept the Cuban economy dependent on U. S. investment and good will, that rich Americans distorted Havana into a playground for prostitution and gambling, and that our government supported a Cuban power elite which grew richer and richer while many peasants remained poorly educated, ill–housed, undernourished and disfranchised.[23] U. S. complicity in the denial of basic human rights for the overwhelming majority of the Cuban people is never discussed. All of the above are subsumed under the phrase "supported dictator." The seeds of Cuban anti-American feelings were planted in those Batista years; that planting was not made evident in even the fullest treatment of Cuban–American relations found in our textbooks.

When the textbooks shift to an explanation of why U. S. sympathy for Castro's Cuba faded in 1959–60, detail upon detail are provided – up to a point. "Castro began to act like a ruthless dictator"[24] who cancelled elections, arrested and executed the opposition, took control of foreign–owned property,[25] collectivized the farms,[26] denounced the United States, declared himself a Communist and turned to the Soviet

Union for support.[27] Discussion of Castro's national policies then ceases. No textbook provides follow–up information regarding Cuba's literacy program, peasant participation in economic decision–making, health and nutrition improvements, or policies aimed at the redistribution of wealth and power among the populace. The student is presented only with a picture of Castro as the communist devil of the hemisphere. Such a protrayal leads the reader toward an easy justification of the Bay of Pigs invasion in 1961. And, had subsequent American efforts to assassinate Castro and destabilize Cuba been treated in the texts (which they are not !), they too might be accepted by readers who have received only the limited textbook presentation of Cuban–American relations. Provided with almost no information after the 1962 Missile Crisis, the alumni of textbooks are generally unaware that Cubans and many other Third World citizens perceive the United States as an imperialist bully. Instead, our readers take from their textbooks an image of America on the side of Right – the champion of freedom and protector of peace. They conclude that those who oppose the United States have either been inspired or duped by the communists.

The truncated textbook treatment of U. S. – Cuba relations is typical of the authors' practice of focusing on international crises and totally neglecting U. S. relations with the nations involved after the crisis has subsided. Looking specifically at Latin America, we find the texts rarely mention the Dominican Republic after U. S. intervention in 1965, Guatemala after the 1954 coup, or Chile after the overthrow of Allende in 1973. In each case, after American power and policy have been reasserted, the country drops from the textbook. The reader can only conclude that peace and order have been restored and the good guys are back on top.

Although this image of International Good Guy permeates the textbooks, even the most nationalistic textbook must deal with the fact that American motives and actions are sometimes less than pure. To do otherwise would be a blind assertion of ideology and a total denial of the educative role of U. S. history textbooks. However, as Frances FitzGerald has noted, textbooks only hint of a "certain level of unpleasantness in (our) history."[28] They include a few paragraphs, somewhere on their pages, stating that the United States has occasionally supported dictators and tyrants. One text asserts that our fear of 'Fidelism' led us to support reactionary oppressive governments elsewhere in Latin America whose policies drove their people to revolt.[29] Another points out that many Latin Americans believed we supported dictators to protect our corporate investments – a very rare reference to U. S. economic interests.[30] A third book states:

> And like earlier Presidents, Nixon largely ignored the denial of civil liberties and other human rights in anti–communist countries that received American military and economic assistance in exchange for military bases.[31]

We have committed "dirty tricks,"[32] as yet another reports, but what these were is left to the imagination of the reader.

These instances of 'unpleasantness' are almost invariably justified by the excuse that when we fail to live up to our professed national commitment to human rights and economic justice in our actions abroad. we do so because of our overriding desire to thwart communist efforts to dominate the world. Thus the Evil Empire is responsible not only for its own bad deeds but for ours as well. Little doubt is left in the readers' minds that if the United States were not forced to respond to the Soviet challenge then American actions in the Third World would, as our text asserts, "benefit the social, political, and economic needs of all nations involved."[33]

These dollops of textbook criticism of American policy and practice are not only lost in a sea of righteousness, but also submerged in a sea of words. Survey texts skip across the historical waters like smooth, flat stones touching as many themes, events, and personalities as they possibly can. This interspersion of critical comments serves two important purposes. First, it protects publishers from the charge of chauvinistic bias. In response to accusations that they have presented an uncritical version of our history, publishers can honestly respond. "What do you mean ? We treated that issue on page 465. We would have liked to have done more, but there are limitations of space." Second, by only touching on less appealing aspects of our foreign policy, publishers avoid the risk of being viewed as anti–American by textbook purchasers and adoption boards and retain their viability in the highly competitive textbook marketing world.[34]

We do wish to note, however, that if one carefully examined the better high school textbooks, pored over them in a scholarly fashion, and conducted a detailed content analysis, one *might* be able to piece together a fairly complete picture of American policy and practice in the Third World. But textbooks are not written for this purpose and are most definitely not read in this fashion. Students' eyes glide across the pages, shifting from one crisis to the next, moving through the decades. Certainly they retain some facts; more importantly, they carry away from their high school textbooks an impression of America and an interpretation of its purposes and practices in the Third World. The impression is undeniably positive and the interpretation is that of the International Good Guy – the champion of freedom and protector of peace.

No More Mr. Good Guy

The textbooks examined do not begin to provide an accurate picture of the nature of American involvement in the Third World since the Second World War. Even a superficial examination of U. S. – Third World relations reveals another Amercia–an America quite different and much more complex than the Good Guy image portrayed in the U. S. history textbooks.

In the area of foreign aid, for example, most Americans generally accept at face value our leaders' declarations that we are the most generous nation on earth. Our textbooks reinforce this comforting self–concept. Few textbooks provide any details about the nature of American aid giving.[35] Other than brief mention of the Peace Corps and the Alliance for Progress, textbooks offer assertions rather than evidence of our beneficence in the Third World. Students are encouraged to feel good about this nation, not think about it.

But the picture of America as generous aid–giver is belied by the facts. While we do provide the most aid in absolute terms, when the amount of our aid is judged in terms of the comparative wealth of nations our contribution is paltry at best. As Table I clearly shows, the United States commitment to providing development assistance to the Third World has not only been low compared to other major industrialized nations but has also actually decreased since 1970.

TABLE 1

U. S. Development Assistance to Developing Countries and Territories and Multilateral Agencies:

Year	% of GNP	Rank among 17 DAC Countries
1970	0.31	10
1973	0.22	13
1975	0.24	12
1977	0.21	12
1979	0.15	16
1981	0.17	17

DAC is the Development Assistance Committee of the OECD and is composed of sixteen Western industrialized nations and Japan. Source: *Handbook on International Trade and Development Statistics 1983*, New York: United Nations, 1983, p. 401.

Nevertheless, the myth of our generosity survives in the minds of Americans. What we should recognize to be a national embarassment, we continue to claim as a virtue.

Exposing the myth of America as generous aid–giver is only the beginning of the process of critically analyzing our government's righteous rhetoric and public declarations of good intent. An examination of American political, economic and military intervention in the Third World reveals a distasteful underside to our foreign policy in practice. To protect American investments and perceived strategic interests, our government has been willing to employ almost any means to prop up friendly dictators or destroy unfriendly governments.

Nowhere is the falsity of America's self–portrait of virtue more evident than in the case of the overthrow of the Chilean government of Salvador Allende. In 1970, Allende, an avowed Marxist, won a fair election in Chile. He had campaigned on a platform committed to redistributing wealth and power among the populace and returning to the peasants control over their own lives. An early step in this direction involved the nationalization of American corporations, such as Kennecott and Anaconda, which Allende saw as exploitative of the Chilean people and destructive to long–term national development.

America, however, would not tolerate the establishment of another (after Cuba) Marxist government, even a fairly elected one, within our historic sphere of influence. As Secretary of State Henry Kissinger said at the time:

> I don't see why we have to let a country go Marxist just because its people are irresponsible.[36]

American foreign policy initiatives moved on many fronts. The CIA had earlier joined with multinational corporations like International Telephone and Telegraph (ITT) in efforts to defeat Allende in the 1970 elections. Failing this, the United States sought to destabilize his government and disrupt the Chilean economy. The U. S. blocked loans through the Export-Import Bank, subsidized opposition newspapers, labor unions and political parties, denied spare parts in industries and trained and financed the military which staged the bloody coup in 1973 in which Allende was killed.[37] The military government that replaced Allende reversed the nationalization of American companies and returned them to private hands, suspended freedom of the press and speech, jailed dissenters and tortured and murdered political opponents.[38] Chile had been 'liberated' from the clutches of an elected Marxist government by a destabilization operation viewed by a U. S government interdepartmental body as a prototype "to test techniques of heavy financial investment — to discredit and bring down a government".[39]

How do our U. S. history textbooks treat the Allende overthrow? One states that Allende had sought to "impose" a Soviet–type socialism, that the economy was in chaos and that the CIA gave help to his opposition.[40] Another reports that Nixon approved funds for the CIA "to make it difficult for the Marxist government ... to govern".[41] These descriptions appeared in texts published in the late 1970's. Other texts published in the 1980's whose authors had access to the House and Senate investigations of 1975–76 documenting CIA covert activities in Chile, provide almost no treatment of the Chilean affair.[42]

When we look at Chile a decade after its U. S. assisted coup, we find another example of those 'crises' threatening American interests and security which appear so often in the textbooks. In 1983, the government ruled by General Augusto Pinochet was killing its own people in the streets of Santiago as they rioted against rising unemployment and the denial of human rights. If this escalates into a full scale revolt, the United States will no doubt blame Cuba or Soviet agitation. Since our citizens never learned from their history texts what our government had done in 1973, they will have no foundation for understanding Chilean events of 1983 or 1993.

The Chilean case is unfortunately a classic, not an isolated, example of American intervention and subversion in the Third World. When we look closely at U. S. foreign policy we do not find an International Good Guy. Instead, we discover a nation which, in the name of "national security interests," "protecting the freedom of our hemispheric neighbors," and "encouraging democratic forces" has intervened in the internal affairs of Third World nations around the globe. To promote an American definition of peace, stability, order and freedom we have: 1) directly intervened with military forces (Dominican Republic, Vietnam, Grenada, Lebanon), 2) provided direct support, including money, weapons and transportation, for CIA–sponsored military forces trying to overthrow unfriendly governments (Angola, Iran, Chile, Nicaragua), 3) attempted to assassinate government leaders (Cuba), 4) trained military and police in counter–insurgency and torture techniques (Iran, Guatemala, Honduras,

Brazil), 5) provided technology used to repress local populations (Iran, South Africa), 6) turned a blind eye to terrorist tactics used by friendly dictators (Chile, Nicaragua, El Salvador, Cuba, Haiti, Brazil), 7) provided protection for American corporations to export products to Third World countries which are banned from domestic markets for being unhealthy and unsafe (almost everywhere) and 8) supported racist regimes with continued trade and military assistance (South Africa, Rhodesia).[43] It will not do to subsume these specific violations of other nations' integrity under such imprecise phrases as "help to overthrow" or "support repressive regimes."

This is the other side of the foreign policy coin – the one that rarely appears on the pages of our high school history textbooks. This negative depiction is not the "true America" any more than the International Good Guy accurately captures the intent and actions of this nation in the Third World arena. Like other nations, the United States looks out first and foremost for its own self–interest. Like other nations, our government wraps its actions in lofty principles and presents them in the most positive light possible. So do our textbooks.

They act as apologists for governmental policy not analysts of it. Our textbooks fail to help students explore the ideological contradictions in our foreign policy. Consequently students are not encouraged to struggle with the fact that their government's actions sometimes violate the very beliefs for which it claims to stand.

Opposing Mr. Good Guy in the Classroom

It doesn't have to be this way. College students who are only a year or two older confront alternative perspectives in their textbooks. These students must evaluate the truth of unpleasant images of America, such as "counter–revolutionary in a revolutionary world" [44] and "satiated, propertied representative of the status quo." [45] High school students who search for explanations and interpretations of their nation's actions in the Third World should not be forced by textbooks to fall back on a type of muffled anti–communism swaddled in the language of peace and freedom. They should be encouraged to reach conclusions not absorb them. Students should be helped to develop the intellectual tools both to analyze past crises and to make informed decisions about future ones. A democracy such as ours should not be afraid to educate its future citizens. It should not mistake socialization for education nor permit ideological indoctrination to substitute for critical inquiry.

We must therefore speak out in the name of democracy. Exposing the narrow textbook view of America as International Good Guy is rooted in our commitment to accuracy, honesty and courage. With the National Council for the Social Studies (NCSS), we argue for instruction which promotes openness, inquiry and intellectual pluralism. In their Social Studies Curriculum Guidelines, the NCSS declares:

> Rationality denotes a critical and questioning approach to knowledge but also implies a need for discovering, proposing and creating; the rational person doubts but also believes. The ultimate power of rational processes resides in the explicit recognition of the opportunity to decide for one-self in accord with the evidence available, the values one chooses and the role of logic.[46]

These guidelines go on to state that social studies curricula should challenge students to reflect on the global problems confronting themselves and their nation and develop their own personal definition of effective global citizenship.[47] Young people must be prepared to become active participants and decision–makers in our nation's foreign policy. The NCSS asks for much more than our textbooks provide–and so do we.

Empowering our students with the analytical skills and knowledge base to understand the nature of U. S. relationships with the Third World will require educators to act in a variety of ways. First, they should supplement textbooks which present only "floating facts" which bob to the surface in the form of international crises, drift around on the textbook page for a paragraph or two, and then sink out of sight.

We have noted that textbook treatments of Latin American relations, for example, rarely mention Cuba after the Missile Crisis of 1962, Dominican Republic after the 1964 intervention, Guatemala after the 1954 coup, or Chile after the overthrow of Allende in 1973. These countries do not go away and the United States does not cease to have relations with them. Although our textbooks no longer have interest in these countries after the crises have passed, teachers must find ways to help students see foreign policy as a continuous process. Students might, for example, do case studies of U. S. relationships with particular countries and as a class develop an aggregate picture of the patterns of American foreign policy in the Third World. Only with such understanding will students be able to make competent judgements when future crises emerge.

Second, teachers should assist students in recognizing that American practices in the Third World are buffeted and challenged by post–war megatrends which are often beyond our control. They should provide students with systematic discussions of decolonization and the concomitant rise of nationalism in the Third World. They should explain to students that the textbook's "floating facts" are often examples of international crises which emerge when Third World people attempt to assert control over their economic and political destinies – an assertion which is often a dialectical reaction to U. S. policies in those parts of the world. The concepts of neocolonialism, economic imperialism, non–alignment, and maldistribution of wealth and power need to be understood by students if they are to become effective interpreters of their world. Without these analytical tools, they must surely remain confused. But, worse than that, they remain hostage to a simplistic interpretation of international relations which places responsibility for Third World crises on Communist machinations.

Third, to broaden our students' understanding of U. S. foreign policy, we must add a most neglected economic lens. Because of glaring textbook omissions, students would be hard pressed to develop an appreciation of the influence of economic considerations on foreign policy in this world of

multinational corporations. One text states in bland, in-
effectual language:

> "Many corporations became billion–dollar corpora-
> tions. Such corporations generally became that
> large by buying a number of different companies.
> ...And many had branches in a number of foreign
> countries.[48]

Several others do mention that the U. S. has supported
oppressive governments in order to maintain access to raw
materials and protect investments, but students need also to
understand why American investments need protecting. There
is more to this issue than an American need to protect
themselves from communists who oppose private property, as
one text is fond of telling us.[49] If private enterprise is good
for a country, if American business helps develop the Third
World, then why would nationalists, leftists, or anyone else
oppose it ?

In the case of Guatemala, for example, our students
should know more than that the government sought to
nationalize United Fruit Company in 1954 and the United
States intervened[50] to bring down a popularly elected leader.
They should be confronted by the fact that indigenous leaders
often view the actions of American companies as contrary to
the achievement of national development goals. Students need
to examine issues related to unequal trade relations, exporta-
tion of capital, low wages for peasants, and foreign ownership
of indigenous resources. Only then will students come to
understand why American companies in the Third World are
vulnerable to expropriation and why U. S. government protection of our overseas investments nurtures anti–Americanism.

To do this we as teachers need not employ the loaded
language of American exploitation or domination. We should
not seek to promote an alternative myth of International Bad
Guy to replace the textbook myth of International Good Guy.
But, in the best tradition of social studies education, we
might raise questions about the appropriateness and morality
of U. S. political and economic intervention in Guatemala and
elsewhere in the Third World.

Fourth, we can challenge the portrayal of the International Good Guy by providing our students with materials drawn from other than officially approved textbook sources. Our nationalistic texts feed our ethnocentrism and present as fact what is in reality only one perspective on U. S. – Third World relations. Additional resources are needed which describe and analyze American corporate behavior, military aid, and CIA covert activities in these countries. These sorts of resources should be in every high school library and familiar to every high school history teacher.[51]

Fifth, teachers can apply pressure on textbook publishers to present fuller, more honest portrayals of American foreign policy. Lobbying through professional organizations for textbook revisions or informing publishers of the reasons for not adopting their textbook can be effective strategies. Also, students who have the opportunity to read alternative perspectives might wish to write to publishers as a class project critiquing their textbook's biases and omissions.

Sixth, and finally, teacher education institutions must assume a major responsibility in the education of present and prospective teachers regarding international issues. Instructional efforts which cite alternative histories, provide or assist in the development of alternative curricula and analyze textbooks for bias and omission are essential to support teachers in their efforts to offer a broader, more honest perspective on U. S. relations with the Third World.[52]

The dynamics of international relations are far more complex than our textbooks lead us to believe and American motives and actions far less pure. We believe that high school students are intellectually capable of examining alternative interpretations of America's role in world affairs. A democracy should trust its young people to sift, explore, and critically evaluate. Certainly our society is not so fragile that it will crumble under the eye of intellectual scrutiny. As educators, we should therefore speak out against textbooks which represent the capitulation of truth–seeking and develop instructional strategies which provide high school students with the intellectual tools and knowledge base needed to understand their nation's actions.

By failing to do so, we contribute to the disempower-
ment of American youth. We deny our students what they
need to define, frame, and evaluate U. S. policy and practice
in the Third World for themselves. We acquiesce to the
fuzzified establishment view of foreign policy presented in
our textbooks and ensure that alternative perspectives remain
"isolated, suspect and only partially developed."[53] We leave
our students vulnerable to nationalistic, unidimensional interpretations of American actions in the Third World which
often serve to justify exploitative international policies.

Notes

1. See George W. Bonham, "Education and the World View," *Change*
    (May-June, 1980) pp. 2-7, for an eloquent argument for the position.
2. The following ten U. S. history textbooks were examined in this re-
    search. Included are some of the most widely used textbooks in
    American schools.

    The American Adventure, Vol. 2, prepared by the Social Science Staff
    of the Educational Research Council of America (Boston: Allyn and
    Bacon, 1977).

    Nancy W. Bauer, *The American Way* (New York: Holt, Rinehart and
    Winston, 1979), annotated teacher's edition.

    Daniel J. Boorstin and Brooks Mather Kelley, *A History of the
    United States* (Lexington, MA: Ginn and Company, 1981).

    Henry W. Bragdon and Samuel P. McCutchen, *History of a Free
    People* (New York: Macmillan Publishing Co., Inc., 1981), annotated
    teacher's edition.

    Richard Current, Alexander DeConde, and Harris L. Dante, *United
    States History: Search for Freedom* (Glenview, IL: Scott, Foresman
    and Company, 1974).

    James West Davidson and Mark H. Lytle, *The United States: A
    History of the Republic* (Englewood Cliffs, NJ: Prentice-Hall, Inc.,
    1981), teacher's edition.

    Harold H. Eibling, Carlton L. Jackson, and Vito Perrone, *Two Cen-
    turies of Progress: United States History* (River Forest, IL: Laidlow
    Publishers, 1981).

    Glenn M. Linden, Elizabeth Aston Wassenich, Dean C. Brink, and
    Wesley J. Jones, Jr., *A History of Our American Republic* (River
    Forest, IL: Laidlow Brothers, 1981).

    Lewis Paul Todd and Merle Curti, *Rise of the American Nation*
    (New York: Harcourt Brace, Jovanovich, 1982), Liberty Union.

    John A. Garraty, *American History* (New York: Harcourt Brace
    Jovanovich Pub., 1982), teacher's edition.

3. For other analyses of U. S. history texts, see Frances FitzGerald, *America Revised: History Schoolbooks in the Twentieth Century* (Boston: Little, Brown and Company, 1979), Martin F. Herz, *How the Cold War is Taught* (Washington, DC: Ethics and Public Policy Center, Georgetown University, 1978), and William L. Griffen and John Marciano, *Teaching the Vietnam War* (Montclair, NJ: Allanheld Osmun and Co., 1979).

4. James P. Shaver, O. L. Davis, Jr., and Suzanne W. Helburn, "The Status of Social Studies Education: Impressions from Three NSF Studies," *Social Education* 43 : 2 (February, 1979), p. 151.

5. *Ibid.*

6. Sherry Keith, *Politics of Textbook Adoption*, Project Report No. 81-47 (Palo Alto, CA: Institute for Research on Educational Finance and Governance, School of Education, Stanford University, April, 1981), p. 1.

7. See Ariel Dorfman, *The Empire's Old Clothes* (New York: Pantheon Books, 1983) for an interesting analysis of the Lone Ranger as an agent of imperialism and neocolonialism.

8. Bauer, *The American Way*, p. 649.

9. Eibling et al., *Two Centuries of Progress ...*, p. 612.

10. Bragdon and McCutchen, *History of a Free People*, p. 717.

11. Ibid., p. 647.

12. Eibling et al., *Two Centuries of Progress ...*, p. 611.

13. Bragdon and McCutchen, *History of a Free People*, p. 697.

14. Todd and Curti, *Rise of the American Nation*, p. 780.

15. Linden et al., *A History of Our American Republic*, p. 700.

16. Eibling et al., *Two Centuries of Progress*, pp. 620 and 626.

17. *New York Times*, March 9, 1983, Section A, p. 18. Speech delivered before The National Association of Evangelicals, Orlando, Florida.

18. Bauer, *The American Way*, p. 664.

19. Linden, et al., *A History of Our American Republic*, p. 570.

20. Ibid.

21. Boorstin and Kelley, *A History of the United States*, p. 736.

22. Todd and Curti, *Rise of the American Nation*, p. 780.

23. According to Martin F. Herz in *How the Cold War is Taught* (p. 51), Robert F. Madgic et al.'s *The American Experience* (Menlo Park, CA: Addison-Wesley Publishing Company, 1975) describes the conditions under Batista in a bit more detail. Unfortunately, this text was not available for our review.

24. Todd and Curti, *Rise of the American Nation*, p. 780.

25. Ibid.

26. Boorstin and Kelley, *A History of the United States*, pp. 620-21.

27. Todd and Curti, *Rise of the American Nation*, p 780; Bragdon and McCutchen, *History of a Free People*, p. 737.

28. FitzGerald, p. 9.

29. Bragdon and McCutchen, *History of a Free People*, p. 756.

30. Davidson and Lytle, *The United States: A History of a Republic*, p. 647.

31. Todd and Curti, *Rise of the American Nation*, p. 789.
32. Bragdon and McCutchen, *History of a Free People*, p. 786.
33. Linden, et al., *A History of Our American Republic*, p. 706.
34. See FitzGerald's *America Revised* and Eric Broudy, "The Trouble with Textbooks," *Teachers College Record*, 77 : 1 (September, 1975), pp. 13–34, for more detailed discussions of textbook adoption.
35. Todd and Curti, *Rise of the American Nation* (Vol. 2, pp. 416–417) provides a rather detailed discussion of U. S. foreign aid in its 1977 Heritage edition. However, this is completely eliminated in the one volume 1984 Liberty edition.
36. Quoted in Thomas G. Paterson, J. Garry Clifford, and Kenneth J. Hagen, *American Foreign Policy: A History Since 1900* (Lexington, MA: D. C. Heath and Company, 1983), p. 589.
37. Ibid.
38. Ibid.
39. *Oversight of U. S. Government Intelligence Functions: Hearings Before the Committee on Government Operations*, U. S. Senate, 94th Congress, Second Session, on S. 317, S. 189 (Washington, DC: U. S. Government Printing Office, 1976), p. 411.
40. *American Adventure*, p. 162ff.
41. Todd and Corti, *Rise of the American Nation*, p. 789, N. B. This reference to the CIA first appeared in the 1977 edition of this textbook.
42. Boorstin and Kelley, *A History of the United States*, makes a brief reference to CIA operations, p. 722.
43. See *Oversight of U. S. Government Intelligence Functions*, Paterson, et al., *American Foreign Policy . . .*, Walter LaFeber, *America, Russia and the Cold War 1945–1980* (New York: John Wiley and Sons, 1980), Noam Chomsky and Edward Herman, *The Washington Connection and Third World Facism: The Political Economy of Human Rights*, Vol. 1 (Boston: South End Press, 1980).
44. Paterson, et al., *American Foreign Policy . . .*, p. 505. Also see Mary Beth Norton, David M. Latzman, et al., *A People and a Nation: A History of the United States, Vol. II: Since 1865* (Boston: Houghton Mifflin Co., 1982).
45. Paterson, et al., *American Foreign Policy*, p. 506.
46. "Revision of the NCSS Social Studies Curriculum Guidelines," *Social Education* 43 4 (April 1979), p. 262.
47. Ibid., p. 267.
48. Eibling, et al., *Two Centuries of Progress*, p. 639.
49. Bauer, *The American Way*, p. 663.
50. Bragdon and McCutchen, *History of a Free People*, p. 737.
51. See Howard Zinn, *A People's History of the United States* (New York: Harper Colophon Books, 1980), William A. Williams *Contours of American History* (Cleveland: World Publishing, 1961), Harvey Wasserman, *Harvey Wasserman's History of the United States* (New York: Harper and Row, 1972), Thomas R. Frazier, *The Underside of American History* Vols I and II (New York: Harcourt Brace Jovanich, 1978). Richard J. Barnet and Ronald E. Muller, *Global*

Reach: The Power of the Multinational Corporations (New York: Simon and Schuster, 1974), Stephen C. Schlesinger, *Bitter Fruit* (Garden City, N. Y.: Doubleday, 1982), Walter LaFeber, *Inevitable Revolutions* (New York: Norton, 1983). Also see sources listed under footnote 43.

52.   There are few alternative curricula which deal exclusively with U. S. - Third World relations. More often, the focus is on development issues. Some useful sources are James and Kathleen McGinnis et al., *Educating for Peace and Justice: Global Dimensions* (St. Louis: Institute for Peace and Justice, 1981), Kenneth A. Switzer and Paul T. Malloy, *Global Issues: Activities and Resources for the High School Teacher* (Denver: Center for Teaching International Relations, 1979), Thomas P. Fenton (ed.), *Education for Justice: A Resource Manual* (Maryknoll, N. Y.: Orbis Books, 1975).
      Rather than looking for a single source, one might contact the following organizations and assemble a packet of materials derived from their publications: Center for Teaching International Relations, University of Denver, Denver, CO 80208; Global Perspectives in Education, 218 E 18th St., New York, N. Y. 10003; American Friends Service Committee, 2161 Massachusetts Ave., Cambridge, MA 02140; New Internationalist Publications Ltd., Stage House, High Street, Benson, Oxon, 0X9 6RP, England; and United Nations Development Program, Information Division, United Nations, New York, N. Y. 10017. Also write to Social Studies School Service, 10,000 Culver Blvd., P. O. Box 802, Culver City, CA 90232-0802 for a list of resources in global studies.

54.   G. William Domhoff, *The Powers That Be: Processes of Ruling Class Domination in America* (New York: Vintage Books, 1978), p. 192.

CHAPTER 12

Worldmindedness:
The Path to Peace and Justice

IDA URSO
University of California
at Los Angeles

Our present educational approaches in multicultural and international education have made us well aware of the diversities existent within the human race. They have also made us well aware of the ethnocentric attitude and the barriers, limitations, and destructive energies such an attitude unleashes among groups and nations. These educational approaches have made available much knowledge about other peoples and places, other customs and languages. This is all well and good. They have given us necessary and useful information, though not sufficient.

Today, we stand at a new cross–roads on the way to improve cross–cultural relations and better human understanding. In order to leave behind the path of our present level of chaos and separateness between groups and nations, we must begin to focus our attention on the unity of one world and on the entity of "one humanity" of which we are all part. We need, not only recognize, but begin to actualize the "brotherhood of man" – the age – old principle to which we have given little more than lip service. The interdependent nature of our world requires nothing less than such a global perspective. Thus, we must begin to use our educational system to help us realize this global perspective. We must begin to teach within our schools the concept of "worldmindedness".

Worldmindedness differs from international and multicultural education in that it is a "value orientation, or frame of reference, apart from knowledge about, or interest in, international relations".[1] The worldminded individual favors a world view of the problems of humanity; his/her primary reference group is humankind rather than, for example, Americans, Arabs or Jews. A review of existing educational approaches to worldmindedness provides the following list of abilities expected of the worldminded individual: she or he possessess the ability to: 1) understand and be compassionate toward those who hold different cultural beliefs or perceptions and participate in human institutions and life situations different from one's own; 2) perceive commonalities in the basic needs of culturally different social institutions and analogies or parallels in the historical experience of different societies or groups; 3) define and develop, as fully as possible, one's own potential, not only for one's benefit, but for the benefits of the one human family; 4) realize and fulfill one's individual responsibility to the rest of the human family – that is, to develop a sense of involvement in and sensitivity to, the problems and needs of humanity; 5) recognize the complexity and variety of human thoughts, desires and activities; see how these affect group and national relations, as well as the "climate" of the planet as a whole and then attempt to adjust personal thoughts, desires and actions within own sphere of influence in such a way as to advance human welfare and contribute to a peaceful world order.

Perhaps these abilities seem overwhelming and even impossible to attain. Yet if we are to move towards a future of peace and progress for the whole human race the attainment of such abilities becomes an urgent necessity which must be accomplished.

We thus become concerned with *how* such abilities can be attained, how worldmindedness can be instilled and developed.

Education for worldmindedness is a relatively new concept. However, in spite of this fact, there already exist several suggested means, perspectives and curricula with the aim of developing worldminded individuals possessing the mentioned abilities. These various approaches can be categorized into the following perspectives:[2] The first perspective can be conceptualized as the attempt to "further the reaches of human nature" – a concept borrowed from the book entitled, *The Farther Reaches of Human Nature*, authored by Abraham Maslow. This perspective includes three components: a) development of the world of the heart, b) development of our subjective inner or self-knowledge, and c) development of the right hemisphere of the brain. Let us briefly consider these.

a) *The World of the Heart.* A quote from Robert Muller, author of the concept, and a well–recognized advocate of worldmindedness, clearly represents the argument for this perspective. He tells us that: "During the last 300 years, humanity's progress has been essentially of an intellectual and material nature. Scientists and thinkers thought that everything could be solved, explained, and furthered by means of pure physical manipulation and intellect. Yet, (it is obvious today that) ... in order to see right, to think right and to act right... we must absolutely restore the great moral force of love, compassion, truthfulness, and hope in the human destiny."[3] In short, within our educational systems, we must emphasize and develop the "world of the heart" as a complement to the present stress on "the world of the mind".

b) *Subjective Inner or Self–Knowledge.* The idea here is to focus inward, to come to the realization – through continued reflection, exercises and experiences – that the state of our outer world is a reflection of our inner nature which is often repressed and chaotic. We often experience conflicts between and among our thoughts, feelings and actions; we "hear" conflicting inner voices, or we simply repress these inner voices, disowning them completely. A focus on the inner self, leading to its development, helps foster harmonious relations and integration within the individual – a state which is then reflected outward in one's relationships, affecting in ripple-like fashion, the group, the nation and the world. The aim of inner development is to reach what Maslow has called, "the full functioning" availability of the human personal essence leading to "full humanness" – a state wherein the individual becomes self–realized or self–actualized. One characteristic trait of such state is that the individual transcends the limits of his / her own culture, and realizes himself / herself as a world citizen – a member of the human family.

c) *Development of the Right Hemisphere of the Brain.* An established belief among many psychologists is that we possess two major modes of consciousness. One mode of consciousness is predominantly a product of the left hemisphere of the brain. This allows us to be rational, analytic, verbal and linear in our thought pattern. The other mode of consciousness is predominantly a product of the right hemisphere of the brain. This allows us to be intuitive, artistic, visionary and meditative. Our educational system in the U. S. has supported, encouraged and even expected a dominance of qualities of the left hemisphere of the brain and, in contrast, belittled, ignored or denounced qualities of the right hemisphere of the brain. Psychologists today tell us that knowledge of the functioning of these two spheres and the development of both is essential in that they complement each other and are equally necessary for creativity. Robert Ornstein, one such noted psychologist, tells us that it is the complementary workings of both the intellect (left hemisphere) and the intuitive (right hemisphere) which underlie our highest achievements.

A second perspective through which to advance world-mindedness places an emphasis on cooperation rather than on competition. This perspective calls for the encouragement of a non–comparative sense of self–worth and it encourages students to assume more responsibility for their own learning and growth.

Today, for the most part, a student's sense of self–worth is dependent upon how the student scores on the scales of evaluation imposed upon him / her by some external authority (teachers, parents or standardized tests). Students are taught that they are only better or worse, smarter or "dumber", as compared to someone else or others. Thus, the student comes to recognize others, in a sense, as "enemies". She / he is continuously competing with others in order to maintain or attain a sense of selfworth. The young person is continuously at "war" with peers in the struggle not to be left behind, not to be left at the bottom of the evaluation scale.

Those who advocate worldmindedness see the need to replace this state of affairs. They emphasize cooperation through group work. They encourage a sense of fraternity through peer responsibility, and peer tutorial systems wherein those who know, help those who don't, and those who can, help those who can't. They encourage the achievement of a non-comparative sense of self-worth through self-evaluations wherein students are encouraged to assess their limitations, accomplishments and behavior in light of their own capabilities and ideal images of themselves. Students thus fail or succeed only in so far as they can or cannot fulfill their own potential and ideal of themselves. Through this process, students become directly involved and assume a greater responsibility in their own growth and learning.

A third perspective through which to advance world-mindedness is to encourage holistic views – to recognize the connectedness of all things and the interdependent nature of our universe. Of particular interest here is the interdependent nature of all groups and nations; for example, the interdependent nature of war and peace, human rights, environmental concerns, economics, international law and resource usage. Thus, this perspective calls for a study of global problems affecting all of humanity. It considers the need for new world order models and global systems of law or resource distribution, for example, and it also stresses a need to study, support and participate in the functions of the United Nations and its related agencies and organizations.

A final perspective on advancing worldmindedness involves encouraging active, experiential learning as opposed to passive and static learning. Much research exists showing that students learn best not by the study of an abstract issue but by tackling a real, concrete problem where both objective and subjective knowledge is required – where both the abstract and personal are involved.

Advocates of worldmindedness place an emphasis on experiential learning through community or group experience or on internships which require relentless self–examination as students are confronted by views of the world often vastly different from their own. Through such experiences, students quickly learn that real–world problems and conflicts are far more complex than either textbooks or political ideologies suggest and that solutions to these problems do not emerge from simple, one–sided formulas. Working in a racially, ethnically, or culturally mixed group or community helps develop a student's sensitivity to others and their positions, thus helping the students develop an ability to empathize with others, particularly across racial, class and cultural barriers.

Through the implementation of these perspectives within our educational system, it is hoped that we can actualize the vision of a world inhabited and managed by worldminded citizens. It is hoped that citizens of the twenty–first century will recognize interdependence as superceding selfish interest, that their concern for humanity will replace self–centeredness and ethnocentrism, and that eventually, they will be able to inhabit a world without war – a world built on trust and love instead of hate and fear. Is this vision a plausible future reality; is it possible? There are a growing number of individuals and groups who not only agree that it is possible but also insist that it is necessary. Let us take a look at a few of these.

In November 1968, with support from the Danforth Foundation, a special, expanded issue of *Social Education*[4] was published wherein several of the authors focused on education for worldmindedness. In an article, becoming a classic in the field, L. Anderson proposed "a world–centered perspective" intended to develop "students' worldmindedness" which he defined as a generalized ability to perceive the world as a whole and hence to see one's own position in time and space from the perspective of the world as a whole".[5] In this same issue, K. Boulding wrote of the need for developing "Education for the Spaceship Earth" while Morris and E. King dealt with "Bringing Spaceship Earth Into Elementary School Classrooms".

The growing interest in this field is well proven by the publication in 1981 of *The Global Yellow Pages* published by a private non–profit organization, Global Perspectives in Education. Identified within this directory are 182 "organizations and projects providing international/global education curriculum materials, teacher training, and consultation at the precollegiate level".[6] This limitation of categories suggests the obvious truth that there are many other groups who are not included in the directory.

The evolving interest in this field is also apparent in the recent convening of a National Assembly on "Global Crossroads: Educating Americans for Responsible Choices" held in May, 1984 in Washington D. C. The event was one of the largest such national assemblies ever convened. Its purpose, as the title indicates, was "to bring together individuals from a wide variety of settings and organizations who are concerned with the state of U. S. Citizens' understanding of international issues and global dynamics" (Preliminary Program).

The inclusion of peace and justice issues as part of teaching worldmindedness is well reflected in the work of the World Policy Institute. In fact, it is this same Institute for World Order[7] which is largely responsible for bringing about a merger between peace and justice issues and the promotion of worldmindedness through their focus on world order studies.

Grenville Clark, a corporation lawyer in New York City, and Louis Sohn, a professor of law at Harvard, collaborated in the publication of "the first piece of modern world order research and writing". Their book became the basic text of the Institute for World Order until Saul Mendlovitz, a professor of International Law at Rutgers University suggested that the Clark / Sohn text be treated as only one of several alternative models for world order.[8] Mendlovitz soon brought fellow scholars into contact with the Institute (for example, Richard Falk of Princeton) and thus began what is currently the 18 year program of "transnational research, teacher training, and publication of educational materials that has spurred the development and spread of the world order approach to peace research and education."[9] This also was the birth of peace and system–transforming world order studies, the overarching goal of which is "the transformation of the present world order of competing sovereign states to a new world order of universal peace, sociopolitical justice, economic well–being, and ecological balance."[10]

True to the definition of a system–transforming approach, those within the world order movement believe that global transformation is an inevitable development; that it will come about either peacefully or through violence and that it will either result in greater global justice or in widespread repression. The goal of the involved academic community, therefore, is to help bring about this transformation as beneficially and successfully as possible for all world's people. Over time, this group of international scholars chose to focus on four overriding global values: peace, economic well–being social justice and ecological balance. Their analysis was based on a perception of the world as an integrated unit materially, ecologically, and spiritually, and the unity of the human species as the starting point for analysis and prescription. The Institute is concerned with the world as a whole and works for the humanity and dignity of each person, aiming at the freedom and welfare of the poor. The globe is seen as a macro–society" and as a "human community".[11]

In keeping with the intent of furthering worldmindedness, the work of the Institute is both normative and value – centered: "The value–centered nature of world order inquiry... makes a substantial difference in how one researches and uses data. For instance, asking what a particular trend means to meeting the basic human needs of the lower one–third of humanity requires a different set of data, than does asking what the same trend means for projected GNP growth."[12] This normative approach to global issues calls for the detached or objective appreciation of values as essential goals of political action.

Richard Falk, authority on international law, argues:

"We favor operational definitions of values that have insight into social costs and benefits (peace in relation to given levels war related casualties and costs, economic well–being in relation to minimum income levels and degrees of inequality in wealth and income) so that it becomes possible to assess tradeoffs between values and to tell whether there has been any progress in a given period of international history with respect to the realization of world order values. Our research here... is for a more detached or objective appreciation of values as goals."[13]

Paralleling the intent to teach subjective inner or self-knowledge, mentioned earlier, is the intent of certain peace and world order scholars to "overcome the dualisms of the rational / scientific tradition, so dominant in the West.[14] Underscored is "the need for a deeper and wider conception of knowledge than is customary according to rationalist canons of higher education. Spiritual traditions and insights become relevant, especially as they shape cultural potentialities that draw on neglected aspects of national and civilizational heritage and posit a sound basis for forms of cultural renewal supportive of economic and political reforms that correspond to ethical and functional imperatives of organizing life humanely on a crowded planet running out of some critical resources."[15] Falk argues that it is "necessary to create a more unified sense of the inner / outer sensibilities that are sometimes differentiated in Freudian terms".[16] Behavior, it is said, cannot be understood if its observation is limited to external planes of existence.

I think it is clear from the examples cited that there exists a substantial network of individuals and groups interested in promoting and teaching worldmindedness for global peace and justice. What is not yet clear, however, is how the presented vision is to be actualized. That is, how can we help sufficient numbers of key administrators and personnel within our educational systems and teacher training centers apply or translate the ideas presented herein into practical and useful programs which would insure a society of world-minded individuals dedicated to the creation of a just and peaceful world?

Notes

1. Personal Correspondence, Academy of World Studies, 1980.

2. Ida Urso, *Teacher's Resource Manual on Worldmindedness: An Annotated Bibliography of Curriculum Materials, Kindergarten Through Grade Twelve,* (Los Angeles: Curriculum Inquiry Center, University of California at Los Angeles, 1981).

3. Robert Muller, Speech at the New York meeting of the New Group of World Servers Festivals Week, 1977 (unpublished).

4. *Social Education* is the official journal of the National Council for the Social Studies published in collaboration with the American Historical Association.

5. L. F. Anderson, "An Examination of the Structure and Objective of International Education" *Social Education*, (1968), p. 647.

6. *The Global Yellow Pages: A Resource Directory*, (New York: Global Perspectives in Education, Inc., 1981), Preface.

7. The change in name occurred in 1983. It reflects an increased commitment to current policy debates affecting the building of a humane and just world.

8. P. Wehr and M. Washburn, *Peace and World Order Systems; Teaching and Research*, (Beverly Hills: Sage Publications, 1976), p. 38.

9. *Ibid.*

10. B. H. Weston, "Peace and World Order Education: An Optimal Design," in Transnational Academic Program, *Peace and World Order Studies: Curriculum Guide,* (New York: Institute for World Order, 1981), p. 59.

11. Saul H. Mendlovitz, "A Look Into World Order Studies," *Macroscope*, 1980 No. 7, p. 3.

12. *Ibid.*, p. 15

13. Richard Falk, *et al., Toward a Just World Order*, Vol. 1 (Boulder, Colorado: Westview Press, 1982), pp. 2–3.

14. *Ibid.*, p. 166.

15. *Ibid.*, p. 167.

16. *Ibid.*, p. 166.

CHAPTER 13

Mutual Aid:
Educational Challenge and Promise

HERBERT S. EISENSTEIN
Pennsylvania State University

Mutual aid is a cooperative act of people voluntarily associating with others because of problems, tasks or needs held in common. Peter Kropotkin initiated the term, providing it with a moral social base – treat others as we would have others treat us.[1] He expanded the concept to form the heart of a political philosophy, incorporating the principles of eqality among people and freedom inherent in each person's existence.

The proposition offered here is that application of the principle of mutual aid to the field of public education would result in arguably beneficial changes in the essential structure, emphases and purposes of education. Colin Ward, arguing the case for "a theory of spontaneous order," an essential component of mutual aid which bears directly on organization, describes the theory in these terms:

> " ... the theory that, given a common need, a collection of people will, by trial and error, by improvisation and experiment, evolve order out of the situation–this order being more durable and more closely related to their needs than any kind of externally imposed authority could provide".[2]

The absence of inherited structures is necessary in order for mutual aid and its inherent component of spontaneous order to flourish. Authority centered structures are necessarily repressive of spontaneous, mutual aid group acts, even when the latter focus on the organization's functions. In particular, organizational arrangements in public schooling provide examples of structure alien to the spontaneous development of teachers' cooperative group formation along mutual aid lines.

Interrelated value perceptions form the foundation for mutual aid and its ongoing consequence, spontaneous order. Together and separately they provide inescapable challenges to inherited structures, emphases and purposes in education and society. Value perceptions concerning equality, autonomy, reflection of self and group, leadership, authority, hierarchy and specialization form the heart of the argument for effecting beneficial changes in formal education. An underlying concern in the following examination will be the attitude of teachers who view the world as fixed, and their attitude toward youth who perceive the world as given. The basic assumption of this chapter is that the secular world is explainable and reasons for its perceived fixities can be illuminated. Changes in social structures, emphases and purposes can be based on renewed perceptions and are within the capabilities of aware people. Formal American education, on the other hand, is an institution with inherited characteristics encountered each year by new teachers and beginning students. The fixed world, the world as given–formal schooling in all its ready–to–be–experienced conditions–can become a constant curriculum: schooling is a given micro–world; the micro–world is a given. The perception of fixedness in the world will be addressed implicitly in the following examination and revealed to be the conditioned assumption from which teacher, student and other educators need liberation.

Equality

To voluntarily participate with others in the performance of tasks and concerns held in common is to perceive entirely new relationship patterns. The task is then perceived as inseparable from the pleasures of group membership. The voluntary commitment is to the group and the task for the conscious purpose of benefiting group membership and self. One's function in completing or continuing the group's tasks is perceived as one's contribution as an equal member of the group. No function makes any member more or less important than any other member. Functions, vis a vis the mutual tasks to be accomplished, may differ in complexity and training required. It is the mutual aid each person performs for the group which equalizes the significance of his or her presence and contribution. The individual's association with a group, each member of which chose to associate for the mutual benefits to be derived from the association, provides an experience among members performing distinct functions. No one is better than another, none is more important. Each is free to leave, and each is free to discuss, to dissent, to persuade as part of the evolving order of the group. Horizontal structure, differential functions with equal status, free choice and free expression derived from open communications among equals are features of the new world.

Schools are not like this. Teachers are not taught to perceive of themselves and others as equals participating in their own mutual aid association. Children encounter schools and teachers whose perceptions, structures and emphases differ vividly from those implied by a mutually beneficial association of voluntary participants. Formal schooling is a set of conditions inherited by new teachers and new students, maintained by veteran teachers and students. Equality is sacrificed to other propositions made perceptible in the daily routines of the school. There is little need to footnote the familiar bureaucratic characteristics of formal school systems. Accommodation is the most favored response–of student to teacher's instructions, administrative mandates and institutional requirements concerning classroom and in–school behaviour. Teachers recognize the need to accommodate to the paramountcy of standards–for student achievement, curriculum coverage, classroom management and formal authority relationships between themselves, principal, central administration and school board. Equal participation by teachers in the establishment of goals or curriculum focus is as absent as student participation in decision making.

The practice of equality is, in the last analysis, the experience of uniqueness. A person openly and clearly considered equal to others regardless of function perceives himself or herself as worthy as another to express and develop personal thoughts, dispositions and judgements. The practice of equality in the pursuit of mutual aid contains the promise of self and social awareness. Teachers participating in equal and joint ownership of formal education would offer new perspectives on equality to their students. The consciousness heightening experiences of teachers would be revealing since they would depart from inherited value of competitive success and external standards and judgements. New and renewed perspectives would be learned within fresh organizational structures which avoid the distancing and divisional characteristics of existing school systems. Centralization of policy and decision–making would give way to fluid, mutually initiating group arrangments of learning. Such arrangements would emphasize regard for self and group as equal owners of evolving learning experiences. The world for both teachers and students would be perceived as possible: as evolving toward human expressiveness and away from institutional rigidity.

Autonomy

One's attitude toward autonomy is crucial. Without belief in the political and psychological values of self autonomy, mutual aid and spontaneous order lack foundation. People whose perceptions of self and society are formed by compliance–featured personal histories will often avoid experiences which risk personal expression. To be an equal is to prize one's presence in a society which often demands the opposite behavior. Deference to authority or to inherited sanctions is a response formally respected in most institutions.

One who chooses to respond differently, to see the world differently, has arrived at an awareness of the distinction between self initiated choice and self as defined by others. Choice that becomes voluntary is choice based on the struggle to perceive what one wishes to see in relation to the powerful, immediate socio–political environment. The struggle for autonomy is the post–industrial society member's struggle for survival. The ability to achieve clarity of vision of the world's capacity to move one's perceptions away from true inclination of self is the attainment of conscious survival. This successful struggle is the attainment of identity of one's authentic self. One must choose autonomy in order to engage in the act of challenging myths of the inherited world. One can only voluntarily choose to view members of a group as equals. One can only struggle to achieve, and then insist on, one's autonomy in perceiving tasks on mutual problems.

The autonomous person can see the value of work in terms of its usefulness to a community's well-being. The autonomous person can perceive a task as a mutually engaged solution–in–process. The solution can be accomplished by a group of equals engaging in a mutually open, experiential give and take. Autonomy thus directly impacts on traditional structures, emphases and purposes of institutions like education.

Teachers do not ordinarily view themselves and their world in these terms. Nor are they typically encouraged to free themselves by the social–technical training in which they are immersed. To become a teacher through the state college or university process of value and curricular imposition is to receive at least implicit instructions in social, political and psychological accommodation. These instructions are justified by measured technique acquisition within a curricular stream of fixed world orientation. The world of the teacher is fixed by successfully implementing the accommodation principle adopted by the training and the employing (public schooling) institutions.

The learned, internalized, given quality of a teacher's world can be penetrated by intentional efforts of autonomous others, themselves a dissenting curriculum within either institution, and themselves achieving, through existential struggle, the condition of autonomy. These liberated efforts lead to reflective experience among people who may become or already are teachers. Reflective experience is necessary for the appreciation of autonomy of thought, choice and action. It equips the individual to perceive self and world independent of shaping forces – by enhancing his or her ability to identify forces alien to self-identification.

Reflection of Self and Group

"By confronting the feelings he experiences when
he is rendered an object by someone else's gaze
or where his sense of himself as a person is
treated as irrelevant, the teacher may become
more sensitive to the importance of encountering
others as individuals".[3]

Unless one confronts the condition of being rendered an
object, there can be no awakening, no recognition of the predicament of one's self in the world. To accept the arrangements of time, space, relationships and accountabilities as
given is unconsciously to declare one's passivity in the face of
impositions and imperatives. The implicit declaration of yield-
ing one's style or one's expectations to powerful, inherited
arrangements for which one has been prepared is to render
the teacher an object. As an object, the teacher sleeps. As
an object expressing implicit accommodation to the "gaze" of
others, the teacher expresses his or her irrelevance to students.
Objects are interchangeable. Accommodation to structure, emphases and purposes becomes the latent curriculum. Those
who learn it well learn to accept the given world, to be objects,
to sleep. Teachers who sleep generate a curriculum of sleep.

To reflect is to confront. To examine time, space and
behavioral mandates demythed of their fixedness by reflection
of self and group is the confrontational experience. The power
of reflection lies in its freeing the self from domination. Once
freed from canalized perceptions of self and society, the
teacher can choose to examine the givens of public education—
its purposes, structures and emphases. The teacher gains the
freedom to question assumptions about self and world and
ways they intersect in the immediate world of work. The
mutuality of teacher concerns becomes a reflective possibility.
The mutuality of school work is seen as consistent with
mutual concerns. The right to think about alternatives to
given work and role assignments forms the foundation for the
right to express one's true convictions about the rightness of
independent thought and expression. Both impact on newer

modes of work arrangement which satisfy the conditions of liberating reflection and independent thinking.

To reflect and confront is to awaken, to become conscious. A conscious teacher is an autonomous person. Conscious autonomy requires structures conducive to the enhancement of free expression. Only equals are free to express themselves. Only undominated teachers can choose new relationship arrangements which guarantee a learning environment in which each participant can perceive each other as mutually autonomous. Reflective teachers are people sensitive to the importance of others and assuredly sensitive to the urgency of individual initiatives and mutual regard. Mutual aid and its spontaneously evolving order represent the ownership of self and destiny through voluntary group endeavors accomplished by equals for mutual concerns. These are as much students' concerns as they are teachers'. The reconstructional impact on inherited pyramidal structures of school authority and compliance is as obvious as implications for social reconstruction. Intentional intervention in the accommodation characteristics of teacher training institutions is necessary to complement and reinforce self and group.

Leadership

Leadership is transformed into a function approved among equals once the experience of mutual aid is underway. In pyramidal structures, in which authority and power are unequally divided among members, leadership is selected by and from the top and vested with unequal power. People in mutual aid groups perceive "leadership" as relating to a large, complex series of functions, or perhaps to a simple, but nonetheless important one. The "leader" is by mutual consent the expert in the particular function called for. But, by no means, is he or she any more important, or "more" equal than others of the group of equals. Each voluntarily, implicitly or explicitly, agrees that the person more expert, or specialized, is in fact more knowledgeable than any other member of the group *in that particular function*.

Of equal importance, the specialist perceives himself or herself in the same philosophical sense: an equal doing a specialized task voluntarily because of mutual respect for the group's membership and purposes. Specialists do what they do for intrinsic satisfaction in the task, including direction and instruction communicated to others mutually involved in the task. Always, group members are free to reflect and dialogue about the need to continue the expert's activities. Always, the expert is free to inform the larger membership about his or her views concerning the need to continue, reduce or expand the duration and scope of expertise. These prerogatives of both experts (specialists) and membership guarantee horizontal, cooperative, mutual, egalitarian, voluntary, non–authoritarian qualities of the mutual aid organization. They also assure the inherent process of "improvisation and experiment" – spontaneous order.

Conclusion

Teachers engaged in a process of spontaneous order would, therefore, perceive themselves as equals owning their own focus and direction by a voluntarily agreed upon horizontal, functional, cooperative structure. Teachers in equal relationship to one another could not abide unequal designations of rank, authority and power. Teachers, in mutual regard for the full expression of each voluntarily cooperative group member, would perceive structure as part of the ongoing curriculum. Hierarchical structures, formal authority layers, specified curricular content or complexity levels and centralized decision-making would be perceived as alien to the mutual aid teacher membership group. The pyramidal public educational organization would be seen as inherited. Ownership of teaching functions, including teaching style, temporal spatial arrangements, expertise, curricular content and educational group size would be perceived as mandatorily granted to unequally powerful people. Each facet of the teaching function would be perceived as a valid object of free reflection – of autonomous thought generating the capacity to confront the given as erroneous and inequitable. Ownership of educational tasks would be perceived as a philosophical possibility for teachers.

Dedicated to the renewal potential of a shared experience of specialists, guaranteeing each other mutual aid and equal worth, teachers would see themselves as free owners of themselves and their shared functions. Inherited emphases would be perceived as fair game for critical reflection. Centrally, decisions concerning emphases and purposes would become the object of autonomous reflection and dialogue among equals sharing mutual concerns. Teachers would be autonomous, conscious, relevant; they would not be passive objects of policies and purposes initiated by others under the protection of a fixed world concept. Such teachers would be examples of cooperative, autonomous, reflective, instrinsically motivated people. They would project a curriculum of vitality to their students. Themselves learning from autonomous people to grow in consciousness, students – like their teachers – would learn the value of free reflection, of the excitement of mutual regard in the group process of mutual aid. Like their teachers, they would find passion in their own worth, passion in the pursuit of reflective strength and unique qualities. Like their teachers, they would not sleep.

College professors who teach teachers would have to distance themselves from the givens of their profession in order to intervene in the fixed world of their students. They would have to reflect on structures, purposes and emphases in the world at large as they impact on those of public education. College professors who teach teachers would have to reflect on the nature and origins of their perceptions of their functions. In order to intervene, they would have to struggle toward the ownership of their own perceptions, of their own functions. Eventually, they would have to choose not to sleep.

Notes

1. Peter Kropotkin, *Mutual Aid* (New York: McClure, Phillips & Co., 1902). See also *Kropotkin's Revolutionary Pamphlets*, Roger N. Baldwin, (ed), (New York: Dover Publications, 1970).
2. Colin Ward, *Anarchy in Action* (New York: Harper & Row, 1974), p. 28.
3. Maxine Greene, *Teacher As Stranger* (Belmont, California: Wadsworth Publishing Co., 1973), p. 82.

PART III

PERSPECTIVES ON WORLD COMMUNITY

Introduction

As the twentieth century comes to a close, world community becomes a reality. But what kind of reality is it, we might ask? Musicians, athletes, business people and diplomats zip around the earth with alacrity. Multinational corporations operate on every continent. Developing countries accumulate huge debts and overdeveloped countries depend upon developing countries for their raw materials. The superpowers make fortunes as arms merchants, while poor countries which buy the newest weapons cannot afford adequate food for their people. Elites worldwide have much in common, but so do the jobless, homeless and hungry. In many ways the world is already a community, but a community which is largely impoverished, unhealthy, unequal and volatile.

Needed today are images of a world community based on social, economic and political justice. We must not settle for the present global community which parallels the sickness and cruel contrasts of most large American cities. Instead of segregation by race and class, high unemployment and crime, an exceedingly wealthy elite basking in precious furs and jewelry while working people struggle just to get through each day, new forms of world community are needed. Diversity must be assured in any design for world order, but diversity based on equitable choice, not inheritance. A transformed world community would relish the differences of multiculturalism, but also cherish the unity of a global order based on equality.

While "world order" or "world community" in the ideal sense may seem difficult to envision, let alone achieve, such a quest should not be avoided. Indeed there has never been a more urgent time to explore the goal of world order, because a peaceful, just world community of nations may be the most practical, realistic key to human survival. When nuclear bombs, so small that they fit in back packs, are carried by U. S. soldiers in Europe and nucleartipped cruise missiles can be stored secretly in barns and garages anywhere, the world is certainly not safe. National and global insecurity are growing daily as launch–on–warning, which leaves genocidal decisions to computers, becomes operational. The only practical alternative to such madness which threatens our earth – a beautiful bubble suspended in space – is a different kind of world.

In Part III, a variety of perspectives on world community and what the world might become are offered. Two leading philosophers, interested in world order for peace, are compared in the opening chapter. Both Brameld and Galtung have the vision of a future global organization which should be realized by transforming the existing social structures. The next chapter provides psychological insights by discussing tea ceremony and the Buddhist world–view. It is followed by a chapter on global hunger urging Americans to assume greater responsibility to reduce the hardships of hunger by making use of their resources. Formation of a world community with a new notion of citizenship is advocated in the next chapter. "Perspectives on World Community" concludes with a chapter of reflections on Theodore Brameld, a world citizen all his life.

CHAPTER 14

World Order for Peace, Philosophical Approaches of Brameld and Galtung

DAVID C. WOOLMAN

Rhode Island College

One of the main concerns of those who study about peace is to try to discover what type of society is needed to reduce violence between humans and how that society might be achieved. Theodore Brameld, an American educational philosopher and Johan Galtung, a Norwegian social scientist, have both tried to describe what a peaceful world would be like. This essay will report and appraise the way that these two twentieth century thinkers have answered this question. Educational as well as broader social dimensions of the issue will be considered.

Theodore Brameld thinks that world peace requires rebuilding of the present social order because important cultural values and behaviors are being lost. He considers schools to be a major instrument for this cultural renewal. To succeed in this reconstruction of society, Brameld thinks that education would have to carry out four roles. These include the restoration of lost cultural values, the preparation of students to adapt to new demands, the transmission of important customs of contemporary culture, and the transformation of culture by teaching students how to recognize and resolve problems of the present society.

Brameld's vision of what a peaceful society should be like can be inferred from the type of social action he recommends to achieve this renewal. For example, he holds that individual growth and renewal should be part of a democratic process. In this way, humans seek their identity through achievements which gain social acceptance through a process of consensus. Brameld also maintains that decisions about future goals and the ways to achieve them should come from group consideration that is based on ideas of common human needs. In this conception of society, peace is thought to result from broad participation in goal setting which will reduce the potential for conflict by enabling most people to achieve their needs.

Johan Galtung is not as positive as Brameld that formal schools are capable of such social reconstruction. Galtung thinks that much schooling supports the general Western cultural system which prevents peace by maintaining social relations based on direct or indirect violence. Some of the ways Galtung thinks that this violence is caused by Western culture and its schools are as follows. First, individuals in schools are mostly taught how to conform to social needs rather than how to develop their own talents; this does violence to each person's individuality and students may grow up without knowing how to develop their own personal abilities. Second, he thinks that the schools promote social inequality by basing learning on competitive activities which produce winners and losers. This again violates the individual's need to develop the self. Even worse, Galtung holds, inequality in education lays the foundation for social and economic inequality based on exploitation rather than cooperation in human relations. Galtung considers that inequality is a major cause of poverty, which he regards as a form of violence. Third, although schools devote much time to preparing students for economic success in life, Galtung thinks that they neglect the subjects of spiritual values, ethics, and democratic living skills which can help to create a cooperative society which controls violence.

Galtung thinks that a new type of education would help to make the world more peaceful. This new school would help people discover and use their personal abilities. It would also encourage people to try many different ways of solving problems rather than just one way as the correct solution. By helping students to develop cooperative skills, the school would prepare them to live in a more equal society. Schools would also have to provide people with skills that would make it possible for them to improve their standard of living once they left school; in very poor countries this might mean learning how to grow food well, to practice health and sanitation, to run a small business, and to contribute to community development projects. In rich societies it might mean rediscovery of spiritual values, community participation, and individual creativity which could make for healthier personal adjustment and outlook on life. In Galtung's theory, achieving peace depends on overcoming such conditions as poverty and personal unhappiness with life which make people more likely to resort to violence because of frustration.

It is clear that both Brameld and Galtung think that education has a job to do in building a new type of society based on peace. The remainder of this essay will be concerned with examining their perspectives on the type of world social order needed to achieve peace and offering some commentary on these proposals.

Goals for a World Based on Peace

Both Galtung and Brameld have a vision that one day some form of global organization will improve upon the present arrangement of nation–states. For example, Brameld speaks of a "world order of nations" directed by "the majority of peoples." Galtung points to the emergence of many international organizations as an illustration of the growing need for global levels of order. However, Brameld differs from Galtung in the way he views the outcome of such a world order. Brameld thinks that peace could result from such an order if participants were to create a world civilization by reducing conflict between cultures and nations and striving for common ideas as a basis for action.

Galtung also agrees on the need for democratic participation in planning for peace and the reduction of conflicts that reach dangerous levels. However, Galtung would argue that uniform ideas about what world culture or civilization should be are a threat to peace because they tend to violate the human need for diversity. He also thinks that any universal world order might try to prevent continuous grassroots social change which is one way people can correct conditions that are harmful to them. Galtung's solution is to have a world order based on pluralistic federalism in which many small countries are free to make any relations they please with other countries and there is tolerance for differences in social and political customs. This freedom also requires restraint from harming any other country through one's associations or activities.

In addition to their ideas of a world political order, Brameld and Galtung also have identified a number of goals which need to be achieved if mankind is to enjoy future peace. Both scholars think that greater social equality is essential to peace. They reason that inequality of opportunity, which produces poverty and discontent, is a major source of conflict in today's world. Galtung considers poverty resulting from social inequality to be a form of structural violence. By this he means that the way society is organized by class actually helps some groups of people take advantage of other people so that the victims are unable to acquire the minimum housing, food, clothing, and freedom necessary to live in peace.

In this perspective, the existence of peace is thought to involve the presence or absence of certain degrees of freedom associated with access to basic living needs. This approach has developed from the concept that peace requires freedom from fear and want. This conception is an important part of the United Nations charter. Wherever there is a lack of this freedom we should expect some conditions which deny either security or basic needs to a group or individual. Three types of conditions are mainly responsible for interfering with the realization of peace. First, internal and external crises which produce wars and other types of armed conflicts clearly obstruct the security and livelihood of many people. Second, social organization based on inequality of opportunity and maintenance of exploitative relationships also promotes differences of security and welfare. Third, national catastrophes such as droughts, earthquakes and floods also threaten the basic needs for life. In principle, all three of these conditions can be modified or alleviated through human intervention and social change. In reality, there are many obstacles which hamper progress against these problems.

Both Brameld and Galtung provide us with a good summary of basic needs that are the foundation for peace in life. The nourishment of good food and balanced diet are critical to man's growth and development; without adequate nutrition in the early years, mental deficiency can result in later life which reduces the human potential for achievement. Proper clothing and shelter are likewise important factors in the physical and psychological well–being of humans; besides the obvious benefit of protection from the elements, clothes and housing provide an opportunity for freedom of individual and cultural expression.

Physical and mental health are other needs stressed by Brameld and Galtung. Physical health depends on the needs of nutrition, clothing, and shelter cited above; maintenance of health requires access to medical and dental doctors with proper facilities for the care and remediation of sickness. Mental health, which is partly influenced by physical health, also depends on having a secure environment with opportunity to grow and develop one's abilities. Other important factors in such health are the need for privacy and sexual expression, the right to work and be self–supporting and the right to associate freely with other people. The latter right is a basic need because humans are social beings for whom participation and belonging to groups is a way to develop social identity.

Another dimension of basic needs depends on access to education which enables self–development and realization of social living skills. One provision that schools can make is for equal opportunity to learn skills and acquire knowledge. Another critical need is to expand the level of literacy training so that most people are able to read and write at a basic level. Finally, education can also provide people with the opportunity to extend themselves into new lines of work so that they can fully develop their creative potential.

Means for Achieving World Peace

In addition to prescribing these goals which are thought to be essential for peace, Brameld and Galtung have also specified various means whereby humankind can strive to achieve a peaceful world order. In many respects, the two scholars are in agreement about these reform strategies. Several economic changes are proposed. First, production would be reorganized to supply basic needs like food, clothing, shelter and health for all the world's people; this would require change in many aspects of the current world economic system which provides many products for the rich and few essentials to the poor. Moreover, many aspects of today's production system are oriented toward providing non–essential luxury goods and armaments which exceed the levels required for self–defense. When governments in poor countries spend heavily on luxury goods and armaments they have less resources to provide for their citizens' needs for nutrition, health and education.

A second economic reform would require that every country provide for full employment which would be guaranteed according to the ability and interest of the workers. The purpose of this proposal is to avoid having anyone get trapped in dead-end jobs which have no relationship to their real potential or desires. Flexibility is required so that employers will allow employees to undergo retraining and encourage them to advance according to their ability and interest. The goal is to avoid having persons who are unfulfilled and dissatisfied with their lives and work, for such people are often not at peace with themselves or the world around them. The fact that one of the most violent political movements of modern times, the German Nazi party, rose to power in an environment of economic depression bears out the point that there is a real connection between peace and economic satisfaction.

A third economic reform would encourage greater worker control of the conditions in which work is done. Participation by workers would include suggestions, a share of decision making and more two-way communication instead of the traditional one-way dictation by management. It is thought that such dialogue has the potential to improve the environment and product of work by tapping experience and understanding from every level of the fabrication process. More important, it may result in more peaceful relations between labor and management by providing opportunities to express frustration and seek remedies for problems before they develop into more serious issues.

A fourth economic reform proposal would provide a guaranteed income to every person so that their basic needs for food, clothing, shelter, education, medical care, and recreation are met. Underlying this proposal is the assumption that poverty is more often the result of bad fortune (being born in a poor country) or social disadvantages (living in a society where education is limited for the poor) than of lack of initiative or industry. Farmers in many poor countries work hard year in and year out but often remain too poor to provide for these basic needs. Another assumption of this proposal is that global resources are sufficient to enable a redistribution to meet the basic living needs of all people. Most famine and disaster relief efforts already operate on this assumption; however, a worldwide program could eliminate the need for relief efforts which often provide too little aid too late to save many victims. The idea of income redistribution could also improve the prospects for peace in many areas of the world by relieving the material insecurity which afflicts many people and is a source of tensions and conflict between and within both rich and poor countries.

Another proposed economic reform is the idea that the general welfare of all humankind is better protected through public control of natural resources and large corporations. One assumption behind this suggested change is that large capitalistic companies do not always operate in the interest of the general welfare of mankind. Another assumption is that control of business by a public interest government agency would manage the enterprise with greater consideration for the needs of all persons. The record of environmental pollution and marketing of products with hazardous ingredients strongly supports the first assumption. However, large public agencies are also likely to grow isolated from concern for the general welfare unless they can be held accountable to some effective democratic body.

Peaceful social relations are also thought to depend on political conditions which ensure wide distribution of resources, democratic participation in decision making, a balance of local and central control and freedom for experimentation. Both Brameld and Galtung think that the present economic system is failing to deliver needed resources to all people. Therefore they propose a new system in which the public would control agriculture; large scale technical production; utilities such as electric power; health services; communication facilities such as radio, TV and telephone; and transportation such as railroads, airlines, and bus service. Through such control they hope that pollution of the environment and depletion of natural resources can be avoided.

In addition, the prospects for peace are held to be improved when there is readily available equal access to political participation for all social groups. The problem of inequality for minorities in the system ruled by the majority is a serious difficulty with this theory of peace through democracy. However, this problem can sometimes be alleviated by allowing local minorities the freedom to be different and self-governing. Flexibility is an important asset of a truly democratic system. If there is too much central control, people in local communities may lose the habit of self-reliance and can suffer from arbitrary rule. If there is too much local control, isolation and narrow viewpoints may obstruct equality and produce social tensions. The solution, according to Brameld and Galtung, requires a balance of central and local control which preserves a tolerance for diversity and experimentation with alternatives.

In addition to economic and political reforms, both Brameld and Galtung envision the need for changes in the cultural organization of life. Cultural pluralism, social security and broad participation by all minorities are common goals of this new social order. Redesign of the environments in which humans live would stress the values of functionalism; freedom of association; uncensored access to art, literature, and music; and planning based on esthetics and quality of life. The interventions of technology in life would be controlled so as to enhance the environment of life. The general idea behind these cultural proposals is that individual and social peace depends on freedom for self–development which can be cultivated by modification of negative social traits. Cultural uniformity, for example, does violence to the idea that there is value in each one of many different cultures. Likewise, automobiles and chemical plants which pollute the air and water we need may shorten our life spans and limit the time we have to make creative contributions to the world.

Finally, the prospect for peace is also thought to depend on reconstruction of the international order, which currently is based on too much inequality and economic exploitation. Both Brameld and Galtung conceive that it is necessary to subordinate national sovereignty to international authority. The reason behind this proposal is that much of the violence in today's world which occurs within or between nations is insulated from international sanctions or intervention by the concept of sovereignty. Sovereignty means a government is the master in its own house; whatever is done against human rights or minorities inside a country cannot be stopped by direct intervention of the United Nations.

The new international order proposed by Brameld and Galtung would include democratic control by all groups; equality in relations between rich and poor countries; and freedom for all peoples to move throughout the world to seek education, cultural awareness, scientific understanding and economic association. The idea behind this proposal is that the many artificial barriers and controls that nations use to separate people in today's world do not serve the goals of human progress or peace. It is thought that peace and resolution of human conflict would be better served by energetic free association and interaction than by the restrictions necessitated by nationalism.

Both Brameld and Galtung recognize that these ideas for reconstructing society to achieve peace are unlikely to come about soon because society is by nature conservative and resistant to change. However, Brameld thinks that change will eventually come because crises will occur which will make society slowly change its customs and institutions. Brameld, like Galtung, hopes that society will move toward a liberal or even radical change in responding to the crisis but he also knows that a backlash or conservative reaction is also possible. Brameld differs somewhat from Galtung in that he rejects the idea of an eclectic response to crisis because he thinks that a unified 'ethos' or set of values is necessary. Galtung, on the other hand, favors greater freedom with eclectic approaches that allow for a creative mixture of ideas and resources according to the demands of the situation.

Commentary

The ideas of Brameld and Galtung represent a model for global reconstruction with the intention of increasing prospects for peace and improving the conditions of life for all the world's peoples. Their ideas belong to a long tradition of idealistic and utopian thought. In assessing these ideas it is not possible to know definitely whether these proposed changes will work in the ways which their authors intended until they have been put into practice and tested. Therefore, evaluation of the ideas at this stage must necessarily focus on logical analysis of their credibility.

There is little doubt that the basic physical needs for human life are essential conditions for peace and security. Both Galtung and Brameld have also proposed that structural political conditions or crises in the present world are mainly responsible for a systematic denial of basic needs. Here there is some room for doubt; the linkage appears to be a partial rather than a complete explanation for the problem. For example, it might be argued from a global structural perspective that nationalism and capitalist economics are responsible for the spread of famine in Africa. No doubt government policy and economic choices (i. e., cash crop agriculture, arms purchases, high interest loans) have contributed to soil depletion and denial of human resource development. However, famine is also influenced by other factors such as overpopulation, elimination of disease, poor natural resources (soil) and traditional farming methods which erode the soil and resist change; many of these conditions are not directly linked to modern global political structures. In short, there is a need to be more specific in linking the causes and effects of global problems. To say that global political structures are entirely to blame is an overstatement which ignores the effects of local political and non–political conditions.

The reform strategies in economics are a mixture of practical and utopian ideas. For example, the idea of worker control is already done in some industries because it has been found to improve productivity and the incentives of labor. On the other hand, the idea of having all jobs fit the interest and ability of workers is problematic in any highly complex industrial economy. Some work is inherently uninteresting because of its tedious or routine nature, but it remains necessary for human survival. A society without sanitary workers would soon run the risk of a public health catastrophe. Likewise, farming is critical to the supply of basic human needs, but it is difficult and relatively unrewarding labor. Suppose no one did these jobs because of insistence on pursuit of interest and fit with ability. Society could mechanize but someone must be found to run machines. Another alternative is dependence on migrant or guest laborers to do jobs that citizens reject. However, this introduces the problem of inequality and exploitation all over again. The idea of work matching ability and interest is a sound basis for positive human motivation. However, the success of this proposal depends on diversity of human abilities and interests so that all necessary work gets done. Perhaps only the small commune with democratic sharing of all jobs can achieve this ideal fit of work, ability and equality.

The proposal for guaranteed income to provide basic needs for all is also meritorious in its intent. However, there are new social problems which can result from the certainties and excessive security created by the social welfare state. In Sweden some alcoholism and apathy among youth has been associated with the rigid environment of cradle to grave social planning. Incentives and motivation appear to be eroded by the absence of some degree of uncertainty which sparks the

will to explore and discover one's own world. There is a need
to balance the guaranteed security with protection of the need
to search for autonomy and self–reliance.

The idea of public control of natural resources and
basic industries is intended to prevent maldistribution and
exploitation. However, such proposals carry the danger of re-
placing corporate monopoly with bureaucratic monopoly.
Neither Galtung nor Brameld is fond of large corporations,
which are the core of the capitalistic economic system, because
they often have such monopoly power. However, the proposal
of global public control would create a greater monopoly than
that enjoyed today by any corporation or government. All the
inefficiencies of large scale centralized bureaucracies would be
multiplied a thousand fold in a global resource board. Moreover, control of such a board would inevitably be concentrated
in the hands of a few experts whose power would be greater
than any present arrangement. Even with thorough democratic
procedures the prospects of resource denial from procedural
delays and/or conflicts are considerable in such a body. In
short, resource management for public welfare is a critical
need which would probably be ill served by a global structure;
local or regional levels of management offer more promise with
some kind of provision for global redistribution.

The concept of a change in culture which would redirect
mankind to basic material and spiritual needs is meritorious
in theory. However, the means whereby such a transition
would occur is a critical determinant of its peaceful potential. In the twentieth century, much culture change has been
achieved through direct and indirect coercion. In such a process, imposition by central planners is often the driving force
behind change rather than self-selection at the grassroots level.
The liberal welfare state is loaded with hierarchical planning
patterns which exert great power on localities through the
power of resource distribution. If the world is to enjoy peace
through diversity, the freedom of choice and initiation needs
to be widely based. An inherent danger in any 'peace planning' process is that the pursuit of a positive objective could

create a singlemindedness of purpose which blocks positive as well as negative forms of human diversity.

A major element in the political proposals of Brameld and Galtung for global planning and peace is that these ideas should be achieved through a democratic process. However, democracy has several structural tendencies which could obstruct some of the other objectives which these planners hope to achieve. For example, a democratic political structure is always vulnerable to the problem of a tyranny of the majority which establishes norms and standards. As such, democracy may pose a threat to pluralism by insisting on levels of conformity and standardization which exclude diversity. On the other hand, genuine democracy also permits different viewpoints to influence the outcomes of decision making so that it is quite conceivable that policies for peace could be compromised by conflicting interests. Therefore, it seems that democracy in itself may be insufficient to assure pluralism and global consensus on peace; some other structural variations within the context of democracy are probably needed. Some kind of quality control moderated through a 'brain trust' which subjects policies to scientific analysis and experimental review might be one option.

There are many examples of international efforts to curb inequality, political injustice, and economic exploitation by alleviating the ill effects of these deplorable conditions. Organizations such as Oxfam and Amnesty International come immediately to mind. However, given the present global structure based on nation–state sovereignty there is a greater need to explore means for alleviating these problems through resources within countries. International intervention is limited for various reasons. On the one hand, countries can bar such efforts from their soil. On the other, international groups may lack depth in their experience with local realities so that their efforts can prove quite ineffective in promoting change at the local level. Galtung's proposals for local self–reliance, which reflect the position taken by Mohandas Gandhi, are an effort to address this need for internal action at the grass-roots level.

A final note is needed about the contrast between the unified ethos sought by Brameld and the more eclectic position taken by Galtung. In an organic conception of the world, with change as a constant reality, it is doubtful that a unified ethos can work unless it too is flexible. Moreover, Galtung asserts that uncertainty and change are essential to sustain the growth and development needed to maintain peaceful conditions of life. He thinks this is true because people are more likely to explore and discover new directions when they are faced with uncertainty. A certain environment offers no incentive for extending the self. However, like the idea of a unified ethos, the notion of uncertainty needs to be more refined; there are some common ethos and certainties which are constructive just as there are others that are destructive. In the quest for peace, restraint from violence is surely a common ethos, whereas the certainty of basic needs is likewise a foundation for human security. As life evolves so do the contexts in which various needs are required. If peace is attached to dynamism and opposed to stasis, there is room for a balance of unity and diversity which would be subject to continual change. There can be no final order of peace because peace must be continually constructed as generations of humans evolve through life.

Selected Bibliography

Brameld, Theodore. *Cultural Foundations of Education: An Inter-disciplinary Exploration.* New York: Harper: 1957.

—. *Ends and Means in Education.* New York: Harper, 1950.

—. *Patterns of Educational Philosophy: Divergence and Convergence in Culturological Perspective.* New York: Holt, Rinehart, and Winston, 1971.

Galtung. Johan *The True Worlds: A Transnational Perspective.* New York: Free Press, 1980.

—. "The Basic Needs Approach." In *Human Needs: A Contribution to the Current Debate.* pp 55 – 125. Edited by Katrin Lederer. Cambridge, Mass.: Oelgeschlager, Gunn, and Hain, 1980.

—. "Schooling and Future Society." *School Review* 83 (August 1975), 73–88.

CHAPTER 15

A Simple Bowl of Tea:
A Psychological Perspective on Peace

FRANCES L. O'NEIL
Tunxis Community College

> If only
> I could throw away
> the urge
> to trace my patterns
> in your heart
> I could really see you.[1]

Continuing research on the psychosocial aspects of peace indicates that it is through the arts rather than through information and logical processing that a consciousness of our present global danger can be reached by larger segments of the population. These dangers are of catastrophic proportion and while the destruction of our life support system and the worldwide disparity of the "have's" and "have–nots" are among them, nothing is more awesome than the threat of nuclear war. This fear is so real to American citizens that studies indicate that the majority expect nuclear war to occur and that it will mean the end of civilization. This is not mere "doom–thinking," for the explosion of a one megaton bomb, which is a small weapon by contemporary standards, would be the equivalent of seventy simultaneous Hiroshima explosions. A twenty megaton bomb would yield the destructive force of 1,600 Hiroshima bombs being dropped at the same time and in the same place. Hiroshima and Nagasaki fail to serve as realistic precedents, however, for we must consider the fact that whereas they suffered under one attack, there might be multiple events in a future war scenario, perhaps within four or five hours of one another. Finally, while in 1945 there was one nuclear power, today there are at least six, with a total arsenal of 50,000 warheads.[2]

> Anyone who inquires into the effects of a nuclear holocaust is bound to be assailed by powerful and conflicting emotions. Prominent among these, almost certainly, will be an overwhelming revulsion at the tremendous scene of devastation, suffering and death which is opened to view, and accompanying the revulsion there may be a sense of helplessness and defeat, brought about by an awareness of the incapacity of the human soul to take in so much horror.[3]

As one person agonized, "Confronting so vast a loss as this brings sadness beyond the telling."[4] An immediate reaction is the marshalling of psychological defense mechanisms against the information in a composite of repression, suppression, isolation, denial, undoing, reaction, formation and projection. Robert Jay Lifton has grouped these mechanisms into a single overall category, which he refers to as "psychic numbing."[5] One can detach oneself from the feelings associated with a holocaust by blocking images, or by having a complete absence of images because one has no prior experience of the event. This is particularly true of the nuclear threat. It is difficult for us to believe that such weapons actually exist, for, other than on film we have never seen a bomb or an explosion.

> In grappling with this issue, people tend to lead "double–lives" — lives that appear as if nothing has changed when, in fact, the very foundations of their emotional stability have shifted.

> Accordingly, we have begun to live *as if* life were safe, but living *as if* is very different from just

living. A split opens up between what we know and what we feel. We place our daily doings in one compartment of our lives and the threat to all life in another compartment. However, this split concerns too fundamental a matter to remain restricted to that matter alone, and it begins to influence the rest of life. Before long, denial of reality becomes a habit – a dominant mode in the life of society – and unresponsiveness becomes a way of life.[6]

As educators and products of our Western culture, our typical response to this crisis is to raise people's consciousness by giving them additional information. Paradoxically, terrifying information only drives people deeper into denial and feelings of futility and despair. As Joanna Rogers Macy says, "We already know we are in danger; the essential question is: Can we free ourselves to respond?"[7] In her workshops on Despair and Empowerment, through imagery, ritual and work with clay and collage, Dr. Macy aids participating members in becoming aware of their deep inner responses to the condition of the world. She concludes these gatherings with "spiritual exercises for a time of apocalypse." One of these exercises is the Death Meditation, used for centuries by the Buddhists, but in this case adapted to a modern age. Members are directed to imagine a person's face, as it changes and disintegrates in the midst of a nuclear holocaust. By way of counterpoint, they also engage in the Buddhist exercise in experiencing the Joy of others known as the Great Ball of Merit, in which all compassionate and altruistic acts are visualized as forming a large pile in front of the participant and he pats them into a great ball and rejoices that no act of goodness is ever lost.

We see in these exercises all the raw materials for more sophisticated art forms. Although the West has isolated instances of art which communicates the horror of war, as in Picasso's "Guernica," or celebrates peace, as in this same artist's later works, we do not have a cultural transmission of peace that serves in the same way as the arts of the Far East. It was no accident that Dr. Macy derived a number of her exercises from Buddhist meditations, since from 300 B. C. onward, the Buddhist message of universal brotherhood affected the lives of billions of people. This message and the practices which accompanied it became the foundation for an extraordinary group of art forms which arose in Japan from the thirteenth to the eighteenth centuries.

There is a legend that during the Tokugawa era, a certain daimyo (lord) was on his way to Yedo (Tokyo) in order to pay an official visit to the shogun. His teamaster accompained him, so that he would be able to participate in the ceremony during his stay. To assure his safe passage, the teamaster, who was also a monk, disguised himself as a samurai, donning the customary two swords at his hip. While he walked through the streets of the capitol one day, he was challenged by a ferocious samurai. Of course, the real samurai had no idea he was challenging a monk to a duel. The monk, for his part, would have been killed immediately if he had admitted his deception. He was not afraid of dying, but only of dying ignobly. Although he had never been trained in fencing, he accepted the challenge and a time and place were chosen.

The monk immediately sought the services of a renowned fencing master, and asked him to demonstrate the first fencing position. He wished to be able to take the correct posture, so that he might face the samurai's death blow with dignity. Although the fencing master was a bit overwhelmed at this request, he did his best to teach the monk. At the appropriate time, the monk appeared before the samurai, held his sword high, bowed his head, and waited for the fatal blow. There was a long pause, after which the real samurai, amazed at the purity of the monk's stance, dropped his sword. The monk's posture was so perfect that the samurai asked to be admitted as his disciple.[8]

This amusing anecdote provides some insight into the influence of Zen on the Japanese do (ways). Whether it be cha-do, the way of tea, kendo, the way of the sword, or da-do, the way of flowers–all are expressions of a deep spiritual state. All aim at the unification of man's spirit with the resulting surrender of the more limiting ego. It is true that the monk was a master of the "way of tea", but the state of mind necessary to master that act was no different from that required to become expert at fencing. With only brief instruction, he was able to assume a perfect fencing stance.

The great Buddhist scholar D. T. Suzuki had this to say of the logical intellect so prized in the West.

> ... it upsets the blissful peace of ignorance, and yet does not restore the former state of things by offering something else .... It is not final, it waits for something higher than itself for the solution of all the questions it will raise, regardless of consequences.[9]

This something higher of which Suzuki speaks is the state of consciousness that the great masters of the haiku, the sumi-ye, and the tea ceremony have attempted to evoke in their audience. Their medium, while taking years to perfect, is but a way of expressing their inner spirit, which is, after all, the same spirit that underlies all reality. When the individual ego is minimized, the unconscious potential is allowed expression, and it is then that the artist becomes the source of wonderful accidents.

The tea ceremony demonstrates on an experiential level that it is possible to express this universal consciousness in the mundane world.

> It is a seated dance, an orchestrated ritual, as delicate, paced and formal as the elevation of the host in a Catholic Mass. All the gestures have been practiced for years, until they fit together in fluid motion.[10]

The tea master is an artist to the core. In Japan, he is an authority on poetry, calligraphy and flower arrangement, as well as an expert on the intricacies of the ceremony itself. Since it is his function as teacher to introduce the student to an environment that expresses the Buddhist world view, he structures the setting so that it will reflect the qualities of harmony, reverence, purity and tranquillity. The tea master, in setting the mood, has attained his first objective. Now, he must introduce the student to a demanding ritual without losing sight of this original psychological set. His own patience and sense of timelessness help to maintain the atmosphere. He also employs humor and anecdote to give a light touch to a difficult exercise in precise movement.

Yet, perhaps, one can place too much emphasis on the complexity of the ritual, for it is the underlying spirit that is all important. As the fiifteenth generation Grand Tea Master said recently,

> Before Buddha we are equal human beings and in
> tea we want to share that common humanity. So,
> we boil water; we offer it to Buddha; and we
> share it with others. Just a simple bowl of tea.

The Japanese frankly acknowledge that this "abode of emptiness" is a retreat from the rigors of everyday life, but it is their conviction that all people need periodically to detach themselves from the mundane world, so that they may later return refreshed. The aim is to capture the spirit of the Taoist sages as they wandered through their mountain pathways. Hung Tzu Ch'eng's collection of sixteenth century poems has this to say:

> If the mind is not overlaid with wind and waves,
> you will always be living among blue mountains
> and green trees. If your true nature has the cre-
> ative force of Nature itself, wherever you go,
> you will see fishes leaping and geese flying.[11]

Tea is more than a rigid format designed to produce cultivated men and women. It is, above all, "a religion of the art of life." As in any religion, first priority is given to the acknowledgement of a fundamental Reality or Ground of Being. The early teamen were strongly influenced by the Buddhist principle of transcendence in immanence. Some commentators claim that it is a lack of recognition of this principle that accounts for the malaise of our present day populace. They express doubt that any civilization can endure without some sense of the transcendental meaning in life. At a time when proportionately fewer people are looking to religious doctrines for answers, they are also losing confidence in the ability of material goals to meet their deepest needs.

The futurist Willis Harman suggests that society may be approaching a crisis similar to that of an alcoholic who hits "rock bottom." At this point the addicted person becomes aware of strengths and capabilities he never knew existed. Yet, it was not until life became completely intolerable that these alternate images arose and made it possible for him to begin again.

> Something like these first two steps of Alcoholics Anonymous may be needed for society. First, admission that we face a set of dilemmas, of thwarted goals and intolerable trade–offs, such that the future of society has become unmanageable. Second, a discovery of a nobler image of man and his potentialities than that which has come to dominate the industrial age.[12]

But where is this "nobler image" to be found? Positive images cannot be manufactured; they often come from the deep inner resources of one's psyche. At times they are collective, such as the one that led so many immigrants to the "land of opportunity" during the early 1900s. More often, they are extremely individualistic, serving as a motivating force through times of hardship. Perhaps, these images will have their foundation in that "perennial philosophy" discussed by Aldous Huxley in which there is an acknowledgement of a "divine Reality substantial to the world of things and lives and minds."[13] This perspective is buttressed by modern scientists who explain that there is, indeed, a fundamental unity underlying all perceived diversity. Harman states that once this basic assumption is affirmed, two corollaries emerge which can serve as a complementary set of ethics.[14] The first is an "ecological ethic," which would concern itself with the husbanding of our natural resources and a greater degree of equity in their distribution. It would also relate to issues pertaining to the preservation of our life support system and a sane policy on nuclear power. If we accept the proposition that there is a single energy underlying all the variations on our planet, then man becomes an integral part of the world around him. This perspective is beautifully illustrated in the Chinese landscapes, in which the viewer sees an expanse of water, surrounded by craggy cliffs shrouded in mist. On the lake is a tiny sailboat with a single passenger at the tiller. The artist's purpose is not to diminish the stature of man, but to show that the subtle force which is responsible for natural phenomena is the same force that animates all humanity.

Secondly, there is the "self–realization ethic," which holds that it is the proper function of man to grow and evolve and that a society can only be called "good," if it facilitates this movement. Maslow spoke of much the same concept when he used the term, "self–actualization." It has most often been applied to theories of motivation and need fulfillment, but Maslow intended it to be used in a broader context. He believed that the self–actualizing person of the past need not be the exception, but could serve as a harbinger of the future's psychologically healthy individual. In this state there is "less differentiation between the world and the person because he has incorporated into himself part of the world and defines himself thereby. He has become an enlarged self, we could say."[15]

Futurists tell us that peace connotes the absence of strife and that this neutral image does not have the motivating power to propel us toward future goals. Perhaps, just as the immigrant had a vision of a land where he and his family could grow and prosper, we should be actively imaging a time thirty years in the future when many of our fondest wishes are realized for ourselves, our children and our co-inhabiters on planet Earth. Before plans and strategies can be set in motion, the image and the vision must be in place. Also, we can look to the arts of the past and the present to serve as guides to the future. The tea ceremony and the arts of the East are, in reality, scenarios, not in form but in spirit. There is a sumi–ye painting done by a Zen Master showing a circle that was spontaneously executed. The brush strokes are very evident and there is an opening at the bottom so that lines never meet. The circle symbolizes tranquillity and completion. When questioned the Zen Master explained, "It represents human consciousness which can be as limited as a pebble on the beach or as expansive as the entire universe."

Notes

1. David Brandon, *Zen in the Art of Helping* (London; Routledge and Kegan Paul Ltd., 1976), p. 47.

2. Ruth Adams and Susan Cullen (eds.), *The Final Epidemic* (Chicago: Educational Foundation for Nuclear Science, 1981), pp. 173–174.

3. Jonathan Schell, *The Fate of the Earth* (New York: Alfred A. Knopf, Inc., 1982), pp. 7–8.

4. Joanna Rogers Macy, *Despair and Personal Power in the Nuclear Age* (Philadelphia: New Society Publishers, 1983), p. 3.

5. Robert Jay Lifton and Richard Falk, *Indefensible Weapons* (New York: Basic Books, Inc., 1982), pp. 103–104.

6. Schell, p. 152.

7. Macy, p. 22.

8. H. M. Enomiya – La Salle, *Zen: Way to Enlightenment* (New York: Taplinger Publishing Company, 1966), p. 59.

9. Daisetz T. Suzuki, *Essays in Zen Buddhism; First Series* (New York: Grove Press, 1961), p. 6.

10. Thomas Hoover, *Zen Culture* (New York: Pantheon Books, 1977), p. 179.

11. Alan Watts, *The Way of Zen* (New York: Pantheon Books, 1957), p. 193.

12. Willis W. Harman, *An Incomplete Guide to the Future* (San Francisco: San Francisco Book Company, 1976), p. 7.

13. Aldous Huxley, *The Perennial Philosophy* (New York: Harper and Row Publishers, 1945), p. 36.

14. Edward Cornish, *The Study of the Future* (Washington, D. C.: World Future Society, 1983), p. 161.

15. Abraham H. Maslow, *Eupsychian Management* (Boston: Dorsey Press, Inc., 1968), p. 6.

CHAPTER 16

Global Hunger: Challenge To America

DEAN S. YARBROUGH, Jr.
Boston Public Schools

The response of the world's press to the famine in Ethiopia is most interesting. [1]

> France, *Le Monde*, Paris (liberal): "When the worst is over and the talk is of hundreds of thousands of deaths in the months to come, everything indicates that the roots of the problem will remain and that little of what has been done will have been effective."
>
> Jean–Claude Pomonti (Nov. 14)

> India, *The Statesman*, New Delhi/Calcutta (independent): "The Ethiopian crisis cannot be seen in isolation from Africa's overall food problem." (Nov. 22)

> Israel, *Ha'aretz*, Tel Aviv (independent): "A five–year drought, destruction of forests, excessive exploitation of agricultural land,... (and) wars in the region have created one of the greatest tragedies in recent times.
>
> (Nov. 16)

> Italy, *Corriere della Sera*, Milan (independent): "The drought (in Ethiopia) is only the straw that broke the camel's back, for in that region the problem (of water scarcity) is one that has existed for years."
>
> Michel Conte (Nov. 20)

Japan, *Asahi Shimbun*, Tokyo (liberal): "Aid that encourages selfsufficiency is more important in the long
term than simply supplying food as a stopgap measure."
(Nov. 11)

Mexico, *Uno Mas Uno*, Mexico City (liberal): "(The
problem) seems directly out of the Dark Ages — something difficult to reconcile with today, when man has
gained control of nature with science and technology.'
(Nov. 11)

Human suffering is at its worst when people starve.
No misery is more alarming than when people die by suffering
the agony of hunger. What is happening in Ethiopia during
the mid 1980's is another appeal to human conscience for
action. Both relief work which gives temporary relief and a
new economic order which brings permanent problem solving
by changing social structures should be strengthened. The
impetus for these types of actions has to emerge out of a
concern for human rights, not just a sympathy for the poor.
The structure of poverty should be knocked down by the
strength of human dignity. The right to eat and live is the
most fundamental of all human rights.

Today this right is denied to four hundred million
people in the world, one–tenth of the world population. More
than half the people do not get adequate food. This happens
at a time when we have the scientific and technical capability
to supply a well–balanced diet to all people. What we need
is the will and radical ideas like world resource sharing. The
first Interreligious Peace Colloquium, which focused on food
and the energy crisis at its meeting in 1975, declared: "The
right to breathe the air and to drink the water becomes
coupled with the right to eat."[2] The Colloquium referred to the
"holiness of bread" and argued that food should be placed in
a separate category internationally. "Food is not just another
commercial commodity among commodities and cannot be so
treated by society or by the world's economic and political
institutions. [3]

Let us examine the problems of world hunger by selecting a few countries.

(A) Ethiopia

The present famine in Ethiopia was not created overnight. Haile Selassie was proclaimed Emperor of Ethiopia in 1930 and ruled until 1974 when a group of soldiers known as the Derg, the word for committee in the ancient language used by Ethiopia's priests, ended his forty–four year reign by revolutionary action. In spite of the efforts of Selassie to modernize Ethiopia, it remained as one of the poorest and least developed countries in the world: Sixty dollars per capita income in 1969, only 7% of the population literate and only 10% of the children in school. By 1973, five hundred people were dying daily as a result of famine due to a three–year drought. Selassie's government attempted to suppress the news of the famine.

Taxi drivers went on strike to protest rising fuel prices in February of 1973. Then teachers and others, including the military, joined in demanding higher wages. A petition to the emperor complained that the ministers had too many Mercedes automobiles. In April of that year, the Armed Forces Coordinating Committee (Derg), arrested two hundred ministers and high government officials and charged that they had "betrayed the emperor, and were responsible for the disastrous famine." [4]

In September of 1974 His Imperial Majesty Haile Selassie, the King of Kings, Conquering Lion of the Tribe of Judah, was deposed from office and died less than a year later. Lt. Colonel Mengistu Haile Miriam became Ethiopia's chief of state in 1977 after his two predecessors died in Derg shoot-outs. Mengistu, like almost three thousand other Ethiopian officers, had been trained in the United States.

But Ethiopia had also developed close ties with the Soviet bloc. Ethiopia's capital, still referred to as the "capital of Africa," now has a granite sculpture of Karl Marx in its Holy Cross Square, renamed Revolution Square by the Derg. Portraits of Lenin, Marx and Engels are strategically located to look down on the square. Yet, under the trappings of Ethiopian socialism, the economy has not improved. Ethiopia is still one of the world's poorest nations. A drought, as severe as the one Selassie tried to ignore in 1973, has left many Ethiopians starving.

United States military aid to Ethiopia continued up until a year after Selassie's death (the United States supplied over $ 287,000,000 in military aid over a twenty-five year period, including F-5 fighter bombers). But in 1977 the White House suspended military deliveries due to public opposition to the Derg's human rights abuses. The Soviet Union jumped in to fill the void, supplying over one billion dollars worth of air-craft, tanks, rocket launchers, armaments and vehicles. This action was in response to Somali troops' crossing the border into Ethiopia. Cuba's Fidel Castro sent 17,000 Cuban troops to support and train the Ethiopians.

The Eritrean People's Liberation Front (EPLF) controls about ninety percent of Eritrea, which became Ethiopia's fourteenth province in 1962. The EPLF which, like the Derg, is a Marxist organization, keeps 100,000 Mengistu troops tied down in the war over Eritrea. Castro will not let his troops fight against the Eritrean guerillas because his troops once trained them. It is also clear that as long as the EPLF conti-nues to fight against Mengistu's forces, the Derg will be de-pendent on Moscow for military aid.

As the people starve the war goes on. There is little doubt that the soldiers are being fed. Before the drought, Ethiopia was the potential bread basket of Africa. Instead of improving agriculture or building industry, Mengistu is using his economic resources to support a 250,000 man army, the third largest in Africa. The Derg is moving toward collecti-vization; Ethiopian peasants are resisting. State farms turn out only six percent of the nation's grain, but receive ninety percent of agricultural investment. The United States alone has supplied over twenty million dollars in emergency food aid in 1984. But the war continues and so does the suffering. [5]

(B) The Sudan

The Sudan is besieged not only by the famine, but also by waves of malnourished, ill and starving Ethiopian refugees seeking the feeding stations set up within the Sudan borders.[6] The government of the Sudan has offered food and shelter to over a million refugees since 1965 when the first Zaireans arrived. But the demand for food has driven prices up greatly. People of the Sudan who have acted in a humanitarian manner must decide whether it is better to close the borders and feed the millions of indigenous nomads, peasants and refugees or to let the refugee flow grow, with the result that less than subsistence conditions may prevail.

But what about the kind of technical aid and equipment which would make clean water available without women having to walk five to ten miles daily to carry water back to their children? What about the tons of seed needed for the next crop? What countries will help the Sudan solve its terrible problems? How will these questions be answered, we might inquire?

(C) Nigeria

Nigeria's plight is considerably different from that of Ethiopia or the Sudan because of many factors, including its oil.[7] In fact, before 1980 Nigeria surpassed South Africa to become the leading country in Africa with respect to its gross domestic product (GDP). Twenty–eight percent of this was due to oil, and fourteen percent to agricultural production. The average Nigerian state (there are 19 states in Nigeria) was equal in resources and finances to the average independent country in Africa.

But the danger of this oil legacy is an over–dependence on it. Ninety percent of foreign exchange, and eighty percent of government revenue, come from oil sales. But Nigeria must use the oil income to support and create industries which will bring in foreign revenue. For instance, Nigeria started producing steel again in 1982 and has a developing petrochemical, as well as motor vehicle assembly industry.

What about food? In 1982 Nigeria imported about one and one–half billion dollars worth of food, but President Shugari campaigned to make Nigeria food self–sufficient. The oil price cuts which Nigeria instituted had a detrimental effect on the economy and Nigeria sought a two billion dollar loan from the International Monetary Fund. As the economy worsened, President Shugari was arrested and replaced by General Bukari, oil minister in the previous military regime.[8]

World's Anticipation and Reaction to Hunger

In 1981 the World Food Council (WFC), a U. N. sponsored agency, forecast prolonged hunger during the 1980's unless considerable changes were made. The U. N.'s Food and Agricultural Organization (FAO) reported that grain imports during the sixties and seventies had about tripled.[9]

In 1982 the WFC again issued a warning that hunger and malnutrition would become far more widespread unless successful remedial action was taken. Both the WFC and the U. N. Economic Commission for Africa pointed out the five major causes for the dire economic condition in Africa:

1. Natural causes (drought, etc.)
2. Absence of adequate infra-structure.
3. Failures of government policies.
4. Adverse terms of international trade.
5. The severe impact of higher oil prices.[10]

The irony of 1983 was that Africa experienced widespread food shortages while major agricultural countries in the developed world experienced expensive agriculture surpluses. In September, the FAO reported that thirty-three countries were suffering from abnormal food shortages. The area south of the Sahara (including Ethiopia, Somalia, Nigeria and Sudan) experienced the worst drought of the century. The usual tropical wet and dry climate simply dried up. Severe hunger and starvation threatened up to seven million people. The United States total food aid to southern Africa amounted to two hundred million dollars in fiscal 1984.[11]

Food or Weapons ?

Yes, we do export some food. However the size of our arms exports must not be ignored. The NATO nations accounted for 53.2% of the total market in export of arms (U. S., 25.2%,

France, 11.1%, United Kingdom, 6.9%, West Germany, 5%, and other NATO nations, 5%) from 1971 to 1980. The United States exported a total of 6.6 billion dollars in arms in 1980 alone. It is an interesting commentary that the Shah of Iran loaned the Grumman Corporation 200 million dollars to save Grumman from bankruptcy; the Shah wished to maintain the Grumman production line which was turning out F–14 Tomcat planes he had ordered. Iran was the first foreign country to order the F–14 and their initial order totalled eighty aircraft.[12]

In 1981 arms trade agreements reached record levels and military assistance – – now given a new name, security assistance – – was increased substantially.[13] If one reaps what one sows, I fear what we will reap from the weapons of death we are sowing. Was Iran an example ? Why not sow the seeds of life: food ? Time may be running out.

Food Aid – – Is It a Band–Aid Approach ?

Theodore W. Schultz, Nobel prize winner in Economics in 1979, points to some interesting facts about U. S. aid to Egypt.[14] American aid to Egypt amounts to about two billion dollars, including large amounts of agricultural commodities under Public Law 480. Economic inefficiency reigns supreme in food production and distribution. Of course, Egypt accepts these agricultural products. Thus cheap food from abroad is available and farmers get low prices for their food. Their incentive to produce efficiently is thus thwarted. The cheap food from abroad produces an anti–market bias which conceals the choice between trade and aid. Dr. Schultz believes that "for most low income countries the opportunities to trade are much more important than foreign aid."[15] He suggests that there is now an emphasis on reducing these economic distortions that hurt farmers. An emphasis is placed on improving incentives to induce farmers to modernize and lessen the exploitation of farmers through cheap food policies.

Global Hunger: Challenge to America !

What are we Americans to do ? We must make a clear, conscious decision as to whether we are going to be our brothers' keepers or our brothers' brothers. If the former, then perhaps our present policies are appropriate. We will rationalize that we helped when the crisis was present. We saved some from starvation today, but will have to play it by ear tomorrow. There will be a new crisis every growing season. If the latter choice is made, to be our brothers' brothers and sisters' sisters, then an entirely different response is in order.

First, we must declare war on malnutrition and hunger anywhere and everywhere on the face of the earth. We must unequivocally guarantee that no one will die of starvation. If we have the means and the power to do anything, we clearly have the means and the power to do this !

Second, we must respond immediately with emergency food for those in need. We must do this with determination and boldness. If a Mengistu, for example, refuses to allow food to be delivered to the rebels in Eritrea, Tigre or Gonder, we must make clear that we will use specially marked airplanes and helicopters to drop food to them. We must establish incontrovertibly that we will not stand idly by and watch our brothers starve and that we will take the necessary risks. We might call this campaign the Berlin Airlift ! Of course we should communicate our intentions to our Russian brothers and sisters and ask them to join us in this humanitarian effort. If they oppose it, we should be prepared to use our fighter planes to escort cargo planes delivering the food. World opinion would be incensed and outraged if unarmed planes carrying food to the starving were shot out of the skies.

Third, a systems approach involving a five–year cycle of funding by Congress should be established. Implementation should be started immediately and renewed each year. The goal of the project, which can be given the code name, "Teach Them to Fish," would be to enable under–developed nations to reach a state of self–sufficiency. Our very finest engineers, scientists, economists, agricultural experts, trade experts and anthropologists would do a most thorough study and recommend a path to self–sufficiency. This study would include a thorough analysis of a nation's resources, water, potential products it could produce and export, food production and so forth. Farming techniques, such as those used in the Negev Desert to grow crops by storing the desert rain in the once barren loess soil, could be used on thousands of square miles of the Sahara.[16] Congress would be requested to fund "Teach Them to Fish" for five year cycles.

Conclusion

The hoofbeats of the Four Horsemen of the Apocalypse are getting louder. They are even now bringing famine and pestilence to Africa, Asia and South America. Certainly, if we choose to let them gallop unhampered, they will cross the United States just as they have crossed Africa. They are bringing hunger and death.

The Bulletin of the Atomic Scientists' clock, symbol of the threat of nuclear doomsday hovering over humanity, stands at three minutes to midnight. The four horsemen are riding hard. But remember, it is we, the people, who must stop them.

Those of us who are educators must prepare a generation of responsible, noble, educated, humane citizens of the United States and of the world. If we restrict our activities to what is good for America, we may very well cause harm to our planet and to other nations. This will invariably reflect harmfully on us. If we base our actions on what is good for our planet, our actions will most certainly reflect favorably on us.

But, above all, we must set the example. We who prepare people for life in a dynamic, democratic society had better start the fires within us. We must draw forth from our society (educate – educo) all those qualities which have made it great and which can continue to make it great.

We must re-orient our goals of education, reconstruct both our ends and our means, so as to give all the people we teach a sense of compassion and responsibility. We must re-direct our focus from local and national issues and move towards needs of the world community. In a larger sense, as educators we must re-orient our thinking so that we become examples, leaders and models of change.

We must even profit from our sins: the sins we perpetrated against Native Americans, the sins we committed under the banner of slavery and finally the ultimate sin of using nuclear bombs to threaten and kill people. Yes, we have known sin and because of that we can repent and go forth to build a more humane, a more knowledgeable and a more just world.

We have reached that time in our development as a nation where a raison d'etre is much needed. We are the envy of the world. We are our own rulers. We have freedoms which few enjoy. If we use our freedom to provide more enjoyment and more ease for ourselves in this world where almost a third of the people are malnourished, then we will have outlived our usefulness and indeed, will deserve to perish. If, however, we use our freedom to guarantee everyone on this earth a minimal standard of living – – enough food, enough water and enough medicine to combat disease – – then, clearly, we will have taken a giant step forward in improving the lot of humanity.

These are crucial hours in our history. If we continue to wring our hands in futility and try to justify all our actions and inactions by pointing to the Russians, then undoubtedly we will use our nuclear weapons in fear and in hatred and we will destroy civilization. We have the weapons. We even have the will. All that is needed is the situation.

If, however, we choose to design and implement a world in which our brothers and sisters do not die of starvation and malnutrition, or from preventable and curable diseases, then we will have raised the dignity of humankind to a new level of love and understanding. We have the means. We have the situation. All that is needed is the will.

Notes

1.   ''The World Looks at Ethiopia's Famine'', *World Press Review*, 32/ No. 1 (January 1985), p. 24.

2. Joseph Gremillion (ed.) *Food/Energy and the Major Faiths,* (Mary-knoll, N.Y.: Orbis Books, 1978), p. 3.

3. *Ibid.,* p. 251.

4. Paul B. Henze, "Ethiopia", *The Wilson Quarterly,* Vol. 8 No. 5 (1984), pp. 98–124.

5. *Ibid.*

6. "Famine Brings Sudan a Cruel Choice," *The Boston Globe* (January 1, 1985), p. 3.

7. Guy Arnold, "Nigeria: Special Report- - Africa's Awakening Giant", *Britannica Book of the Year 1988,* pp. 556–557.

8. "Nigeria", *Britannica Book of the Year 1984.*

9. "African Affairs- - Social and Economic Conditions", *Britannica Book of the Year 1982.*

10. African Affairs--Social and Economic Conditions", *Britannica Book of the Year 1983.*

11. "Agriculture and Food Supplies", *Britannica Book of the Year, 1984.*

12. James Perry Stevenson, "Grumman F-14 'Tomcat'", 25 (Fallbrook, California: Aero Publishers, Inc., Aero Series, 1975), p. 35.

13. Mary Kaldor, "Flourishing, Worldwide, Deadly--The Open Market in Arms", *Britannica Book of the Year, 1984,* pp. 35–40.

14. Theodore W. Schultz, "The Economics of U. S. Foreign Aid", *Bulletin of the Atomic Scientists* (Oct. 1983), pp. 21–27.

15. *Ibid.*

16. Michael Evenari, "Farming the Negev Desert", *Science Year, 1980- The World Book Science Annual,* pp. 126–139.

CHAPTER 17

Civic Responsibility to a World Community*

BETTY REARDON
Teachers College, Columbia University

The fortieth anniversary of a world organization brought into being by "We the people of the United Nations" makes 1985 an appropriate year to reflect upon the concepts of world community and global citizenship and what those concepts demand of education. The United Nations, while subject to much severe criticism and largely ignored by the politics of the major powers, has provided the only significant arena for the construction of world community and the exercise of global citizenship. For peace educators the notion of global citizenship and the structure of the United Nations constitute essential dimensions of the framework of education for civic responsibility to a world community.

The concepts of civil order in the UN structure are fundamental to most visions of a peaceful and just world society which inform the efforts of peace educators. They are especially central to the conceptual frameworks used by those educators who hold a dynamic concept of peace. Peace within such a framework constitutes a public order in which the range of economic and social values comprising justice can be pursued

* This essay is based in part on talks given at the University of Bridgeport in December 1983 and at the Midwest Regional Meeting of the National Council for the Social Studies in April 1984.

and conflicts can be resolved without violence. In such an order peace is the product of active exercise of the skills and arts of peacemaking; indeed, any just and viable civic order derives from the practice of these arts. The United Nations, as a world structure, has struggled to provide this function on a global basis as national governments conditioned by democratic values have struggled to do on a national basis.

Democratic values have led citizens to expect their rights and interests to be protected by the laws which regulate the public life of the society. They also expect these same laws to "promote the common welfare". Maintaining civil order is, therefore, a balancing act between promoting the common good and defending particular interests. What sustains the civil order, i. e., keeps the peace, is the observance of procedures for maintaining that balance and dealing effectively with cases of imbalance. That such procedures could contribute to the achievement and maintenance of world peace has long been recognized by advocates of international law, particularly by those who advocate law to settle international disputes and those who espouse world government.

Such advocates of law as the basis of a global civil order assume that world law of necessity would be based on fairness and that, at the very least, rudimentary justice would be a criterion in the balancing process. Without fairness, civil order can only be imposed upon, not elicited from, the majority, such imposition being itself a form of violence or war against some segments of the population. Most who advocate law as a means of achieving world peace conceive of law as an instrument of justice and a mechanism for the resolution of conflict. What is espoused is the concept of law as it has evolved in the Western political tradition. It may indeed be that this tradition can provide a significant contribution to world peace. Certainly it has won advocates and adherents in all parts of the world, ordinary people and leaders from nearly all cultures and many different societies.

While most proposals for world government seem too Western in origin and concept to be fully applicable to a culturally diverse and ideologically conflictual world, the politics of advocacy which their proponents pursue are primary demonstrations of the civic responsibility of global citizenship. In the Western tradition it is assumed that the fairness of the civil order depends largely on the political participation of the citizenry. Order may be *imposed* on *subjects*, but it is *derived and defended* by *citizens*. The fundamental differences between the notions of subject and citizen lie in the concepts of political participation and civic responsibility.

A further contribution to the notion of global citizenship made by the advocates of world government and world law is the specification of the notions of global polity and the functions of citizens. If indeed the concepts of global citizenship are to have any effect on world politics and contribute to the development of an authentic world community, there is a need to specify and substantiate the concepts. They need to be grounded in a sense of commitment to a world community, but especially to be manifest in a set of values and sub–concepts that call forth from the global citizen a repertoire of political behaviors conducive to the development of a just and viable global civil order. World community is itself such a sub–concept of global civil order. Community derives from recognition by any group that common interests are more significant to individual survival and well–being than conflicting and competing interests. It is a widely recognized fact that world survival now depends on the peoples of the world recognizing that common human interest should become the basis for development of practical concrete concepts of global citizenship. A primary purpose of global citizenship, then, is to support and further develop the recognition and manifestation of the common interests of all the peoples of the earth.

In most national societies, however, there is still a widely held misperception that the national interests and the global interests are not in true harmony and that to place a higher priority on the global interest would erode the interests of the nation. While virtually every nation derived from smaller subgroups has had an historic experience of nation–building which directly contradicts this notion, the application of the historic lesson to the global case is generally resisted.

This resistance runs counter to the reality of inter-dependence and to the imperative of global integration for human survival. Actual and practical global citizenship is both necessary and possible. Upon the viability of the world community depends the viability of all component communities. It is possible because most peoples of the world are citizens of nation–states which have had an experience of positive integration of smaller groups. And most peoples of the world also have some notions of the universal common good and of universal human values.

While few people today actually advocate world government or any kind of global central guidance system, even fewer would deny that there is a burgeoning world society which requires some systematic regulation; however, today's global order–in which economic and political affairs are dominated by the major industrial powers and the strategic balance and issues of war and peace are largely determined by the two superpowers–is rejected by the vast majority of the earth's people. They do not see the present order as the protector of their rights and interests. Indeed, few would accept the present order as either desirable or democratic. There is a profound struggle over the reordering of the world. The East–West competition for world hegemony is augmented by the North–South struggle between industrial and developing nations over a new international economic order. Within regions and political systems there is equally fierce competition for control over the power to make policy which will determine the global order. The intensity of political struggles and armed conflicts which abound throughout the world–the life and death competition among ideologies, visions and values–is basically over what leaders, what standards and what purposes will guide the formation and maintenance of the emerging global polity.

Most of the significant political struggle and much of the conflict over world politics, however, is still conducted within individual nation states. Global citizenship, at least at this period, is exercised at the national level, making that level even more significant than either the global or local level for the exercise of public responsibility and participation. This does not mean to impute the necessity to "think globally and act locally", but to observe that decisions and policies which will most effect the emerging global polity are made at the national level and those who would now exercise the responsibilities of global citizenship must also do so at the national level. This most emphatically means that global criteria need to be introduced into all political discourse which effects national leadership and national as well as local policy. Citizens of all nations who hold a commitment to the global community must become familiar with the relevant global criteria and how to apply them to local and national politics in their own countries.

Such global citizenship requires an education for global citizenship. The concepts of participation and responsibility devolve upon education a special duty in the deriving and maintaining of a global civil order. The skills and arts of peacemaking necessary for the exercise of civic responsibility at any level of social organization must now become the basis of education for civic responsibility at the global level. Planning and implementing structures and means for the pursuit and protection of citizen rights of all peoples, and procedures and processes for resolution of conflicts among peoples, are learning tasks for the global citizen. The tasks of asserting universal human rights and maintaining international peace are assumed tasks of the United Nations. Familiarity with that institution and commitment and creativity in using the institution to pursue the values of a world civil order based on peace and justice are central to education for global citizenship.

The centrality of the United Nations to the exercise of civic responsibility to a world community poses a special challenge for American peace educators at this time when there is a serious tension between the nation's responsibility to the world organization and its playing the role of a superpower in a volatile, conflictual, war-prone world. The fortieth anniversary of the United Nations might serve as an appropriate opportunity for Americans to reflect upon the role and significance of the political values and traditions of our own system which were manifest in the charter of the United Nations and in the aspirations which that organization sought to pursue on behalf of humankind. Indeed, the fortieth anniversary might provide an occasion for many peoples of the world to review their own traditions and concepts conducive to universalism, to human dignity and to peace as the social condition in which human dignity is best realized. A truly democratic global civil order can be derived only from a world community which, while recognizing its common interests, honors and nurtures cultural and other differences among the world's many peoples. In fact, one of the primary tasks of a global civil order would be maintenance of the richness of human differences and diversity. It is important to emphasize this point as we look at the sources and traditions of American political values which are in harmony with the aspirations of a just and peaceful world community.

Americans must understand that first and foremost in the pursuit of such a world order our primary need is the application of our own democratic values to our own behavior, and not the application or imposition of our institutions–either political or economic–in other areas of the world. The essential argument here is that Americans need to understand thoroughly their own traditions in order to be effective global citizens. A true understanding of the fundamental political values which are basic to this society would lead us toward more democratic behavior in the world and help us to be a nation which contributes more to peace and justice than some peace advocates and educators believe our present policies are doing. Peace and global educators who advocate such a reexamination of American political traditions and values assert that these traditions and values are totally consistent with the needs of the world planetary society.

There are six basic points to support this argument. First, the fundamental point is that American political values are consistent with the concepts of a peaceful and just global community and a fair planetary civic order because they are basically peace–making values and because they were conceived in universalist terms, intended to apply to all citizens. Granted, the notion of who qualified as a full citizen was narrowed by the white Western male bias which still plagues us to a large degree. Nonetheless in their universalist expression the basic principles of the Declaration of Independence and Constitution laid a foundation for the universal concept of citizenship which has informed all of the struggles for human rights undertaken since the end of the eighteenth century.

Second, America's role in the twentieth century has had potential to provide leadership and example in the development of an authentic global community and in the design and structure of a world civic order. There have been, however, two basic thrusts -- contradictory and in conflict with each other -- to American history in this century. One has been the trend toward more democratization, toward providing full citizenship rights to all of our own people (e.g., the civil rights movement and the women's movement) and the other, the trend toward intervention and dominance in other parts of the world.

The third point is that, given the fact that we have had to struggle to extend full citizenship rights to all of our peoples, it is evident that our values have always been in tension and conflict. But it is apparent that the tension has developed into an outright distortion of our most fundamental values during our past thirty years as a super power.

Fourth, the rapid pace of technological change and the consequent imperatives of a computerized society and technical arms race in pursuit of ever more sophisticated weaponry have overtaken the evolution of our values development and have misdirected America's purpose in the world. We have moved from a people – centered to a product–centered society and from the extension of democracy to the extension of national power. Americans have sold their democratic birthright for a mess of imperial pottage. We have sacrificed our traditional political values for control of enough of the world's resources to support a large "upwardly mobile" middle class while contributing to the impoverishment of millions of others in the developing world, and tolerating hunger at home. We need to reverse these trends and return to the values of our political historic roots.

The fifth argument is that this historic generation has the capacity and the responsibility to fulfill the potential of the United States to contribute to a fair global order by reclaiming our traditional values from the distortion they have suffered during this period of global hegemony and applying them to U. S. behavior in the world. We need only go back to the "Manifest Destiny" argument and resulting debates of the last decade of the nineteenth century to understand inconsistencies between a democratic republic and a world imperial power.

Sixth, it is the responsibility of American education to prepare citizens to apply themselves to this task of reclamation; to enable them to learn to function as authentic global citizens; to help them become involved in envisioning, planning and acting for a world civic order consistent with American values, one which provides full citizenship rights and opportunities for the exercise of civic responsibility equally to all the earth's peoples. Contrary to contemporary popular political culture, fundamental American values are not the Norman Rockwell, *Saturday Evening Post* values of a comfortable white America frequently extolled by the present leadership, but the values of a people engaged in struggle for the dignity of all persons. Our most fundamental values and basic political principles are the self–evident truths upon which this nation was founded: the equality of persons; the concept of unalienable human rights; the notion that the purpose of government is to secure such rights, among them the right of citizens to choose their own government as well as the right to dissent or disagree with the government; if necessary to "alter and abolish" a government which abuses their rights and "set up new governments in forms that seem to them most likely to effect their safety and happiness." It is important here to comment upon that notion of happiness. It should not be interpreted as ego satisfaction or the kind of materialistic hedonism which passes for happiness in our society today. It seems that "happiness" in this sense is a civic value, more the notion of *shalom*, of communal well–being, of the right to fulfillment within a framework of a positive, constructive community and social responsibility.

Another significant related political principle is that the civil order, the maintenance of a peaceful society, is the combined responsibility of citizens and the government. For governments get "their just powers from the consent of the governed." The function of government, therefore, is to assure the greatest possibility for the security and well–being of the citizens. The process of assuring security and well–being is essentially the task of peace–making. In the words of the Constitution, the task of government is to "establish justice, ensure domestic tranquility, provide for the common defense and promote the general welfare." These are the conditions which make for peace, and these are the very goals for which we need to struggle at this historic juncture on a planetary as well as national level. Today, these values are not even assured within our own country.

The United States played a major, positive leadership role in articulating the goals for a just and peaceful world in the closing and immediately post–World War II years. It seemed in those years as if we had matured beyond the imperialist adventures of the Spanish–American War and Caribbean intervention to see ourselves as authentic democrats, participants in an emerging world community, striving for equality and equity among all participants. We recognized the rights of other peoples of the world to aspire to the same blessings of liberty, security and well-being we believed to be our own birthright. We had truly assumed the responsibilities of global citizenship.

Many Americans received their early global socialization and their perceptions of America's intended role in the world from Franklin Roosevelt's 1941 State of the Union message, in which he articulated the four freedoms that became the objectives which this nation claimed to pursue in its involvement in World War II. In this address, he reiterated the basic American political values in a global context. He said, "there is nothing mysterious about the foundations of a healthy and strong democracy. The basic things expected by our people of their political and economic systems are simple. They are equality of opportunity for youth and others; jobs for those who can work; security for those who need it; the ending of special privilege for the few; the preservation of civil liberties for all; the enjoyment of the fruits of scientific progress in a wider and constantly rising standard of living."[1] He also noted that "the strength of our systems is dependent upon the degree to which they fulfill those expectations." Then he stated some long–range goals for the world community: "in the future days which we seek to make secure, we look forward to a world founded upon four essential freedoms." Those he identified as speech and expression, worship, freedom from want and from fear: "We seek to secure to every nation a healthy peacetime life for its inhabitants. We seek also freedom from fear, which we will pursue by reducing armaments to such a point that no nation is in a position to commit an act of aggression."[2] What the President was telling his "fellow Americans" and the world was that the policy of the United States was to be based upon the assumption that all people of the world had rights to the basic necessities of life, to freedom and to peace. The notion emerged that these were rights of world citizens. It was a reassertion and an extension of the universalism of the "founding fathers."

It was these notions and values that Americans took to their participation in the San Francisco conference at which the United Nations was established. The delegates in San Francisco were trying to envision a better life for the people of all the planet and a more peacefully regulated international order, an order which might overcome what they called "the scourge of war." The Preamble to the Charter of the United Nations echoes the very rhythms and concepts of the American constitution as it begins with "We the people of the United Nations, in order to..."[3]

The significance of these values and principles in the formulation of the vision of a peaceful and just post–World War world was no better reflected than in the struggle to formulate and bring forth the Universal Declaration of Human Rights. This declaration sets forth basic notions of what citizens should expect from a civil order and by inference what they should be prepared to contribute to it. Further, it calls attention to the equality of all persons, including the equality of women and men. And, most significantly, it is a reflection of the universalism of those earlier documents, the Declaration of the Rights of Man of France and the

Bill of Rights of the United States. Its purpose is to "serve as a common standard of achievement for all peoples and all nations to the end that every individual in every organ of society keeping this declaration constantly in mind shall strive by teaching and education to promote respect for these rights and progressive measures, national and international, to secure their universal and effective recognition and observance."[4] In this statement of purpose the declaration can be read as an exhortation to assume some specific civic responsibilities to the global community. As such it is a document with which every global citizen should be thoroughly familiar. It further recognized that the fulfillment of these rights was necessary if we were to avoid future violent struggles, if we are to overcome the need for armed force and assure the reduction of armaments envisioned in the Four Freedoms speech. In fact, it states that we have a right to peace. "Everyone is entitled to a social international order in which the rights and freedoms set forth in this declaration can be fully realized."[5] It has become clear that without peace there is no possible fulfillment of these rights. Peace therefore becomes a fundamental human right and peacemaking a general civic responsibility, a responsibility which demands citizen participation at the local, national and global levels.

It is these concepts of participation and responsibility which devolve upon education a special duty in the deriving and maintaining of a civic order. In that the process is essentially one wrought by the skills and arts of peacemaking, education for civic responsibility calls for training and instruction in these arts, especially those which depend upon the pursuit and protection of citizen rights and community interests and those related to the recognition and resolution of conflict. To focus education on these arts and skills and on the tasks of building appropriate structures for the maintenance of a just and peaceful planetary order would be a most fitting observation of the fortieth anniversary of the United Nations.

Notes

1. Franklin D. Roosevelt, "State of the Union Address", (Washington, D. C., 1941).
2. *Ibid.*
3. Preamble to the Charter of the United Nations", 1945.
4. "Universal Declaration of Human Rights".
5. *Ibid.*

CHAPTER 18

WORLD CITIZEN: REFLECTIONS ON THEODORE BRAMELD

(In this chapter three authors share their personal views of Theodore Brameld in whose honor this book is published. A profile of his life and contributions are discussed in the first article. Brameld's emphasis on cultural renewal for the creation of a world community is noted in the next. The last article discusses the Society for Educational Reconstruction which carries on Brameld's vision of a new social order.)

Brameld as Visionary Educator

DAVID R. CONRAD
University of Vermont

Historian W. Warren Wagar refers to Theodore Brameld as a "prophet–father of the coming world civilization."[1] Educational philosopher George Counts wrote that "throughout his professional career Theodore Brameld has been a challenging force on the educational frontier in the United States and the world."[2]

Some scholars have not been as kind as Wagar or Counts in their assessments, but it is clear that Brameld deserves a place of honor in the history of educational philosophy. Throughout the nineteen fifties when liberal and radical ideas were continually under attack in the United States, Brameld developed and taught his "reconstructionist" philosophy of education. In the 1960's, many students began to appreciate his lifelong commitment to broad social and political change through education. In 1970, Brameld was recognized by a major educational journal as "the leading proponent of the hopeful reconstructionist theory of education which encourages the schools to take an activist position with respect to social and political ills."[3]

After receiving his doctorate in philosophy at the University of Chicago, Brameld's distinguished career in philosophy of education began in the early 1930's at Long Island University and Adelphi College in New York. Continuing at the University of Minnesota, New York University and Boston University (where he is now Emeritus Professor), Brameld taught at Springfield College and the University of Hawaii after his formal retirement. He has lectured at universities throughout the United States and around the world. Brameld is the author of more than a dozen books and several hundred articles and book reviews. He also co–authored or edited a dozen other volumes.

Reviewing Brameld's prolific scholarship from the 1930's through the 1970's, it is easy to see his wide range of concerns. In the 1930's, he wrote a characteristically controversial article called "Karl Marx and the American Teacher" for the lively progressive journal, *The Social Frontier*, and "American Education and the Social Struggle" for *Science and Society*. During the following decade, Brameld completed manuscripts on teachers and organized labor, workers' education and planning for a more equitable post–war America. He authored *Minority Problems in the Public Schools*, beginning a long commitment to intercultural (or multicultural) education. At this time, Brameld started developing his own philosophy of education which focused on education for personal and cultural transformation. One of the key tenets of this philosophy is education for world community, so it is not surprising that he wrote an article called "The Human Roots of World Order" for the journal *Progressive Education* in 1948.

Brameld further developed and refined his philosophy in the 1950's, culminating in *Toward a Reconstructed Philosophy of Education* in 1956. Several other books comparing and contrasting educational philosophies helped establish Brameld as a leading figure in his field. As he began exploring relationships between philosophy, education and anthropology during this decade, he placed philosophies of education in a conceptual framework which he later called "culturology" or "an anthropological philosophy of education." By this, he aimed to interpret varying educational philosophies as orientations of culture. All theories could be examined from this perspective, he argued, but his own view of "culturology" had a definite orientation: "This orientation is an anthropological philosophy that is frankly naturalistic, experimental and radically democratic."[4] Late in the 1950's, Brameld published a complex volume called *Cultural Foundations of Education: An Interdisciplinary Exploration* which demonstrated his debt to various anthropologists and then completed a field study based on his research, *The Remaking of a Culture: Life and Education in Puerto Rico.*

During the 1960's, Brameld hit his stride with books like *Education for the Emerging Age: Newer Ends and Stronger Means, Education as Power, The Use of Explosive Ideas in Education* and *Japan: Culture, Education and Change in Two Communities.* A series of lectures originally delivered in Korea and Japan, *Education as Power* focused on critical contemporary issues in education. Two chapters, one on "Values: Educator's Most Neglected Problem" and the other on "World Civilisation: The Galvanizing Purpose of Public Education," were particularly timely and provocative. One of Brameld's most influential books, *Education as Power* was translated into Korean, Japanese, Spanish and Portuguese.

In the 1970's, Brameld analysed four major philosophies of education in *Patterns of Educational Philosophy: Divergence and Convergence in Culturological Perspective.* In his discussion of reconstructionism, one of the four, he explored the historic contributions of utopian thought as well as normative designs for a reconstructed society. He admitted that reconstructionism borrowed much from other philosophies, particularly pragmatism and progressivism, but also found fault with progressivists:

> "Too often ... they soft-pedal, even circumvent, the impact of cultural forces upon the individual; only rarely do we find them providing incisive analyses of class structures and cleavages or of the phenomena of mass believers."[5]

Reconstructionism is, most of all, a crisis philosophy which acknowledges the perilous nature of life in a world saturated with weapons of nuclear warfare. It is a philosophy of values, ends and purposes which goads each of us to find intelligent solutions to critical problems confronting humankind. Brameld introduces concepts like "defensible partiality" which suggests a search for answers to human problems by exploring alternative approaches and then defending the partialities which emerge from a dialectic of opposition. "Social–self–realization" becomes the supreme value: "It is a dynamic fusion of economic, political, educational and personal goals," Brameld argues, "as well as of scientific, esthetic and religious goals-all to be sought, interwoven and achieved."[6] Educationally, social–self–realization is seen both as means and end: a process which encourages individual and group learning in democratic environments and a goal of education for world citizenship. Stressing the democratic value orientation of reconstructionism, Brameld maintains that "world civilization is the great magnetic purpose which education requires today."[7]

In the mid 1980's, considerable attention is being directed to improving the preparation of teachers in the United States.[8] Brameld has been concerned with teacher preparation and the quality of teachers all of his professional life. In the early 1970's, he shared the first draft of a book called *The Teacher As World Citizen* with students in a summer course at the University of Vermont. Appropriately, this university, the alma matter of John Dewey, several years later awarded Brameld an honorary degree.

The Teacher as World Citizen is a visionary little volume which outlines many of Brameld's beliefs and hopes. Looking back from the year 2000, the teacher–narrator recalls global transformations of the preceding quarter century. Radical changes had occurred, especially establishment of the World Community of Nations based on a global Declaration of Interdependence. As education became globally oriented and ethnocentrism disappeared, a World Education Authority and strong Teachers Union of World Citizens were formed. The quality of teaching had improved vastly since teachers now received a minimum of six years of professional preparation after high school: two years in a general education program which examined and evaluated vital issues and four years of arts and sciences bearing on problems of world order. Prospective teachers during these years became involved in community life, local, regional, national and transnational. The sixth year featured a vigorous internship to demonstrate that the student " ... not only deserves assignment as teacher–citizen of the world, but has attained professional qualifications at least equal in thoroughness and competence to those of any doctor of medicine." [9]

Though Brameld embraces the world as his home, he has shown special interest in Japan where in the 1960's he was Fulbright Research Scholar at Shikoku Christian College. His deep affection for Japan has never waned. Several Japanese assistants helped him in his research in two communities, one a fishing village and the other a segregated community which suffered from considerable discrimination. Later, Brameld helped two of his assistants come to Boston University for doctoral study. Shigeharu Matsuura, who wrote his dissertation on Edward Bellamy, became the first blind Japanese to earn an American doctorate in education. Until his recent untimely death, Professor Matsuura was Professor of education and Dean of the Faculty at Shikoku Christian College. Nobuo Shimahara, another of Brameld's aides in Japan, completed his doctorate and is now a distinguished professor of educational anthropology at Rutgers University. Midori Matsuyama, a third assistant, worked with Brameld on his major book on Japan and some years later they were married. Since the late 1970's, Ted and Midori Brameld have lived in New Hampshire, Hawaii and now North Carolina near Ted's youngest of three daughters. Besides being co-author and editor of several publications, Midori has been a loving, devoted wife as Ted's health has worsened in recent years due to a series of strokes.

In the late sixties, Ted Brameld's former doctoral students and others inspired by his ideas founded an organization centering on reconstructionist principles. The Society for Educational Reconstruction (SER) published a journal *Cutting Edge* and continues with a newsletter called *SER in Action*.

Many conferences on educational and political issues have been sponsored or co-sponsored by SER over the years. Ted Brameld took an active part in such activities as a member of the executive committee. To honor Brameld, SER established the Theodore Brameld Lecture series on education and social change. Outstanding scholars like Michael Harrington and Rene Dubos have delivered lectures in this series.

An impressive scholar who demanded much of himself for a half century, Ted Brameld also demanded much from his students. As a beginning student in a master's of education program in the foundations of education at Boston University, I remember well my first course with him, "Cultural Foundations of Education." Like others in the class, I felt overwhelmed by the complexity of the issues and especially the difficulty of the text he had written himself. But I also recall with great pleasure his drawing upon Japanese education and culture to illustrate points or define concepts. Professor Brameld, as I called him at the time (he encouraged his graduate students to call him Ted if and when they became confortable doing so), had just returned from a sabbatical in Japan and the glow of that experience permeated his teaching.

As he always did in his courses, Ted required group projects which integrated academic and experiential learning. My group decided to study educational and cultural conflict in an American Indian community in Maine. At the conclusion of our project, we decided to take Professor Brameld out to dinner to discuss our results in an informal setting. He consented, and we all had a wonderful time sharing ideas with each other. I realized this distinguished scholar and tough teacher was also a warm human being. He agreed to be my faculty advisor and later encouraged me to pursue doctoral study. We have remained good friends and colleagues ever since.

It should not have surprised me as a graduate student to see Ted Brameld at an early anti-Vietnam war rally in New York. After all, Ted always argued that philosophers of education must act on their beliefs. Seeing Ted there, however, was both enlightening and inspiring since I had seldom come across an activist professor. Later, I learned about Ted's courage when he refused to be intimidated by Senator Joseph McCarthy's anti–communism. Here was a teacher, I found, who held high intellectual standards for himself and others, but also dared to speak out forcefully and become immersed in the political struggles of his time.

Of course, Ted was not always easy to get along with, nor did we always agree. Ted could be quite stubborn and strong–willed at times. Yet, as a teacher he always respected his students as fellow learners in a common effort to make sense of the world. He welcomed opposing viewpoints and provoked others to argue with him, but naturally he loved it when they found agreement with his position. Ted remains devoted to his former doctoral students and their families — and they to him. His country home in New Hampshire, "Hardscrabble," became a marvelous gathering place for those who shared his reconstructionist vision. For years, Ted and his wife Ona were gracious hosts to visitors and Ted was a charming "uncle" to the children. Many a lively discussion, perhaps spiked with a shot of whiskey, carried into the late evening around the fireplace in Ted's cozy living room.

During several summer weekends in the late 1970's, "Hardscrabble" was home to "Hardscrabble Seminars" sponsored by the Society for Educational Reconstruction. Gathered under a large striped tent on a terrace just below Ted's red clapboard house, participants hotly debated urgent problems confronting education and society while children played blithely nearby. But time was always set aside, too, for swimming in the cold brook Ted had dammed some years earlier, playing volleyball on the sloping lawn or taking a refreshing walk through the surrounding woods. Ted loved the large "extended family" of the Hardscrabble Seminars and hoped it would be possible someday to build a permanent round structure on a high meadow above the house. Always impressed by his friend Myles Horton and the Highlander Education and Research Center he founded in Tennessee in 1932, Ted, Midori and some SER officers dreamed of starting a northern New England conference center for activists in social/educational change. But the dream was never realized because "Hardscrabble" was sold in the early nineteen eighties and Ted and

Midori moved to Hawaii where the climate was much more agreeable.

Shortly before his retirement, Brameld was asked to deliver the Boston University Lecture for 1968–69. Entitled "Imperatives for a Future–Centered Education," he called for a shift away from traditional investigations of the past and present to the future and its vast potential. Human beings, he affirmed, have the capacity to direct and shape the course of their evolutionary future. They *"can* achieve an international order strong enough and democratic enough to eliminate war" he claimed; they *"can* commit themselves to individual as well as cooperative life–affirming values," he asserted.[10] At the conclusion of his lecture, Brameld argued that a future–centered education can and must fulfill an urgent prophecy, a prophecy, which seems to encapsulate Brameld's lifetime of scholarship and teaching: "This is the prophecy of a converging, peace–maintaining, yet ever evolving and adventuring community of mankind."[11]

Notes

1. W. Warren Wagar, *Building the City of Man* (New York: Grossman Publishers, 1971).
2. George S. Counts, rear of book jacket of *The Climatic Decades: Mandate to Education* by Theodore Brameld (New York: Praeger, 1970).
3. See editorial note accompanying "A Cross–Cutting Approach to the Curriculum: The Moving Wheel" by Theodore Brameld, *Phi Delta Kappan* (March, 1970), p. 346.
4. Theodore Brameld, *Patterns of Educational Philosophy* (New York: Holt, Rinehart and Winston, 1971), p. 15.
5. *Ibid.*, p. 359.
6. *Ibid.*, p. 421.
7. Theodore Brameld, *Education as Power* (New York: Holt, Rinehart and Winston, 1965), p. 35.
8. See Gene 1. Maeroff, "Improving Our Teachers," *The New York Times* (January 6, 1985), Section 12, p. 1.
9. Theodore Brameld, *The Teacher as World Citizen: A Scenario of the 21st Century* (Palm Springs, California: ETC Publications, 1976), p. 60.
10. Theodore Brameld, "Imperatives for a Future–Centered Education" in *The Climatic Decades* (New York: Praeger, 1970), p. 31.
11. *Ibid.*, p. 41.

Cultural Transformation for World Community

NOBUO SHIMAHARA

Rutgers University

Since the publication of his first work in 1933, *A philosophic Approach to Communism*,[1] Theodore Brameld's chief concern as the foremost reconstructionist educator has been the problem of human order. Succinctly stated, the problem of "what kind of world can we have and do we want?" has been his relentless pursuit throughout his brilliant and colorful career.

In the early 1940s, Brameld turned to education as a domain of inquiry and action to articulate his growing preoccupation. He sought an explicit and active avenue of exploring the problem by joining the "social frontier" group of educators and scholars centered at Teachers College, Columbia University. One of his early books, *Design for America*,[2] reveals the formative process of Brameld's philosophical vision later known as reconstructionism. His acceptance of a professorship in educational philosophy at New York University in 1947 ushered in probably the most creative decade in terms of the development of his thought and publications. It was during this decade that reconstructionism was systematically formulated as a philosophical position recognized by educational philosophers and educators in general. In 1974, Brameld epitomized the reconstructionist vision that he had originally crystallized in his major work, *Toward a Reconstructed Philosophy of Education*, published in 1956.[3] Reconstructionism, he contended, "stresses far-reaching, future-directing, and thorough-going, redesigning and renewing of cultural dynamics as well as of cultural structures and processes."[4]

In the late 1950s and 1960s, Brameld further turned to anthropology to understand the enculturative process of society through which culture is transmitted and also "renewed." He viewed education as the enculturative process removed from sterile, conventional notions of schooling. For him, it is a universal process endowed with "virile" power and is most indigenous to cultural evolution. He insisted on a close partnership among three disciplines – education, philosophy and anthropology – as most crucial to articulate the reconstructionist position. Brameld saw education as a pervasive process of human renewal in which philosophy is perceived as a symbolized system of beliefs guiding the dynamics of culture.

This emerging perspective led him to explore empirically Puerto Rican culture in the 1950s[5] and Japanese culture in the first half of the 1960s[6]. He endeavored to consider education as enculturation in these specific cultures and to discover especially its transformative functions. These two major studies produced empirical support for his assumption that education is an invariant culture–building process that is understood in the entire context of culture.

In 1974, reflecting upon the evolution of his philosophical outlook, Brameld suggested: "If I were asked to pinpoint my outlook upon the world, I should call it 'an anthropological philosophy of education.' "[7] His anthropological philosophy is predicated upon two explicit assumptions, among others. First, humanity is faced with a critical planetary transformation and second, education ought to and can serve as a major instrument of cultural transformation toward the establishment of a global order of human societies. It is this philosophical position that has singularly contributed to the definition of education essential to the emerging world.

Notes

1. Theodore Brameld, *A Philosophic Approach to Communism* (Chicago: University of Chicago Press, 1933)
2. Theodore Brameld, *Design for America* (New York: Hinds, Hayden and Eldredge, 1945)
3. Theodore Brameld, *Toward a Reconstructed Philosophy of Education* (New York: Dryden Press, 1956)
4. Theodore Brameld, "Culturology as the Search for Convergence", in *Mid-Century American Philosophy,* Peter Bertocci (ed) (New York: Humanities Press, 1974) pp. 78–79.
5. Theodore Brameld, *The Remaking of a Culture: Life and Education in Puerto Rico* (New York: Harper, 1959)
6. Theodore Brameld, *Japan: Culture, Education and Change in Two Communities* (New York: Holt, 1968)
7. Theodore Brameld, "Culturology as the Search for Convergence", *op. cit.,* p. 62.

Ser: An Organization
Committed to Global Peace

JAY M. SMITH
Adelphi University

In 1969 The Society for Educational Reconstruction (SER) was founded in Boston, Massachusetts as an organization committed to personal, social and political transformation through education. Its purpose was to put into practice the reconstructionist philosophy of education advocated by Professor Theodore Brameld of Boston University who saw education not only as a transmitter of culture, but as a powerful initiator of social change. Among Brameld's many books were: *Patterns of Educational Philosophy (1971)*, *Education for the Emerging Age (1950)*, *Education as Power (1965)*, *The Climactic Decades (1970)*, *Japan: Culture, Education and Change in Two Communities (1968)* and *The Teacher As World Citizen (1976)*.

The idea for The Society for Educational Reconstruction was born out of a series of informal discussions, written communications and meetings involving a group of Brameld's doctoral students in the foundations of education at Boston University. As an author of many books on the philosophy and anthropology of education and as a teacher, Brameld had argued that public education should teach critical thinking and democratic decision–making, advocate peaceful solutions to conflict and world community and support economic and social justice. Given the crisis situation which existed in the United States in the late 1960's as a result of the Vietnam war, urban problems, the assassinations of Martin Luther King Jr. and Robert Kennedy, the cries for school reform and the movements for equality and participatory democracy on campuses and throughout American society, the time was ripe for Brameld's young graduate students to act on their reconstructionist ideals by establishing the Society for Educational Reconstruction.

Since its beginnings, SER has been in the forefront of efforts to humanize education and to make it a force for political and social change. Through its annual conferences and more recently through the Theodore Brameld Lecture Series on Education and Social Change established in 1977, SER has brought together scholars, classroom teachers and educational administrators for dialogue on such issues as global education alternative schooling, educational futurism, peace studies, civil rights and democratic socialism. Past Brameld Lecturers have been Michael Harrington – social critic and author of *The Other America*; the late Rene Dubos – internationally renowned environmentalist and author of the Pulitzer Prize winning *So Human An Animal*; Herbert Gintis, radical economist and co–author of *Schooling in Capitalist America*; Maxine Greene, Professor of Education at Teachers College, Columbia University and author of *The Teacher As Stranger (1973)*; and Jonathan Kozol, school reformer and author of *Death at An Early Age (1967)*.

In 1983, The Society for Educational Reconstruction co–sponsored a symposium with Adelphi University, Educators for Social Responsibility and the World Education Fellowship entitled "Schooling in the Nuclear Age." Participants at this meeting discussed such concerns as "education for the 21st century," "the back–to–basics movement," and "the classroom teacher's role in addressing the threat of nuclear war." In 1984 SER co–sponsored a symposium on the struggle to maintain human values in the face of rapid technological change, particularly that being brought on by the computer. This symposium was entitled "The Search for Humanistic Perspectives in a Technocratic Society."

Through SER's quarterly journal, the *Cutting Edge*, and more recently in its newsletter *SER In Action* Theodore Brameld's vision of education for peace and justice has been continued and amplified. These publications have provided a forum for educators both within the United States and beyond who wish to share both reconstructionist perspectives and concrete examples of reconstructionist teaching as they address SER's four goals: cooperative power, global order, self–transformation and social democracy. In addition, the Gertrude

Langsam Educational Reconstruction Award recognizes the achievements of individuals or organizations that further SER's goals.

Members of The Society for Educational Reconstruction are utopians who envision a world of peace, brotherhood, equality and freedom. But at the same time SER members are activist–educators struggling in their own communities, schools and universities to help pave the way for those changes. Currently, SER members are engaged in such diverse projects as designing curriculum units for global education and peace studies, organizing for disarmament, leading workshops for teachers on conflict resolution, researching the impact of computer education on today's children, advocating for financial support of multicultural education, teaching literacy skills to the poor, developing teaching strategies for reducing prejudice, writing on world hunger and examining educational systems in other countries.

As The Society for Educational Reconstruction moves toward the completion of its second decade as an organization committed to social change through education, it remains true to the vision of Theodore Brameld and its founders. Today, SER continues to function as a communications network and support group for its members. Though its meetings, conferences and publications, SER initiates and supports education for peace, justice and global consciousness.

NOTES ON CONTRIBUTORS

KEVIN J. CASSIDY, Assistant Professor of Political Science at Fairfield University in Connecticut, has published articles and presented proposals on economic conversion and related topics. He is on the Justice and Peace Commission of the Catholic Diocese of Bridgeport. Professor Cassidy is very active in Connecticut Campaign for Nuclear Arms Freeze and other peace movements in the region.

DAVID R. CONRAD, Professor of Education at the University of Vermont with specialization in philosophy of education and peace education, serves as co–director of the Center for World Education and co–chairperson of the Society for Educational Reconstruction. Dr. Conrad is author of *Education for Transformation: Implications in Lewis Mumford's Eco-humanism* (1976) and a variety of articles in American and Japanese journals.

HERBERT S. EISENSTEIN, Associate Professor of Education Programs at Capitol Campus of the Pennsylvania State University, has published articles in *Urban Education, Cutting Edge, Education* and *Phi Delta Kappan*. His monographs and books include *Higher Education's Faculty Characteristics* (1976) and *The Same Chance to Fail* (1977). Dr. Eisenstein has several years of experience in academic administration.

GERTRUDE FEINSTEIN LANGSAM, Professor of Education (Adjunct) at Adelphi University, is co–chairperson of the Society for Educational Reconstruction. Her articles have appeared in *Educational Studies, Cutting Edge, Focus on Learning and High School Journal of Behavioral Science*. She is a contributor to the Biographical Dictionary of American Educators. Professor Langsam is recipient of several awards for her services to education and the community including a major award from SER: the Gertrude Langsam Educational Reconstruction Award.

JAMES W. LOEWEN is Professor of Sociology, with specialization in race relations, at the University of Vermont.

His revisionist history text, *Mississippi: Conflict and Change*, won the Lillian Smith Award for Best Southern Non–Fiction. Professors Loewen and Shiman are working on a book, *Lies My Teacher Told Me*, about cultural myths in American education.

RICHARD G. LYONS, professor of Educational Philosophy at the College of Education, University of Lowell, has published in *Social Education, Focus on Learning, Educational Theory* and *Cutting Edge.* He is co–editor of a book of readings on the relationship between working and schooling in American society which will be published later this year. He is former president of the New England Philosophy of Education Society and is currently an active member of the faculty union at Lowell.

ROBERT J. NASH, Professor of Education (ethics and philosophy) at the University of Vermont, is author of more than sixty journal articles, book chapters and monographs, including a recent article entitled "Where There Is No Vision, the People Perish: A Nation At Risk."

FRANCES L. O'NEIL, teaches psychology at Tunxis Community College Farmington, Connecticut. She has published several articles and has spoken widely on issues relating to the psychological theories of the East. In the Summer of 1984, she presented a paper at the international meeting of the World Education Fellowship in The Netherlands. Dr. O'Neil recently received a Mellon Foundation Grant to pursue advanced studies at Yale University.

BETTY REARDON, Co–ordinator of Peace Education at Teachers College, Columbia University, is also Director of the Peace–making in Education Program of the United Ministries in Education. She is the author of a number of articles and monographs. Her recent book is *Sexism and War System* (1985). She directs the annual International Institute on Peace Education.

MARY–LOU BREITBORDE SHERR, Assistant Professor of Education and Co–ordinator of Elementary Education at Curry College, Milton, Massachusetts, has written in the area of teacher professionalization, teaching as a woman's occupation and teacher self–esteem. Dr. Sherr is currently exploring notions of literacy in the light of the new conservatism in education.

NOBUO SHIMAHARA, Professor of Anthropology of Education at Rutgers University, is currently a full–time researcher on Japanese education at the National Institute of Education, Washington, D. C. His interest in the crosscultural theory of education resulted in publication of *Adaptation and Education in Japan* (1979). Dr. Shimahara is author of several other scholarly books including *Educational Reconstruction: Promise and Challenge* (1973).

DAVID A. SHIMAN, Professor of Education with a speciality in Comparative Education at the University of Vermont, is author of *The Prejudice Book* and articles in various educational journals. Professor Shiman taught in Africa for four and a half years and is currently co–director of the Center for World Education at the University of Vermont.

JAY M. SMITH, Associate Professor at the Institute for Teaching and Education Studies, Adelphi University, is co-author of *The Teacher as Learning Facilitator* (1979) and former chair-person of the Society for Educational Reconstruction. Dr. Smith is director of the Center for Male Development at Adelphi University.

FRANK A. STONE, Professor of International Education and Co–director of the I. N. Thut World Education Center at the University of Connecticut, Storrs, spent a dozen years as an educator in Turkey before moving to Connecticut in 1968. Dr. Stone was chairperson of the Society for Educational Reconstruction from 1979–1983 and Editor of its journal *Cutting Edge*. He has written more than forty journal articles and several books and monographs including *Academies for Anatolia*, (1984). He is currently President of the World Education Fellowship, United States Section.

T. MATHAI THOMAS, Associate Professor at the University of Bridgeport, teaches courses in sociology, philosophy of education, international education and peace studies. He served the Society for Educational Reconstruction as its first Secretary–Treasurer (1969-73). He is a former president of the New England Philosophy of Education Society. Dr. Thomas is author of *Indian Educational Reforms in Cultural Perspective* (1970), *Images of Man* (1974) and *Kerala Immigrants in America* (1984).

DATE DUE

IDA URSO is a recent Ph. D. graduate
and international education at the Univers
Los Angeles, where she taught courses i
Prior to pursuing her degree, she works
national organizations, including the Uni'
She is author of the *Teacher's Research*

DAVID WOOLMAN, Assist
and Adjunct Professor of Histor
vice–chairperson of the Society for
His publications include *Mass Media*
Modern Egyptian Literature, Music and Visua.
Social Functions of Iranian Education: An Historica.
and *Education and World Order: The Thought of Joha.*
and Nine American Reconstructionists (1984).

DEAN S. YARBROUGH, Jr., Principal of the McKay
Elementary Science Magnet School in the Boston Public School
system, started his career as an engineer after studying at
Boston College and Northeastern University. Later, he left
engineering and became a teacher.